The *Jewelry* of Southeast Asia

ANNE RICHTER

The *Jewelry* of Southeast Asia

with 357 illustrations, 353 in colour

On pp. 2–3: Yao (Mien) bride of Lao Cai, northern Vietnam, adorned in silver torques (cf. Pl. 155), early 20th century.

Above: A man from the south of Nias island, north Sumatra, photographed before World War II, displays an unusually diverse array of ceremonial ornaments. They include a gold crown with central tier of leaf ornaments which indicate high status, and a torque of gold wire spirals. A brass and coconut shell torque marks him as a successful headhunter and, together with the upward-pointing gold moustaches and the metal jacket, is intended to convey fierceness.

Opposite: A young Balinese dancer, early 20th century. Her gold crown embellished with fresh flowers and her gem-set belt buckle are especially opulent. Her jewelled collar is similar to that shown in Pl. 191. Her armlets are of a traditional Balinese type, with Garuda motifs.

A longer version of this book, containing a detailed text, was first published in hardback in 2000 in the United Kingdom by Thames & Hudson Ltd, 181A High Holborn, London WC1V 7QX

thamesandhudson.com

First paperback edition 2010

British Library Cataloguing-in-Publication Data
A catalogue record for this book is available from the British Library

ISBN 978-0-500-28866-5

Printed and bound in Hong Kong by Paramount Printing Company Limited

Acknowledgments

I am greatly indebted to the following institutions and individuals for their assistance, encouragement and support: **Belgium** At the Etnografisch Museum, Antwerp, Els de Palmenaer and Mirielle Holsbeke • **Burma (Myanmar)** The Minister for Culture, H.E.U. Win Sein; the Director of the Library, Museum and Research Branch, Daw Nanda Hmun; U Khin Win and U Kyaw Win • **Cambodia** His Royal Highness, King Norodom Sihanouk; Madame Kech Sisoda, Director of Royal Protocol; the Minister of Culture, Samdech Preahream Norodom Bopha Devi; the Head of the Department of Museums, Pich Keo; the Director of the National Museum of Cambodia, Khun Samen; the Royal Cambodian Ballet • **China** Professor Li Kunsheng, Director of the Yunnan Provincial Museum • **France** At the Musée National des Arts Asiatiques Guimet, Paris, Pierre Baptiste, Conservateur • **Germany** At the Linden-Museum, Stuttgart, Professor Dr Peter Thiele • **Indonesia** The Director of the National Museum, Jakarta, Dr Endang Sri Hardiati, and staff, and the former Director, Dra Suwati Kartiwa; Dra H. Aminah Pabittei, Museums Department, Ujung Pandang; Sungguminasa Palace Museum, Ujung Pandang; and the Sultan of Bima, Sumbawa • **Malaysia** The Director of the National Museum, Kuala Lumpur, Dr Kamarul Baharin bin Buyong, and the Curator, Encik Kamarul Kassim, and also Encik Mohammed Kassim and Zubaidah Shawal; the Director of the Sarawak Museum, Mr Sanib Said, and the former Acting Director, Mr Ipoi Datan • **The Netherlands** At the Museum voor Volkenkunde, Rotterdam, Heleen Bjil; at the Tropen Museum, Amsterdam, Mr David van Duuren, collections manager, and Ms Janneke van Djik of the photography department • **The Philippines** The Director of the National Museum of the Philippines, Manila, Father Gabriel Casal, and staff; the Director of the Ayala Museum, Manila, Ms Sonia Ner, and staff; the former Governor of the Banco Sentral, Mr Gabriel Sinsong, and Ms Frances Arespakochaga; Mr Kenneth Esguerra of the Banco Sentral Museum, Manila; the Director of the Geronimo Berenguer de los Reyes (GBR) Museum, Cavite, John Silva • **Singapore** The Directors of the National Museum and National Heritage Board of Singapore; Irene Lee, Christie's, Singapore • **Thailand** Department of Fine Art in Bangkok, Mr Somkid Chotigavanit; the Director of the Chao Sam Phraya National Museum, Ayutthaya, Ms Patcharee Gomonthiti; the Director of the Uthong National Museum, Suphanburi province, Mrs Manita Keunkan • **United Kingdom** At the City Museum and Art Gallery, Bristol, Sue Giles; at the British Museum, London, Department of Oriental Antiquities, Janet Newson; John Guy, then at the Victoria and Albert Museum, London, Indian and South-East Asian Department • **United States of America** At the Asia Society, New York, Merantine Hens; Honolulu Academy of Arts, Hawaii; Ms Pauline Sugino • **Vietnam** The Minister of Culture and Information, Nguyen Khoa Diem, and Vu Thi Tuyet Thuy; the Director of the History Museum, Hanoi, Pham Quoc Quam; the Director and staff of the Thay Nguyen Ethnographic Museum, Thay Nguyen, northern Vietnam; the Director of the Museum of North Vietnamese Women, Hanoi, Dao Thi Nhien; the Director of the Museum of Ancient Objects, Hue, Le Phu Hap; the Goldsmiths' Co-operative, Hue; the Director of the History Museum, Ho Chi Minh City, Trinh Thi Hoa; the Director of the Museum of South Vietnamese Women, Ho Chi Minh City, Tran Thi Hong Anh.

I would also like to thank Jeannie and Michael Backman, Thomas Bodmar, Ruth Bottomley, the Chantikavan family, Simeon Gilding, Madame Mekhala Inthavong, Veronica and Christopher Hazzard, Russell Howard, Stanley Hram Uk, Caroline Kashemsant, Ms Kyi Kyi Than, Chris Lambert, Susie Lebassi, Ian Matthews, Katherine Millikin, Jean Nicholls, Mrs Liz Oley (President of the Indonesia Heritage Society), Angela Parker, Nelson and Angie Tan, Margaret Tan, Louis Richter, Issare Surachestpong, Haji Syamsuddin, A.M., Jenni Von Tempsky, Andrew Trahair, Paul Trahair, Ramon Villegas, Daw Yin Yin (Saw Mon Hyin), and Dr H. Muh. Hayom Widagdo.

Anne Richter
Melbourne

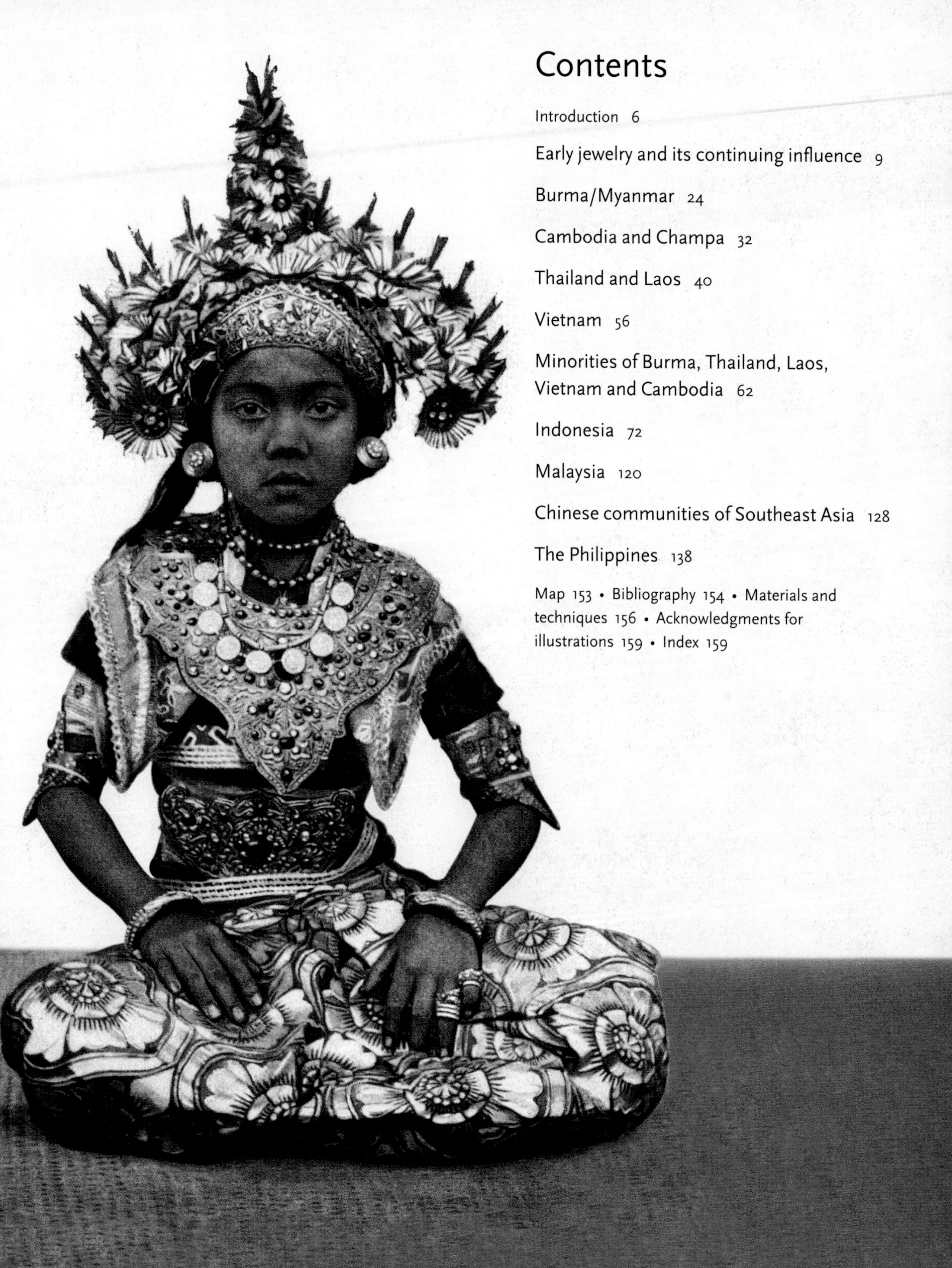

Contents

INTRODUCTION

National museums and royal and private collections throughout Southeast Asia contain jewels which are remarkable for their outstanding beauty and technical skill. These jewels are also expressions of political power and markers of social and religious status, and some served the talismanic function of deflecting ill fortune. Many techniques, forms and motifs come from India, the Islamic world, China and later Europe, transmitted at various times and places through trade and diplomatic and religious contacts. However, imported styles were often transformed and ornaments accorded different purposes. Underlying these foreign influences remains a deep and ancient set of cultural meanings and aesthetic preferences that are also reflected in Southeast Asian architecture and textiles.

Ancient Traditions

Some styles which were still being made and worn in the 20th century have their origins in the Neolithic and Bronze Ages. The first section, 'Early jewelry and its continuing influence' [**1–34**], shows ornaments from a diversity of sources and periods which derive their forms, motifs and worldview from ancient traditions. The earliest Southeast Asian jewelry was made of shells [**2**], and these are still used to adorn the body. Ancient graves containing ornaments of shell, and later of stone [**3**, **5**, **6**], also reveal a concern with indicating differences in social status, gender and age. The inclusion of imperishable ornaments among ancient grave goods may imply an early belief in life after death, and possibly in the existence of a supernatural realm of ancestral spirits and deities capable of exercising power over the living.

The ethnologist Robert von Heine-Geldern identified three current Southeast Asian tribal art styles that he believed had very early origins. The first is associated with the construction of megalithic monuments and the ritualized feasting typical of stratified societies. Valuable horned cattle were sacrificed and precious works of art such as jewelry and textiles were displayed to enhance the prestige of warrior aristocrats and their ancestors. Horn and cosmic tree forms occur [e.g. **1**, **3**, **10**, **30**, **237**], but these often coalesce into images of crescent moons or boats which in splendid gold ornaments of the eastern islands of Indonesia recall the mythic journeys of ancestors who founded communities [**30**, **231**]. Horned gables are common in architecture [**241**]; the horn form in jewelry may also refer to clan lineages and households composed of ancestors and living members [**30**, **231**, **235**]. Other motifs include human faces and figures [**22–26**, **30**, **238**, **242**, **246**, **248**, **249**, **336**], which may represent ancestors celebrated in myth and ceremony, or the slaves and decapitated heads associated with warfare.

The second style is related to the advent of bronze technology. The bronze drums of the Dian culture (400–100 BCE), excavated in Yunnan, southern China, show people engaged in feasting and dancing and indicate aristocratic styles of adornment that include feather headdresses and the grandiose belt buckles [**12**] and large earrings that have been found in excavations. Bronze ornaments of the Dong Son culture of north Vietnam (1000–100 BCE) are notable for their coiled forms [**10**] which once sheathed limbs in gleaming metal, and also for the use of surface patterns with geometric and spiral motifs [**8**].

The third style is based on the dynamic curvilinear art of the late Zhou dynasty of China (1045–256 BCE), which according to Heine-Geldern influenced the distinctive Dayak art of Borneo [**18**, **20**, **22**, **246**, **273**, **274**].

On the mainland, some minority groups have worn metal coiled limb ornaments until very recent times, and also bells of cast metal, torques, wire pendants in double spiral form, peacock- and hornbill-feather headdresses, ivory bracelets and ear plugs [**129**, **137**], tusks and teeth [**7**, **276**, **277**], ornaments constructed of horn or in the shape of horns, and necklaces of glass beads [**129**, **131**, **132**, **134**, **276**, **277**] and shells acquired through trade [**135**, **136**, **277**]. Metal bracelets, sometimes decorated with geometric and spiral motifs, may signify promissory bonds with the human and spirit worlds [**19**, **129**, **130**, **134**]. These ornaments were typically favoured by speakers of Austronesian languages related to those of the Philippines and Indonesia, and also speakers of Austroasiatic languages ancestral to Mon, Khmer and Vietnamese, who live in the forested uplands and plateaux of Laos, Cambodia and central and south Vietnam. Some speakers of Sino-Tibetan languages in Burma/Myanmar, such as the Naga and Chin [**7**, **24**, **28**, **136–138**], share these styles.

Ornaments worn in the Philippines and the outer islands and in remote inland societies of Indonesia also include beads, bells, shell, ivory and animal teeth and tusks [**276**, **277**, **333–337**, **340**, **343**]. Coiled forms adorn limbs and ears [**16**, **17**, **21**, **222**], and some jewelry is beautifully decorated with applied geometric and curvilinear elements [**232**, **239**, **249**] and surface patterns [**231**, **239**, **241**, **242**, **245**, **246**, **338–343**]; among the finest examples are the magnificent brass belts, boxes and jingling anklets of the Bagobo and Monobo in Mindanao in the Philippines [**338**, **339**], the coiled brass bracelets of the Toba Batak of north Sumatra [**29**], and the silver bracelets of Timor [**241**, **242**, **245**]. However, island jewelry is often more complex structurally and richer in symbolism than that of the mainland. Much of it displays motifs and forms that evoke a cosmology in which a tiered universe with an upper realm of air, spirits and ancestors, heat, masculinity and nobility is in perpetual interaction and dynamic tension with a lower world of water, coolness, human and agricultural fertility and femininity. Some jewels display feminine motifs that contrast with obviously masculine symbols. The gold pendants of the mountain peoples of northern Luzon, for example, resemble stylized female genitalia and are elaborated with heads of animals and of victims of headhunting and warfare [**25**]. Ornaments of this type were also produced in Indonesia [**13**, **15**, **227**, **228**]. An art work in which signs and symbols of upper and lower worlds, feminine and masculine, are brought together can become a representation of the cosmos in its entirety – a microcosm. Such a jewel may express complex human relations with the supernatural realm and be seen as radiating enormous spiritual power in its own right.

Indian Influences

By about the 2nd century CE, influences from the Mediterranean, Western Asia and especially India become apparent. Excavations conducted at Oc Eo, in what is now south Vietnam, revealed an abundance of gold jewels, seals, imported and locally made glass beads and a few Roman ornaments [**32–34**]. It is believed that this site was part of an empire known as Funan, which was described in detail by Chinese visitors in the 3rd century CE. Funan was famed for its trade in perfumes, ivory, brightly coloured birds and every imaginable type of rare and precious merchandise. There were extensive libraries and archives. Wooden houses were built on stilts. Surrounded by bejewelled young women waving ornamental fly whisks, the king of Funan sat on a carved *naga* (Indian serpent/ dragon) that served as a throne, with a vivid scarf the colour of the dawn sky draped over his bare shoulders. His high pointed crown was adorned with golden flowers and set with precious stones. He wore a golden belt, cords and necklaces. An identifiable cultural style had evolved. Chinese visitors recognized this in other early court cities in Southeast Asia and described it with precision. Their accounts are not only extremely vivid, but also consistent with those provided by European observers more than a thousand years later. This is not to suggest that Southeast Asia was unchanging, as kingdoms and empires fell and were replaced, but simply that Indianized styles of personal adornment were firmly established.

Excavations of first-millennium cities throughout the region have revealed jewelry, jewellers' tools and moulds similar to those found at Oc Eo [**32**, **59**]. And it is in court cities that resembled Funan to a greater or lesser extent in architecture, costume, religious practice and ceremonial style that the spectacular gold jewelry and beads shown in the Burma/Myanmar, Cambodia, Champa, Thailand and Indonesia (Java) sections of this book were made and worn.

The *naga* and floral motifs such as the lotus were widespread [**60**, **104**], and links in the form of jasmine flowers were employed in magnificent Khmer chains [**65**]. The gold ornaments of Java dating from the 10th–15th centuries are notable for their extraordinary sculptural expressiveness and imaginative use of motifs based on Indian mythology and epic literature [**158**]. Extensive use of coloured gemstones, often set according to Indian conventions, appears to have been more common in the courtly jewelry of the mainland; nevertheless, surviving Indonesian crowns are also richly encrusted with precious stones [**181**, **251**, **256**]. The employment of diamonds, in particular, was further encouraged by the migration of Indian jewellers to Burma/Myanmar and the Straits Settlements under the British colonial regime.

Many large and spectacular gold ornaments have been excavated in the Philippines that display extraordinary skill in the techniques of wire weaving and gold beating [**323**, **325**]. Highly skilled geometric granulation work recalls that of the ancient Mediterranean [**1**, **323**, **329**]. Some pieces suggest Indian influence possibly acquired via contacts with Indonesia [**327**], but the degree and extent of engagement with Hindu–Buddhist ideologies remains unclear. Many of these extraordinary jewels may have been produced in polities not dissimilar to those of other sophisticated Southeast Asian societies prior to Indianization.

Chinese Contributions

Vietnam did not adopt an Indian courtly style, because Chinese occupation of the north from 111 BCE until the 10th century CE, and the acculturation of its elites to Chinese norms, tastes and Confucianism forestalled any such development. The torque was favoured in Vietnam, but was also worn at the Chinese imperial court and by minority groups of mainland Southeast Asia [**125**, **126**, **132**, **149**, **151**, **153**, **155**, **156**]. Bracelets were the traditional betrothal gift [**126**, **127**]. Vietnamese pieces are distinctive, however, in that silver ornaments were typically worked in a refined style possibly derived from that of the Tang (618–907 CE); this may have been introduced during the Chinese occupation. Motifs such the seasonal plants [**128**] and the Eight Precious Objects are also of Chinese derivation. While the jewelry of Hue, the old royal capital, is comparatively ornate [**125**], Vietnamese traditions of personal adornment are notable for their elegance and restraint.

Chinese jewellers migrated from southern Chinese cities to the cosmopolitan courts and coastal ports and towns of Southeast Asia over many centuries. They may have introduced coloured enamelling to the Thai capital of Ayutthaya (1350–1767), although West Asian and Indian influence is also very likely in the introduction of that technique, as in that of niello in Indonesia, Malaysia and Thailand. Rural communities sometimes commissioned Chinese artisans to make their traditional ornaments. The Chinese were expert in filigree work and also made many of the ornate metal belts worn on the mainland. It is likely that some wedding crowns and hair comb styles of Malaysia and Indonesia were strongly influenced by Chinese models.

Minorities from southern China also migrated into the north of Southeast Asia. The dispersion of the Tai and Shan probably occurred between the 7th and 11th centuries, but many groups speaking Sino-Tibetan and Tibeto-Burman languages, including the Akha and Hmong, did not settle until about the 19th century. The latter are noted for their colourful costumes and bold silver ornaments. Torques are forged and beaten in gleaming silver. Forms such as the stylized lock which binds the soul to the body [**157**], silver buds, flowers and butterflies, and the use of coloured enamels, are related to Chinese jewelry traditions [**148–150**, **157**]. While the Tai cultivate rice in the high valleys, the Sino-Tibetan and Tibeto-Burman groups typically occupy the steeper mountainsides.

In the British Straits Settlements of Penang, Melaka and Singapore, a distinctive creolized culture evolved from the marriages of Chinese men with local women, in which social customs and traditions of cuisine and adornment were blended into a unique style that is usually referred to as Peranakan or Nonya [**295**, **296**, **314**]. Although wedding attire remained fundamentally Chinese, elaborate belts, buckles and brooches in precious metal drew not only on Chinese but also on Malay and Indonesian jewelry traditions, which, over centuries, had evolved from a mixture of indigenous, Indian and Islamic influences. Peranakan communities benefited from the economic stability provided by the British colonial regime, and in the late 19th and early 20th centuries many could indulge in extravagant displays of family wealth. They commissioned magnificent jewels from Hong Kong and Shanghai as well as from local firms. Some types of Peranakan jewelry were also worn in Chinese communities in Indonesia.

Islamic Ideals

Marco Polo at the end of the 13th century recorded conversions to Islam and the presence of Arab traders in north Sumatra; however, the process of Islamization in Southeast Asia was gradual and occurred over centuries. Islamic ideals of modesty led to changes in clothing, notably the adoption of upper body garments, especially for women. Jewelled collars, buttons and sets of brooches decorated the blouses, tunics and jackets of Muslims living mainly in coastal trading areas of Indonesia and Malaysia. Motifs representing living things such as animals and people were eliminated, although local variations on Indian mythological creatures survived in parts of Indonesia, and a deeper substratum of animist thought can sometimes be detected in the persistence of abstracted visual references to horn and house forms. Decoration was mostly restricted to vegetal motifs, often worked in repoussé [**262**, **212**, **216**, **221**], engraving [**253**, **258**, **278**], niello [**214**, **215**, **278**], or applied filigree and granulation [**185**, **210**, **257**]; belt buckle forms and necklace elements were based on the leaf; Arabic numerals were employed in talismanic ornaments [**278**, **261**, **254**].

Sumatran forms and styles, and to a lesser extent those of Java, are similar to those of coastal Borneo and Sulawesi and the Malay Peninsula. Artisans working in fine metals were essentially based in and around regional courts. Malay ornaments are distinctive for their unusual refinement and beauty and for the wide range of vegetal motifs – drawn, in the main, from local tropical plants – which are shown to great advantage on the surfaces of large belt buckles, betel and tobacco accoutrements and modesty plaques [**279–294**]. In the southern Philippines, the Muslim (Moro) rulers shared Malay traditions of court jewelry, including imposing buckles of precious metal worn by noblemen, whose garments were extensively decorated with buttons worked in filigree and granulation [**353**]. Women were adorned in the varicoloured pearls of the Sulu archipelago, gold filigree ear ornaments, and hairpins.

European Incursions

The first Europeans to attempt control over the lucrative Southeast Asian spice trade were the Portuguese. They conquered the international trade emporium and royal city of Malacca (Melaka) on the Malay Peninsula in 1511. The designs of heart-shaped brooches and sets of hairpins tipped with cockleshells worn on the Malay Peninsula may be based on Portuguese or Dutch models.

After the Spanish conquest of fertile lowland areas of the Philippines in the 16th century, conversion to Christianity became essential for local elites who wished to survive and prosper, and many eventually intermarried with Spanish and Chinese Christian families. Exquisite rosaries, crucifixes, reliquaries and scapulars announced their wearers' piety and also their wealth [**344–349**]. Earring and hair comb styles drew on Spanish models [**350–352**].

By the late 19th and early 20th centuries, as the power of colonial regimes reached a zenith, growing fascination with modernity led to greater interest in European motifs and forms, and, among royalty and the very wealthy, the occasional commissioning of jewelry from important European firms.

More about Southeast Asia's magnificent jewelry traditions can be found in the books and articles listed in the bibliography, and in the original edition of this book.

EARLY JEWELRY AND ITS CONTINUING INFLUENCE

1 Three ornate conical gold necklace finials with exceptionally fine granular decoration, from Butuan, Mindanao island, the Philippines, 500–1300. The motifs articulate fundamental Southeast Asian concerns expressed in jewelry for over two millennia: the larger finials show human figures, perhaps guardian ancestors, wearing horn-like headdresses, and waving long banners as they dance ceremonially around the cosmic Tree of Life.

2

3

4

5

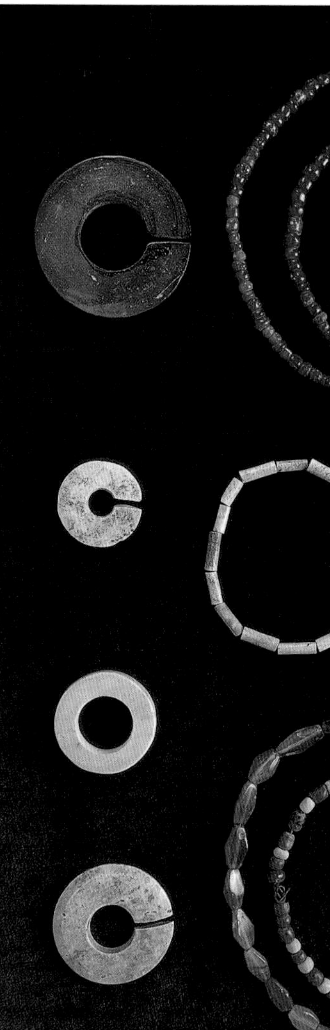

2 Shell bracelet and necklace, found in the Tabon caves complex on Palawan, the Philippines, *c.* 1500–1000 BCE. Imperishable funerary ornaments imply belief in life after death and the existence of a supernatural realm of ancestral spirits. Shells were ascribed high intrinsic value.

3 Stone earrings, a button, and jewelry fragments from Dong Dau, northern Vietnam, *c.* 1500 BCE. The horned pendant may signify aggression and protection. Cattle were important as symbols of prestige, and as sacrificial animals they provided a link between the human domain and that of ancestors and spirits.

4 Glass bracelet and ear ornament (cf. Pl. 5) from the Tabon caves complex on Palawan, the Philippines, *c.* 200 BCE–100 CE.

5 Stone ear ornaments of the Sa Huynh people, central Vietnam, *c.* 300 BCE. The two-headed design (bottom left) the may depict horned deer or cattle. The split-ring types have conical projections; similar ornaments have been found in Hong Kong, Taiwan, Thailand, Borneo, and the Philippines (Pl. 4), testifying to cultural and economic exchange within Southeast Asia.

6 Stone ear ornaments and beads of the Sa Huynh people, central Vietnam, *c.* 300 BCE. The carnelian beads were imported from Gujarat, while those of opaque red, blue and yellow glass may have been made by Tamil beadmakers in Arikmedu, southern India.

7 Helmet of the Kalyo-Kengyu Naga people, on the Assam–Burma/Myanmar border, early 20th century, of rattan, orchid fibre and bear's fur. The boar's tusks are emblems of warrior status.

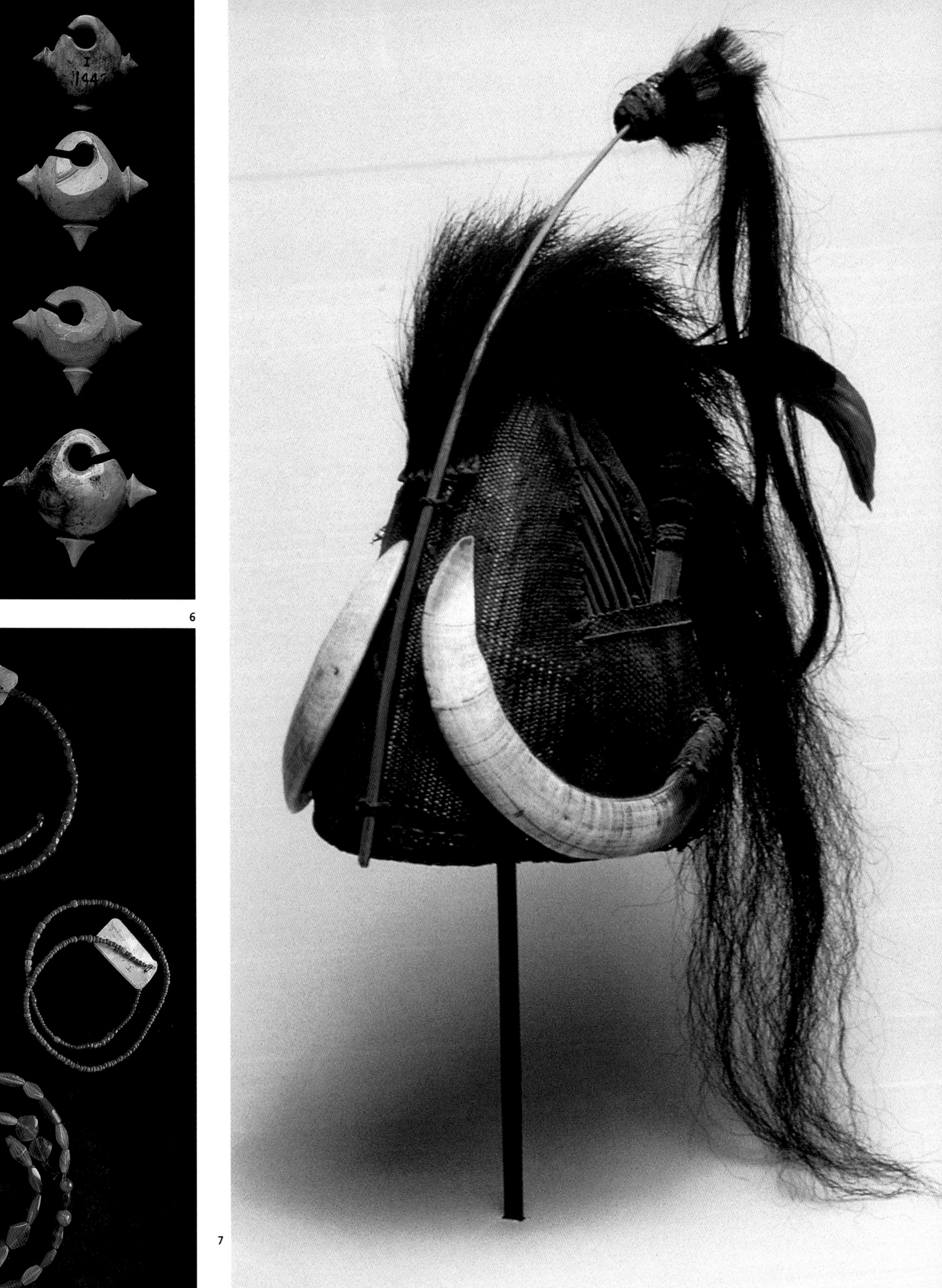

6

7

8

8 This bronze belt buckle with attached bells exemplifies the decorative style of the Dong Son culture of northern Vietnam, *c.* 400–300 BCE.

9 Bronze torque elaborated with bosses, from the Ban Chiang area of north-eastern Thailand, *c.* 500 BCE.

9

10 Bronze arm ornament in coiled form found at Ban Chiang, north-eastern Thailand, *c.* 500 BCE, and three bracelets; one has decorative bosses, while the others have stylized bull or buffalo horns and loops that may represent butterflies or dragonflies.

11 A bronze bracelet found on the Laos–Vietnam border, of 400–200 BCE, shows typical Dong Son motifs of frogs and a procession of cold- and warm-blooded creatures. Reptiles inhabit the underworld realms of earth and water and also the earthly domain shared by mammals and human beings.

12 Bronze belt disc set with malachite and a central agate bead, Dian culture, Yunnan, southern China, *c.* 200 BCE.

10

11

12

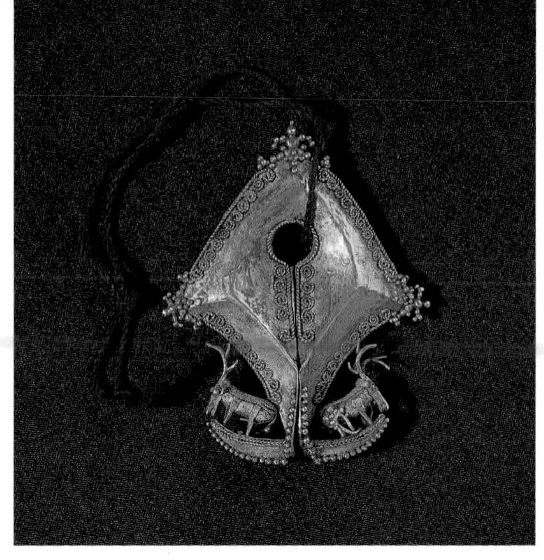

13

13 Gold *mamuli* from east Sumba, eastern Indonesia, 19th century. The deer symbolizes the protective power of horns and also magical royal potency. *Mamuli* are thought to represent female genitalia in stylized form.

14 Gold repoussé ear ornaments with spiral patterns that may allude to the scales of a *naga* (serpent/dragon) or crocodile, and a gold split-ring ear ornament, from the Philippines, 800–1300. One has breast-like terminals signifying fertility and prestige.

15 In the gold *taiganja* ornament of the Kulawi or Kaili people of central Sulawesi, Indonesia, an evocation of female genitalia is accompanied by symbols of status and fertility such as horns, shooting plants and rice grains. Surrounding it are necklaces of gold and coral beads (*manik ata*) and fine gold discs of the Toraja people of south-central Sulawesi. All are 19th-century in date.

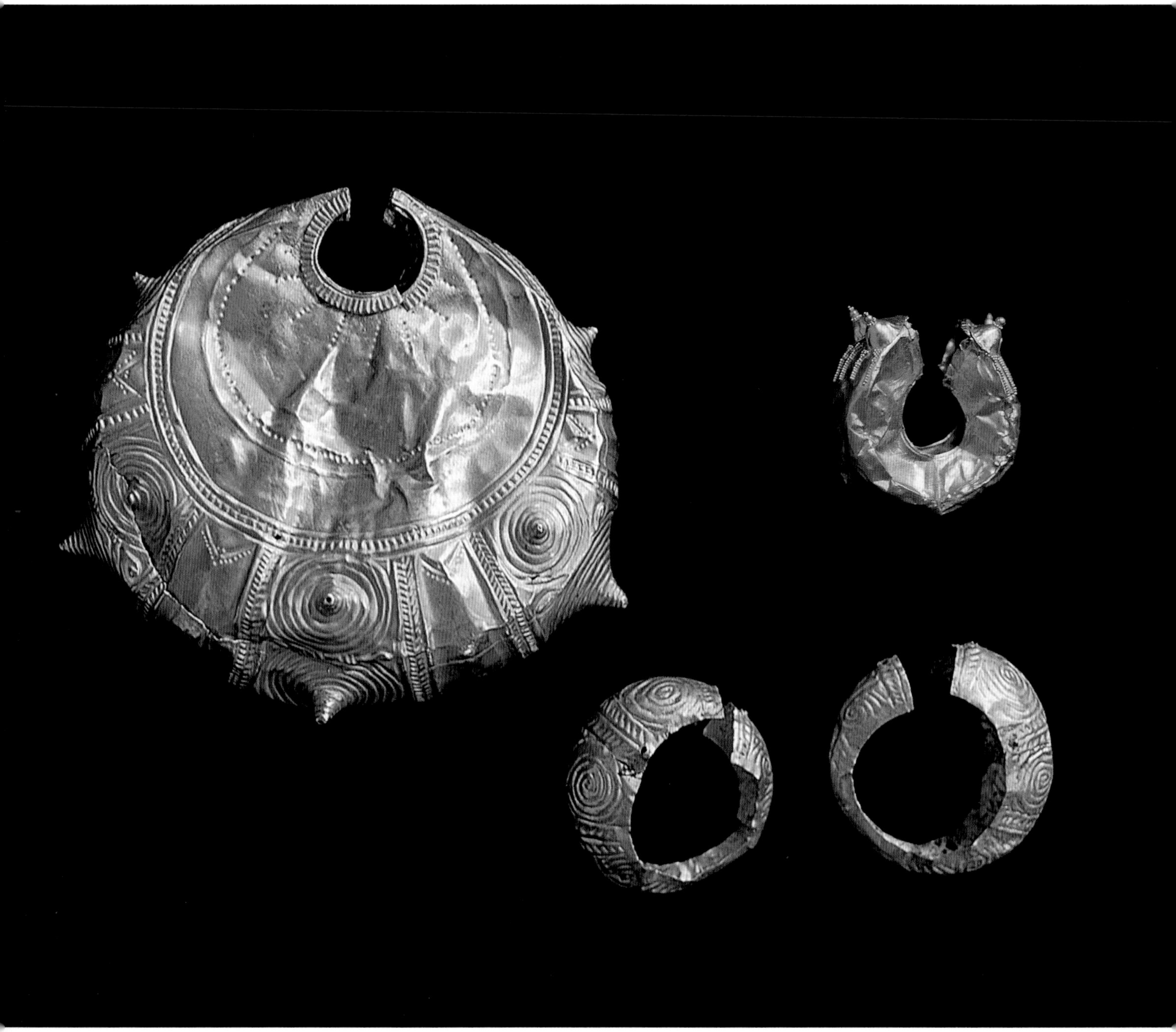

14

16, 17 The enormous silver ear ornaments known as *padung-padung*, worn by Karo Batak women of north Sumatra, Indonesia, and the brass spiral anklets of the Bontoc people of northern Luzon in the Philippines demonstrate the persistence of spirals in form and motif in the 19th and early 20th centuries.

18

18, 20 Broad hairpins and thin loom pins of carved and blackened bone, Kelabit and Iban Dayak people, Sarawak, Malaysia, early 20th century. The spiral, geometric, and dynamic curvilinear motifs may derive ultimately from the art of the Dong Son culture of northern Vietnam (*c.* 500 BCE) and that of the later Chou dynasty in China (before 221 BCE). The large whirling spirals represent the underworld *naga* fertility goddess.

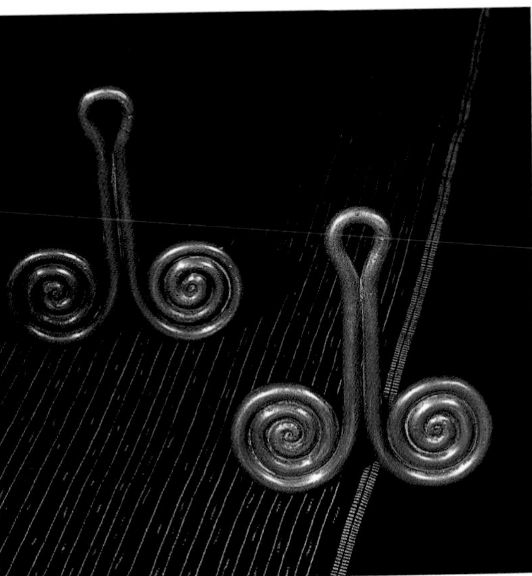

16

19

19 Bronze bracelets from Cambodia, of uncertain date. The deployment of spiral patterns suggests possible manufacture in late prehistory or the earlier centuries of the first millennium.

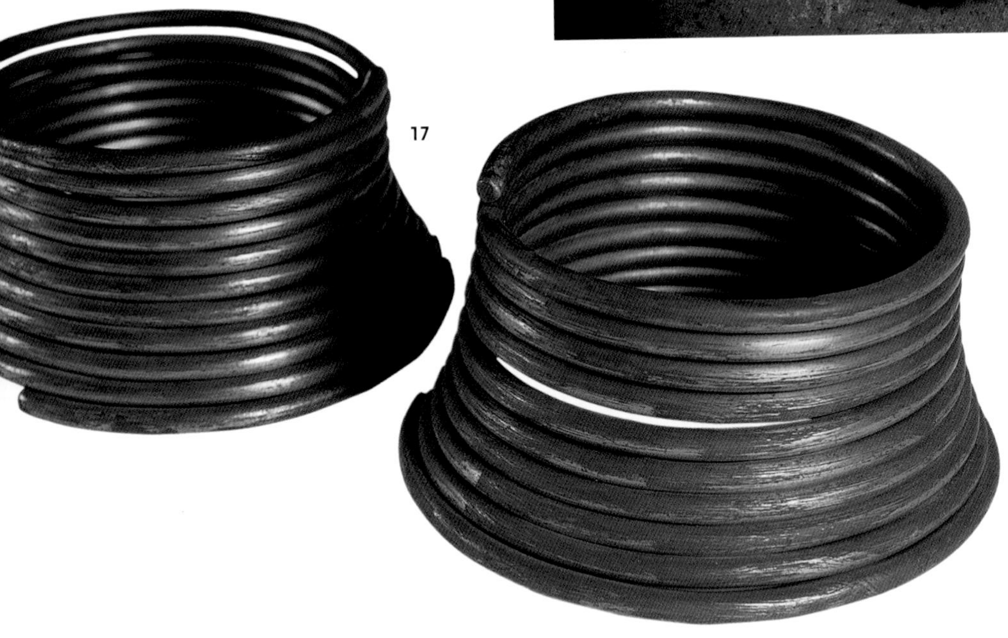

17

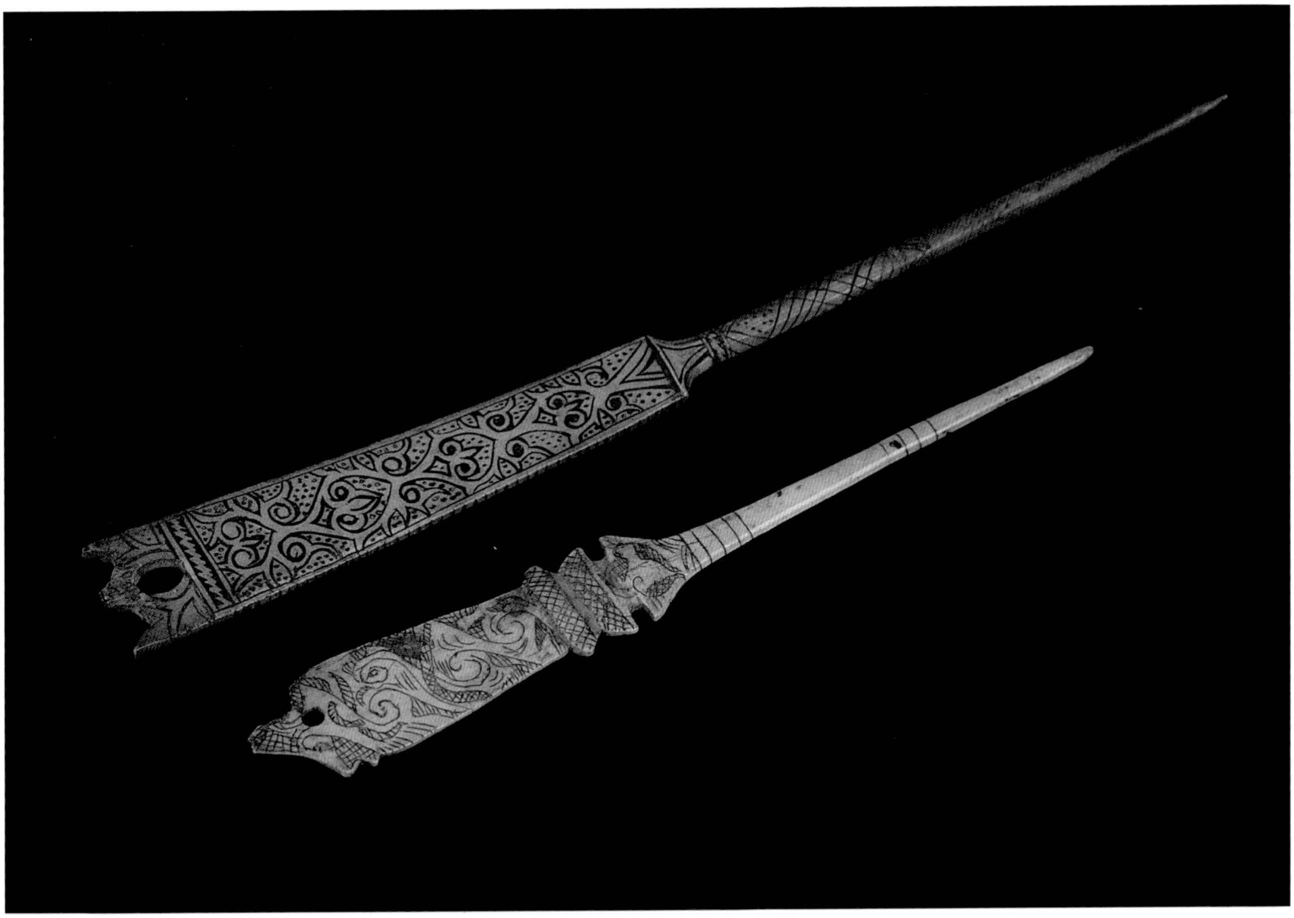

20

21

21 Copper alloy *sanggori* head ornament, Kulawi or Kaili people, central Sulawesi, Indonesia, 19th–early 20th century. Its spiral form represents a magical serpent. *Sanggori* were worn in ceremony and warfare because their gleam was thought to deflect harmful influences.

22

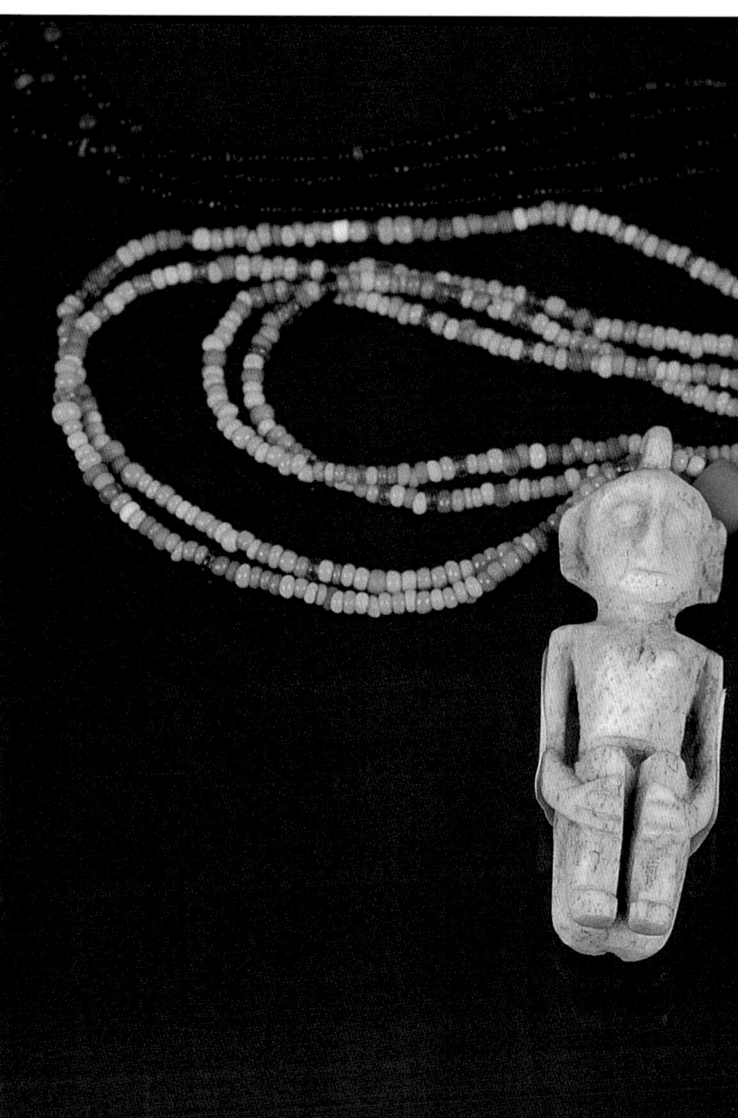

22 A pair of ear-pendants made of hornbill casque, Kayan Dayak people, Sarawak, Malaysia, early 20th century. The motifs of squatting human figures may represent deities but they may also be slaves, since ear ornaments of this type were worn by slave-holding aristocratic warriors of high status whose possessions often displayed motifs of captives. The sides are decorated with whirling motifs of the underworld *naga*/dragon fertility goddess.

23 Strings of glass beads with attached figurines of spirit guardians of carved bone or wood, Dayak people, Sarawak, Malaysia, early 20th century. These were attached to baby carriers and also worn as necklaces by shamans engaged in healing and propitiatory ceremonies.

24 Warrior's brass pectoral ornament, Naga people, north-western Burma/Myanmar, early 20th century. It depicts the number of human heads taken by the wearer. Heads symbolize fertility and prestige.

25 Gold pendants from northern Luzon in the Philippines, 18th–19th century, with motifs including human figures and horned deer. Their basic form also alludes to female genitalia. They express several ancient and widespread concerns about horns, warfare, prestige, the human head and body, the world of the ancestors, and fertility.

26 Toba Batak brass necklace with massive links, woven cotton balls, dangling bells, and a plaque elaborated with two male figures supporting a central disc. It formed part of the ceremonial regalia of the Rajah of Tonggeng in north Sumatra, Indonesia, and was still worn in the 1930s.

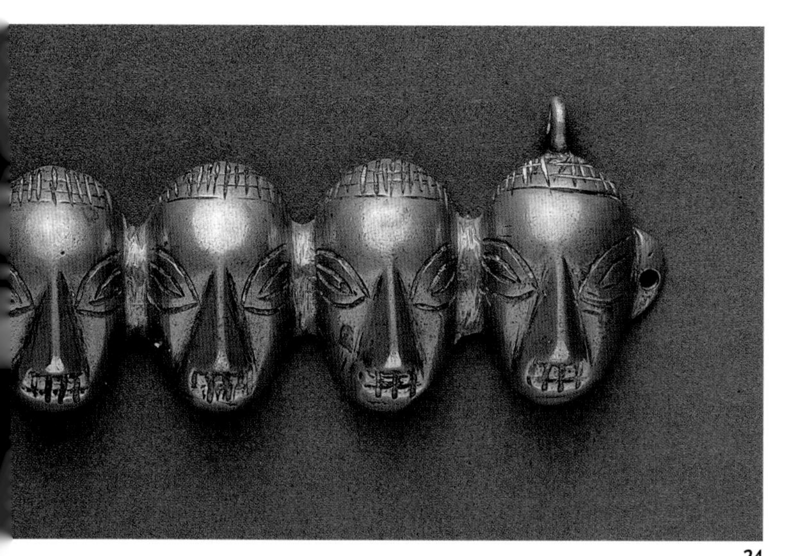

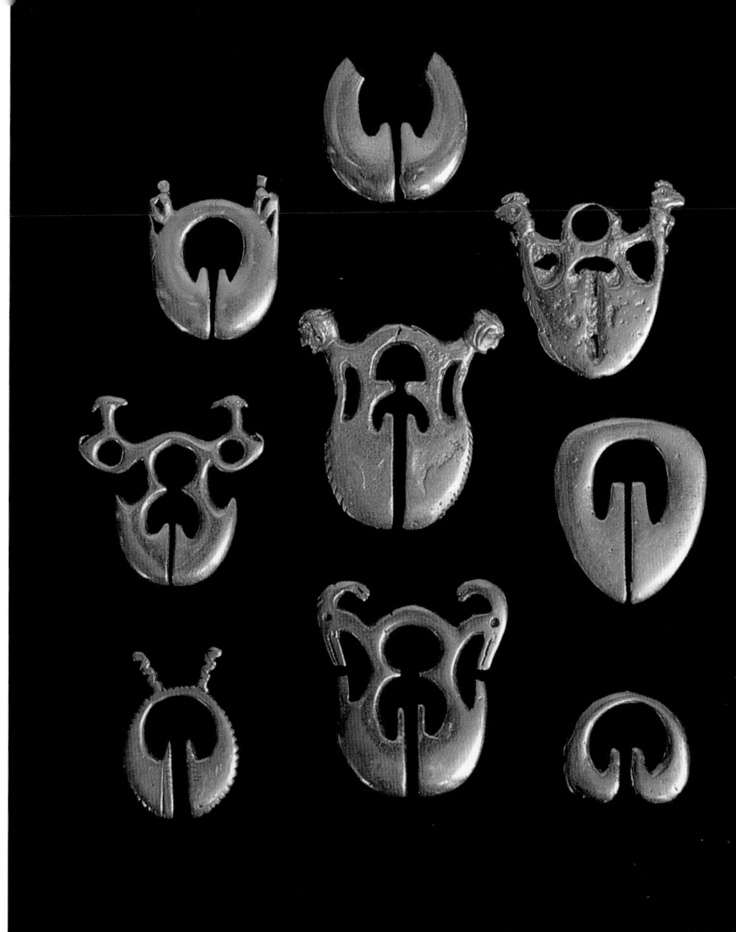

24

25

23

26

28

29

27 Gold burial ornaments for the eyes, nose and mouth, from the Philippines, 10th–13th century. Such ornaments have been found at several sites in island Southeast Asia. The bird images at the sides were probably attached to clothing.

28 A bronze bracelet decorated with spirals and surmounted by a pair of hornbills, Chin people, north-western Burma/ Myanmar, 19th–early 20th century. Hornbills are widely associated with high status and warrior prowess and regarded as spirit messengers.

29 Brass bracelet inlaid with copper, tin and iron, formed as the powerful and protective *singa*, whose body is composed of *naga* and elephant elements. Toba Batak people, north Sumatra, Indonesia, 19th century.

30 Two gold pectoral ornaments. The upper one shows a human figure wearing a necklace and a crown resembling the tree-like headdress worn on Sermata island, Maluku, eastern Indonesia. Trees extend from beneath the earth into the sky and thus symbolize the tiered cosmos. The lower pectoral, from Maluku, 19th–early 20th century, depicts a boat and its passenger, the ancestral founder of the community and the community itself. Embossed motifs include bird and breast images.

30

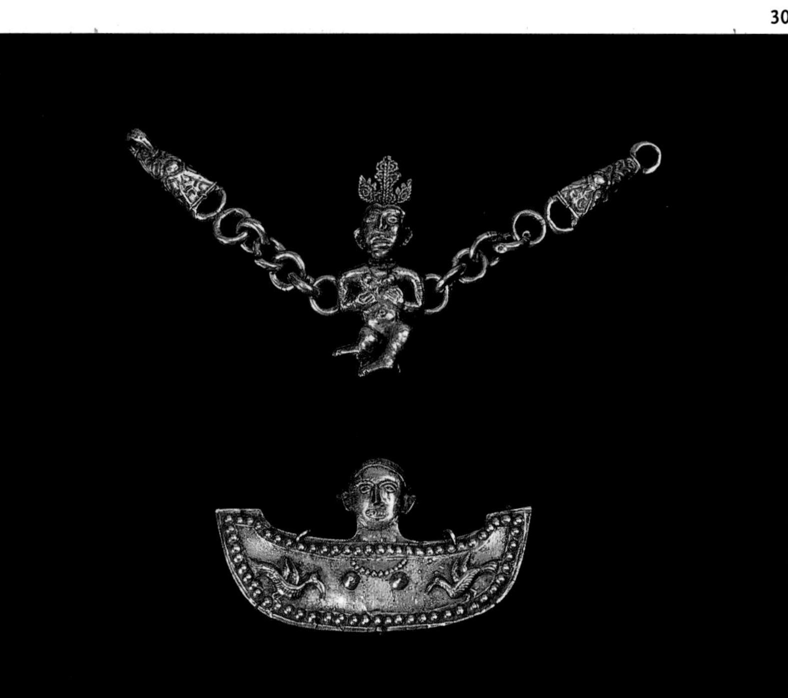

27

31 Blue and white beads with motifs of birds and sunbursts, found at a Sa Huynh site in central Vietnam, *c.* 300 BCE – 100 CE. Similar beads have been unearthed at Oc Eo and elsewhere in Southeast Asia as well as in India, where they are thought to have originated.

32 Objects found at Oc Eo in southern Vietnam, 2nd–5th century. The bronze pointed shaft (bottom) is probably a hairpin, while the stone block carved with leafy patterns may be a mould or a container for cosmetics. All the rest are goldsmith's tools: a large stone mould for producing split-ring ear ornaments, beads, and a medallion depicting a seated royal figure; a smaller mould; and a hammer-head and crucible.

33 Gold ornaments found at Oc Eo, 2nd–5th century. Applied filigree, the use of gemstones and flower motifs, and seal rings are of Indian and West Asian inspiration. The large spiky pendant (top centre), of gold sheet over a tin or lead cast core, resembles earlier stone and glass ornaments of the Sa Huynh type and ornaments later found in Indonesia and the Philippines. The small coronet (top right) is decorated with lotus motifs. The split-ring ear ornament (lower right) is hinged to permit easier fitting. The motifs of nippled breasts on the small ornament below that are typical of archaic Southeast Asian art. The bull ring depicts Nandi, vehicle of the Hindu god Shiva. The boldly moulded ear ornament is typical of first-millennium pieces found in the region.

34 Glass, rock crystal, agate and gold beads found at Oc Eo, 2nd–5th century. They show the advanced state of bead manufacture in early Southeast Asia. The agate beads may have been imported from India or made at Oc Eo from imported stone; it is likely that the others were made locally.

31

32

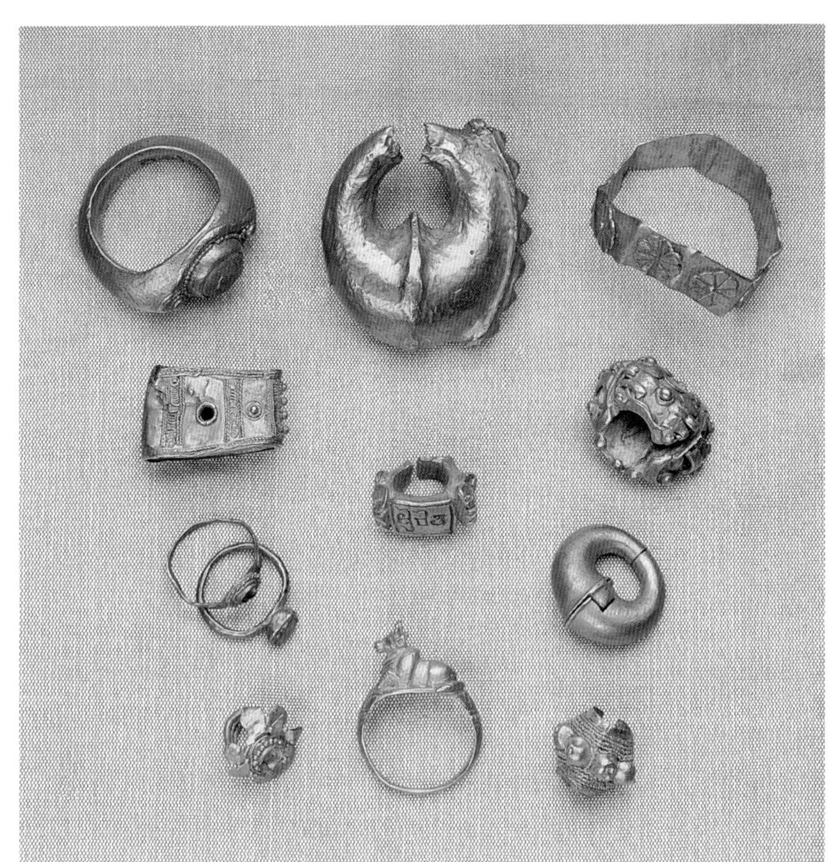

33

34

35

BURMA/MYANMAR

35 Royal crown worn by the last Burmese king, Thibaw (1878–86), from upper Burma/Myanmar, 19th century. It is constructed of leaves of gold sheet applied to a linen backing and supported by a rattan frame, and set with gemstones and iridescent insect wing-cases. Southeast Asian Buddhist crowns, like religious architecture, represent aspects of the cosmos. The fundamental shape evokes Mount Meru. The upper section of this crown is formed as a swelling banana bud (*amalaka*); the gem-studded umbrella above symbolizes royalty; the upper cone is surmounted by a gem at the pinnacle. The bell form is variously interpreted as a womb, the cosmos in miniature, or an upturned beggar's bowl evoking the ideals of poverty and chastity.

36 Pyu gold ornaments, including filigree, granulated and repoussé beads, seal and ruby-set rings, small pendants, and a gold ear-cylinder, 5th–9th century. The gold coins resemble those of silver found at the Pyu city of Beik-thano, at Mon sites in Thailand and at Oc Eo in southern Vietnam, and may date from the 1st–6th century. The floral stud with a long separate shaft attachment is similar to those worn in the Pagan period (1044–1287).

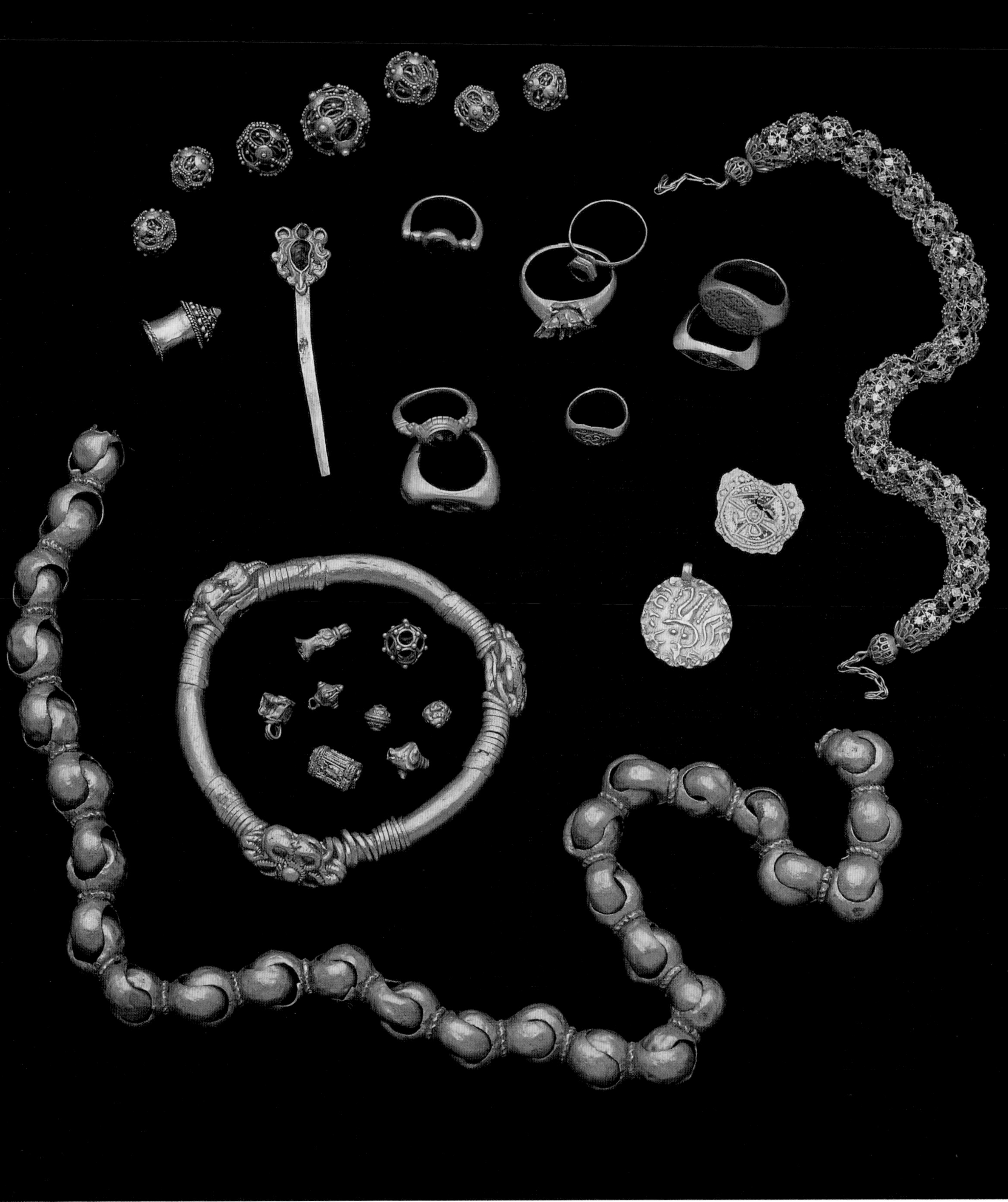

36

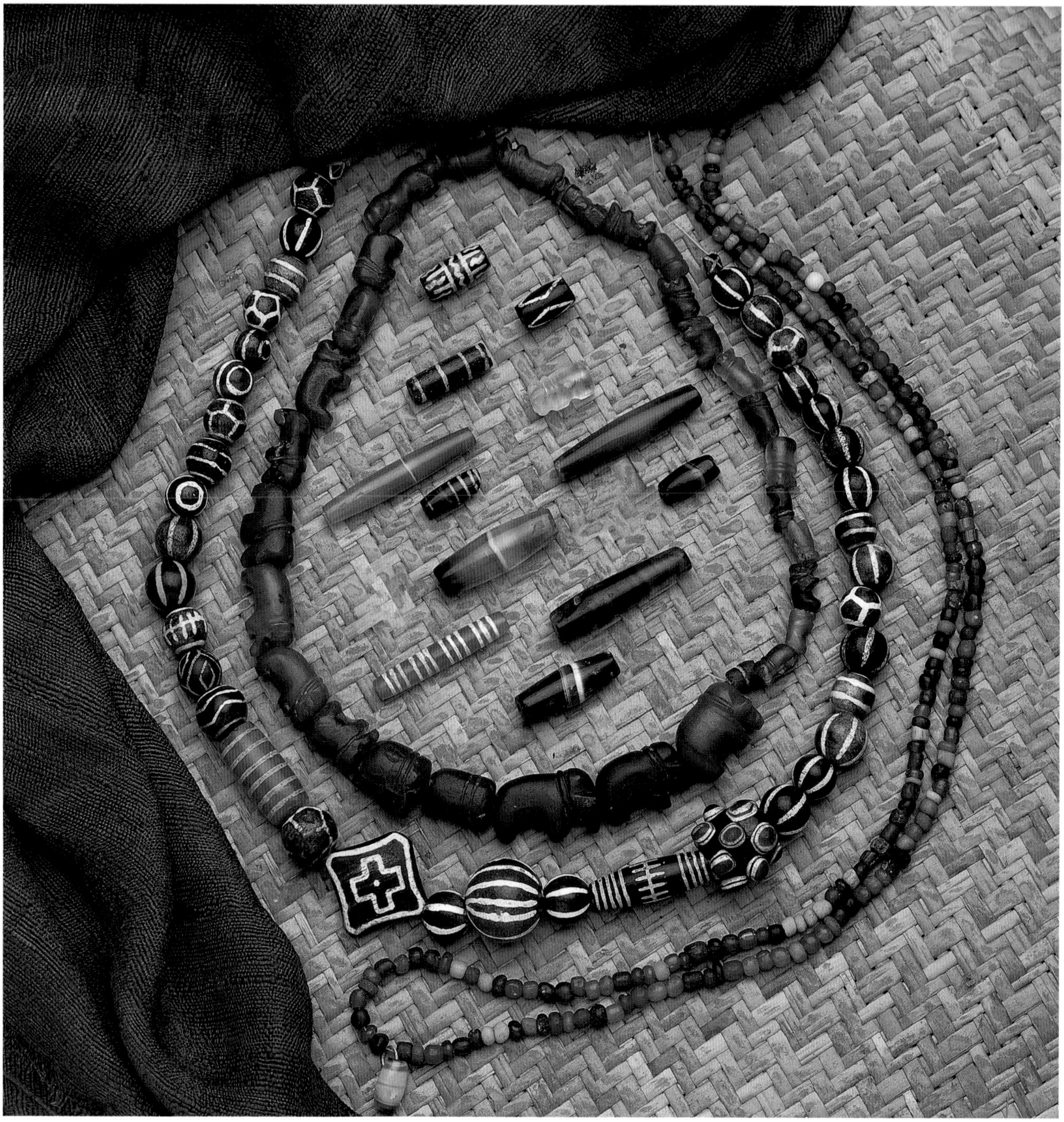

37

38

39

37 Beads found at 1st-millennium sites. Those of etched agate were undoubtedly imported from India. The black and white decorative beads known as *pumtek*, made from fossilized palm wood, were worn by the Pyu people *c.* 4th–9th century. Green jade and white rock crystal beads in animal form were worn by the Pyu and also in the Pagan period (1044–1287). Glass beads have been found at several Mon sites of southern Burma/Myanmar and in Thailand. The multi-eyed blue bead may have been made in China in the period of the Warring States (481–221 BCE) or later and acquired by trade.

38 Fine Pagan period ear-cylinder of gold sheet, decorated with granular ornament.

39 Seals of semi-precious stones, one engraved with an elephant and two with bulls, found at Pyu sites, *c.* 2nd–9th century. They were probably intended for rings.

40, 41

42

40, 41 Gold chain of crescent discs with very finely worked gold tassels, 19th century. This replicates in metal the long garlands with tassels of flower buds worn for some religious ceremonies, including that of the sacred thread held in Burma/Myanmar and Thailand for novices on their entry into a monastery. A chain of such magnificence may have been worn for ceremonies involving royal participants.

42 General's gilded helmet ornamented with gold wire netting, diamonds and rubies, from upper Burma/Myanmar, first half of the 19th century. Like the Burmese crown (Pl. 35), this also includes banana bud, umbrella and cone motifs and gemstones, and its bell form is similarly subject to various interpretations. Brimmed helmets were worn by senior officials at Buddhist courts throughout Southeast Asia.

43

44

45

43, 44 *Da-li-zan* necklace, of gold filigree stained red, with the peacock of the Kon-baung dynasty, and a gold necklace with dangling strings of pearls and gold elements, both mid-19th century. The late 19th-century gold ear-cylinders from Assam (then ruled by Burma/Myanmar) have opaque and translucent enamels, and lotus flower fronts set with rubies and emeralds in an Indian manner.

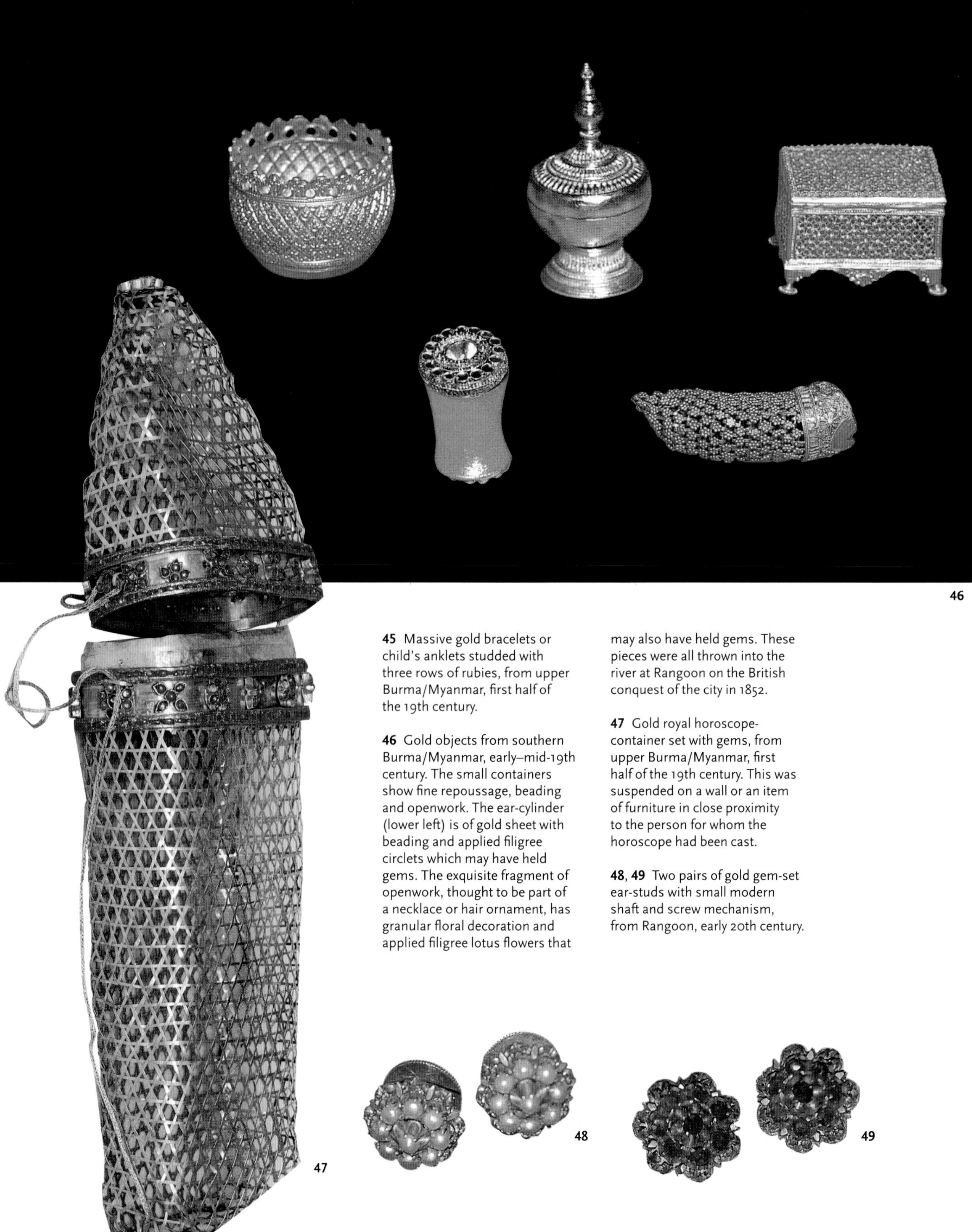

46

47

48

49

45 Massive gold bracelets or child's anklets studded with three rows of rubies, from upper Burma/Myanmar, first half of the 19th century.

46 Gold objects from southern Burma/Myanmar, early–mid-19th century. The small containers show fine repoussage, beading and openwork. The ear-cylinder (lower left) is of gold sheet with beading and applied filigree circlets which may have held gems. The exquisite fragment of openwork, thought to be part of a necklace or hair ornament, has granular floral decoration and applied filigree lotus flowers that may also have held gems. These pieces were all thrown into the river at Rangoon on the British conquest of the city in 1852.

47 Gold royal horoscope-container set with gems, from upper Burma/Myanmar, first half of the 19th century. This was suspended on a wall or an item of furniture in close proximity to the person for whom the horoscope had been cast.

48, 49 Two pairs of gold gem-set ear-studs with small modern shaft and screw mechanism, from Rangoon, early 20th century.

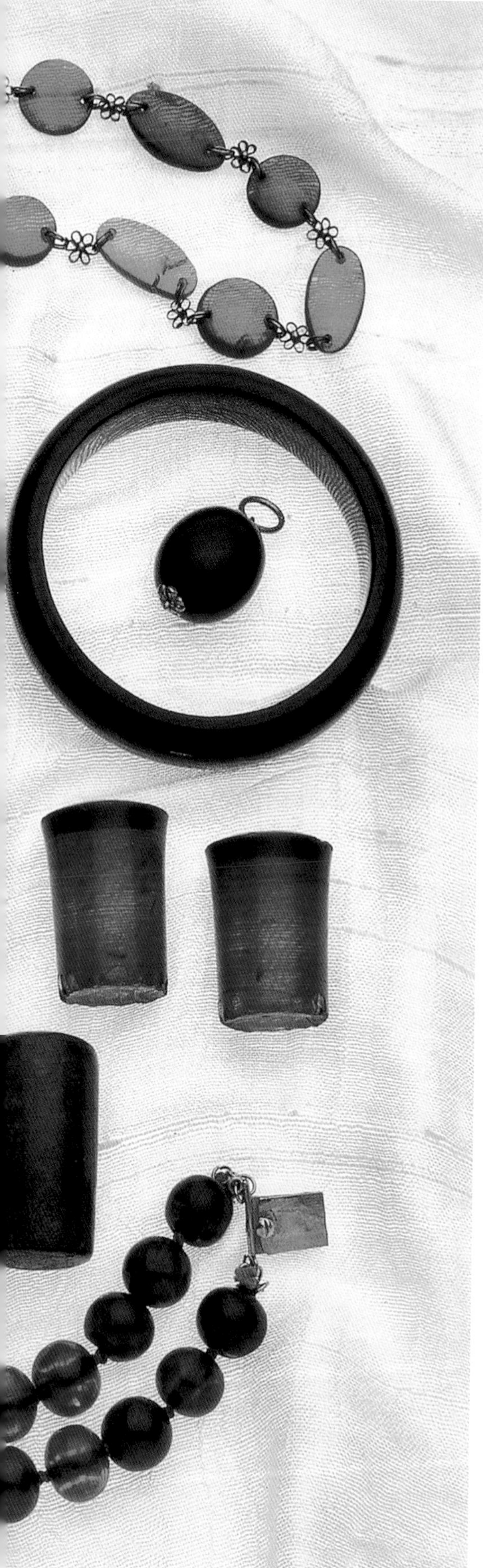

50

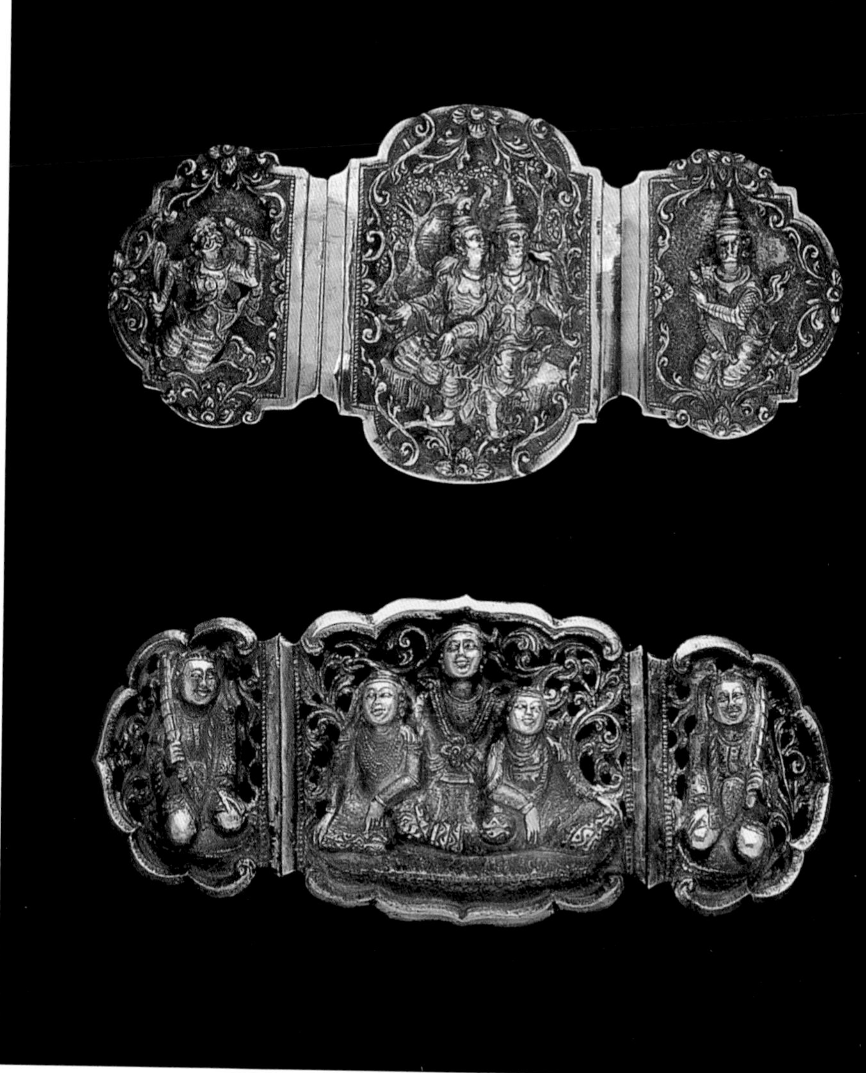

51

50 Amber jewelry, 19th century. Solid and hollow ear-cylinders were worn in the 19th century by Burmese; the long pointed types are still worn by the Kachin people. The buttons served to fasten the upper garment of Burmese women. One bracelet is carved from solid amber, the other made of beads linked by gilded spacers.

51 Two silver belt buckles, made in the northern Sagaing district but worn by men in the south with cloth sashes to secure the voluminous ceremonial *pah-so* lower garment. The upper one, of the early 20th century, depicts characters from the *Ramayana* epic; the lower one, of the 19th or early 20th century, shows a scene from the *Jataka* tales.

52 Jade ear-cylinders, Taung-ngu dynasty period, 18th century.

52

53 A Cham crown, necklace, bracelet and ear ornament of the 10th century, probably intended for the statue of a deity, were found at the temple complex of Mi Son in central Vietnam. The predominant motifs are lotuses and vegetation. The pyramidal forms surrounded by curling vegetation on the necklace and bracelet evoke Mount Meru. The bird ear ornament is thought to represent the phoenix, but may allude to Garuda, the eagle steed of Vishnu. The location of the originals is not known; these precise replicas were made by French colonial authorities in the early 20th century.

54 Cham ring from central Vietnam, 10th century (left), and two Cambodian gold rings, 7th–10th century.

55 A magnificently crafted Cham gold chain necklace of unusual richness and complexity, from central Vietnam, 10th century.

56 Gold ear ornaments which range from the plain split ring to elaborately moulded forms evoking fruit and plant forms, from Cambodia, 7th–10th century.

57 A pair of gold ear ornaments with beading, from Cambodia, *c*. 10th century. Each spoke is formed as a *naga*. Similar ornaments adorned the sculpted *devatas* (celestial female deities and guardians of Hindu mythology) at the 10th-century complex of Banteay Srei.

53

54

55

56

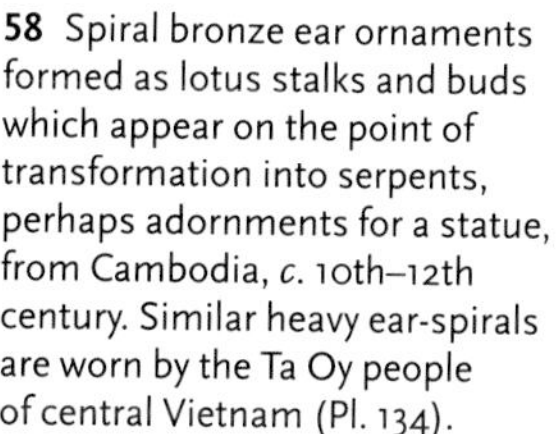

58 Spiral bronze ear ornaments formed as lotus stalks and buds which appear on the point of transformation into serpents, perhaps adornments for a statue, from Cambodia, *c.* 10th–12th century. Similar heavy ear-spirals are worn by the Ta Oy people of central Vietnam (Pl. 134).

59 Two Cambodian stone jeweller's moulds. One, from late 12th-century Angkor Thom, was used for casting bracelets, rings and beads. The other, found at Phnom Penh, may be 15th-century or later; gold sheet was probably beaten into it to make light pendants.

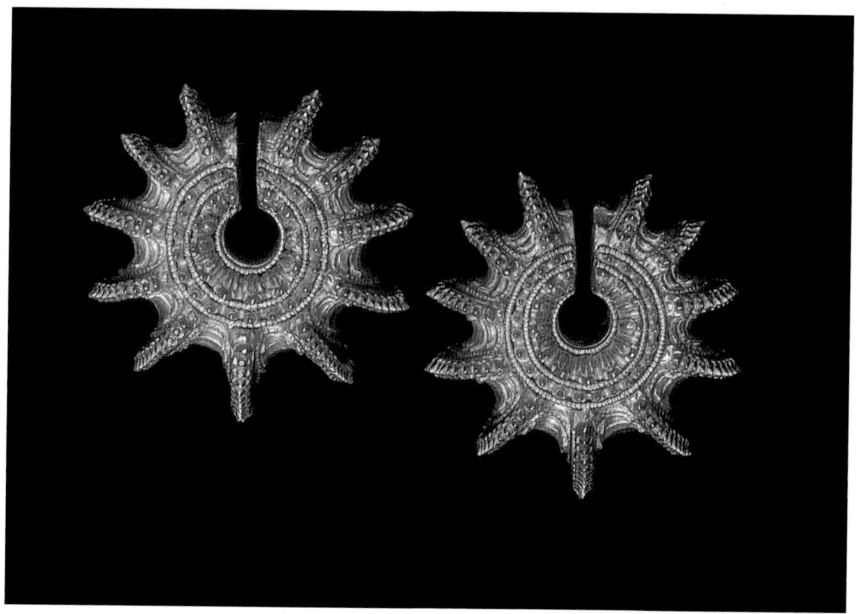

57

59

58

62

Cambodia

60 Gold pendant, 12th century or earlier. This magnificent piece, formed as an open lotus flower supported by stylized *nagas* and set with a rock crystal, resembles those worn by figures at 12th-century Angkor Wat.

61 An outstanding gold chain necklace, *c.* 12th century. Each terminal is formed as a *makara*, the mythical water monster composed of elephant, fish and crocodile elements, which symbolizes aquatic fertility and regeneration; their trunks are looped to form the clasp.

62 A 10th-century gold ring set with a rock crystal bears on each side the fearsome but protective mask of a *kala*, associated with Shiva and with Rahu, the demon of eclipses who symbolizes the death and rebirth of the world.

63 Gold ring with a rainbow arch supported by scrolls that suggest emerging *makaras*, 12th century.

64 Gold ring found at Angkor, with a split shank supporting a bezel with filigree decoration set with an amethyst, 12th–14th century or later.

65 Gold bracelet, 10th–12th century, composed of complex three-dimensional links formed as jasmine blossoms. Necklaces and bracelets of this type recall the wreaths of fresh jasmine noticed by the Chinese envoy Chou Ta-kuan (Zhou Daguan) in the late 13th century, and the floral garlands still worn today.

65

61

63

64

Cambodia

66 Small silver box for cosmetics or lime, 20th century. It depicts Micheno, the fish-tailed offspring of the monkey warrior Hanuman and the mermaid Supanamacha in the *Ramayana* epic, a very popular theme for containers since the 19th century.

67 Silver bracelet, boldly engraved and embossed with motifs of stylized birds and foliage, early 20th century.

68 Painted wooden sculpture of a richly adorned worshipper, originally at Angkor Wat; the low crown suggests emerging Thai influence, 15th–16th century. The fine gold chain is late 20th-century, but of traditional Cambodian style.

66

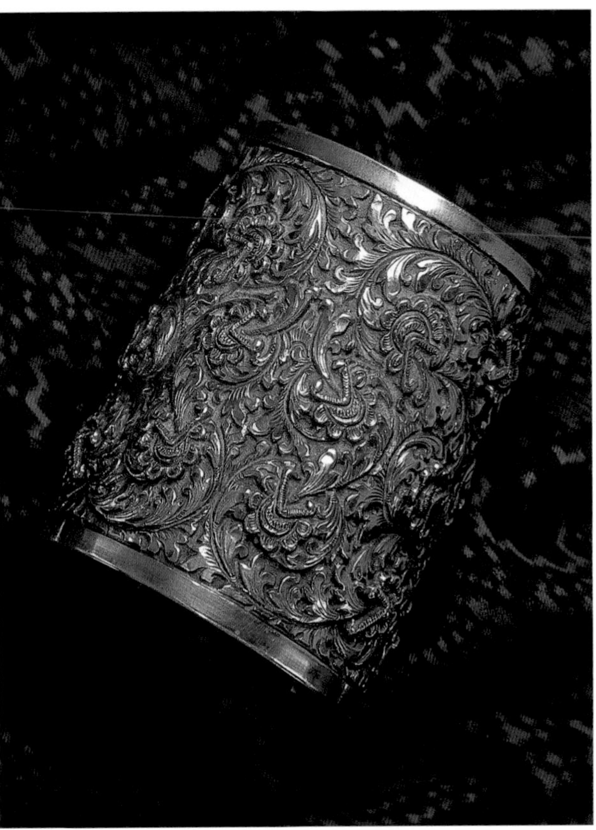

67

68

69

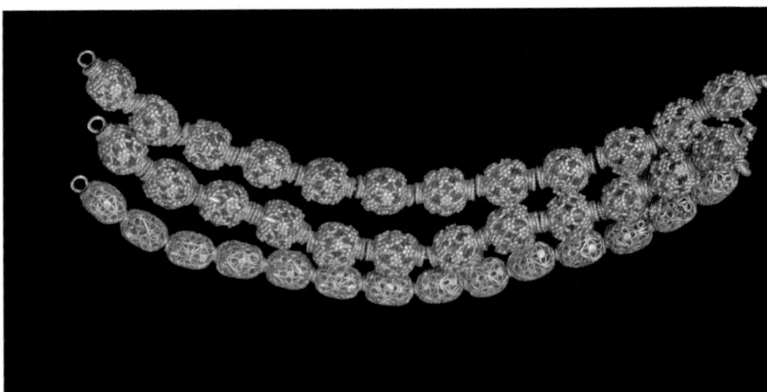

70

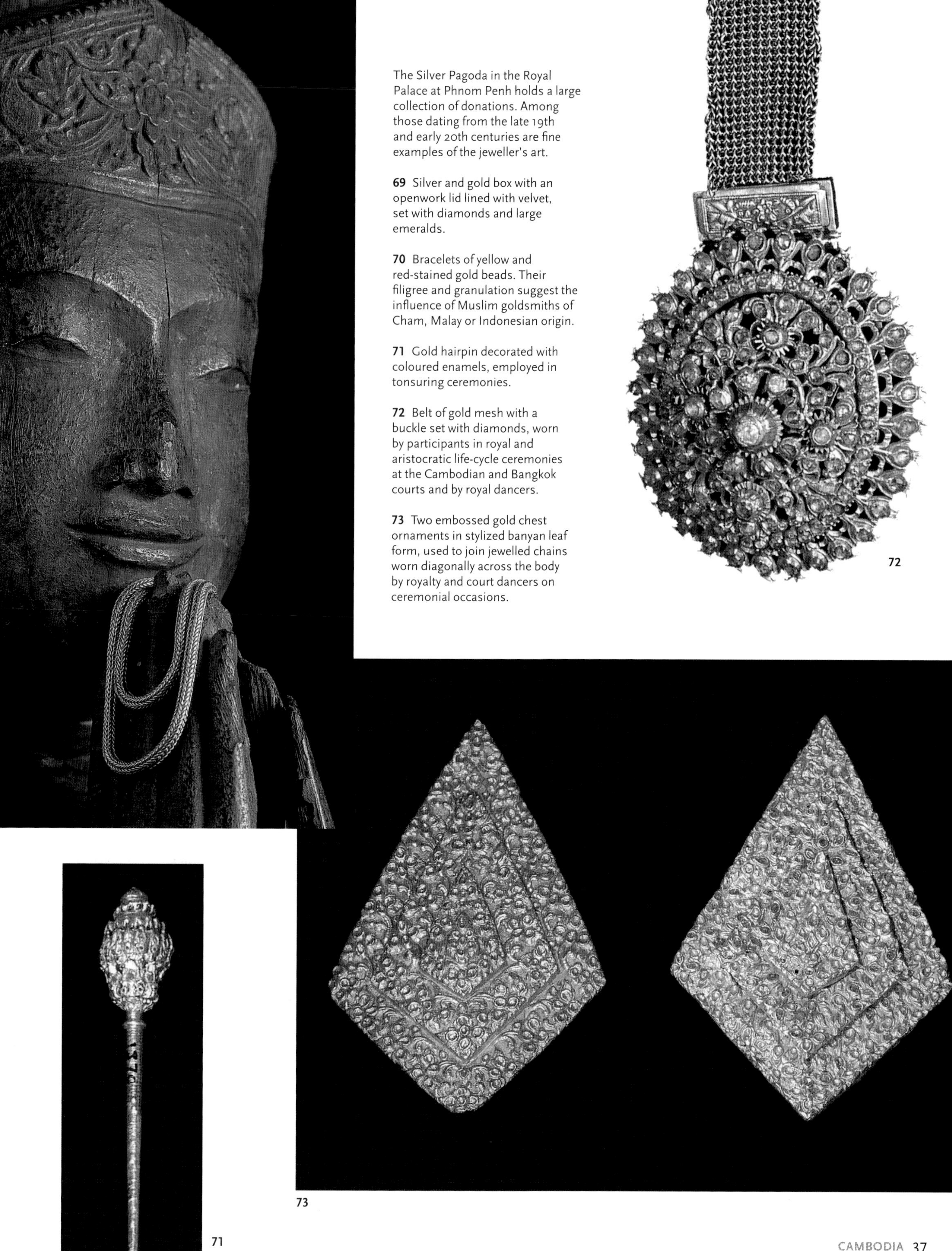

The Silver Pagoda in the Royal Palace at Phnom Penh holds a large collection of donations. Among those dating from the late 19th and early 20th centuries are fine examples of the jeweller's art.

69 Silver and gold box with an openwork lid lined with velvet, set with diamonds and large emeralds.

70 Bracelets of yellow and red-stained gold beads. Their filigree and granulation suggest the influence of Muslim goldsmiths of Cham, Malay or Indonesian origin.

71 Gold hairpin decorated with coloured enamels, employed in tonsuring ceremonies.

72 Belt of gold mesh with a buckle set with diamonds, worn by participants in royal and aristocratic life-cycle ceremonies at the Cambodian and Bangkok courts and by royal dancers.

73 Two embossed gold chest ornaments in stylized banyan leaf form, used to join jewelled chains worn diagonally across the body by royalty and court dancers on ceremonial occasions.

72

73

71

75

76

77

Cambodia and Champa

74 Collar of a bridal tunic worn in Cambodian communities in Soc Trang, south-eastern Vietnam, mid–late 20th century. The tunic shows Vietnamese influence, but the decoration of beads, spangles, iridescent beetle wing-cases and pompoms draws on ornamental traditions seen in sculpture at Angkor and in more recent court costume. Mirrors deflect ill fortune.

75 The four gilded bridal bracelets worn in Phnom Penh today are similar to those worn by a princess in Cambodian classical dance (cf. Pl. 77).

76 Cham gold ear-studs ornamented with filigree and cotton tassels, and a gold ring, all seen within a tinsel and cotton circlet worn on the head to support a large ceramic pot in which adolescent girls carry offerings at temple festivities for the New Year (*Kate*), mid–late 20th century.

77 The ornaments worn today by dancers playing regal characters in the Royal Cambodian Ballet reflect the forms and decorative styles current for court ceremonies in the 19th and early 20th centuries.

78

79

81

THAILAND AND LAOS

Thailand

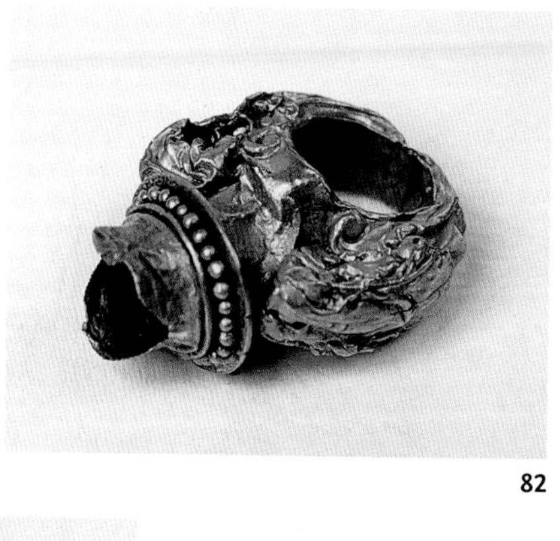

82

80

84

83

85

78 Gold ear ornaments with knobbed projections set with blue glass, Dvaravati period, 8th–11th century or earlier. Like other ear ornaments with spiky or knobbed projections from Oc Eo, from Java, north Sumatra and Maluku in Indonesia, and from the Philippines (Pls 33, 223, 243, 324), these may represent stylized *nagas*. The hinge mechanism is similar to that on some ear ornaments found at Oc Eo.

79 Split-ring ear ornaments, Dvaravati period, 8th–11th century or earlier.

80 Small gold split-ring ear ornaments, Dvaravati period, 8th–11th century or earlier. They bear the projecting spheres and hemispheres also found on ornaments from Oc Eo (Pl. 33) and Java. The piece on the extreme right was composed by soldering together a series of small discs (cf. Pl. 164).

81 Dvaravati beads, 8th–11th century or earlier. Some may have been made locally, but others, such as the dark blue bead with the white sunburst, are probably Indian (cf. Pl. 31).

82 High-shouldered gold repoussé ring, Dvaravati period, 8th–11th century.

83 Gold ornaments found at Uthong, Dvaravati period, 8th–11th century or earlier. Thought to have been fitted to the upper helix of the ear, they are formed to resemble the *vajra* (thunderbolt) of Hindu and Buddhist symbolic traditions; the same type was worn in central Java (Pl. 164).

84 A gold finger-ring set with coloured stones and a small hinged ruby-set earring, both embellished with granulation and filigree, from central Thailand, 12th–16th century. The gold mango-shaped pendant with granular ornament is thought to have originated in Sukhothai.

85 Gold ear-cylinder from north-western Thailand with exceptionally fine applied filigree decoration and granular beading, 10th–14th century. The style suggests Burmese influence.

86

Thailand

86–88 The Burmese attacked the Thai capital, Ayutthaya, in 1549 and subsequently conquered it in 1596. During this period a number of magnificent 15th-century royal ornaments were covered in bitumen and hidden from the invaders in Wat Ratchaburana. Among the pieces recovered later by the Thai Antiquities Department are many gold rings (Pl. 86), a gold gem-set nobleman's helmet which was supported with a rattan frame (Pl. 87), and fragments of royal chains, a chest ornament and bracelets (Pl. 88). They are worked with great skill in the techniques of applied filigree, openwork and beading. Many still hold the original precious and semi-precious stones, which provide a rich polychrome effect. The broader gem-set chain fragments in which twining ribbons, buds and shoots appear to overlap to form a textured three-dimensional effect are masterpieces of the jeweller's art.

87

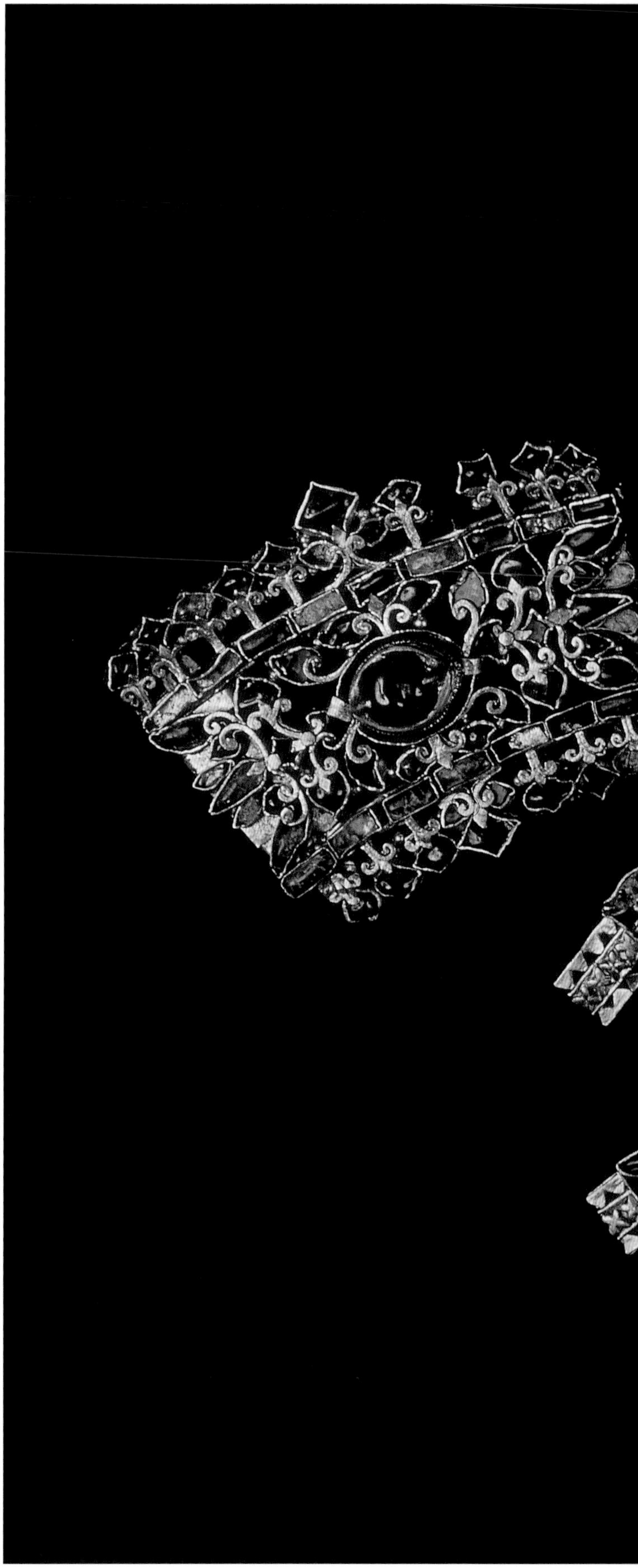

88

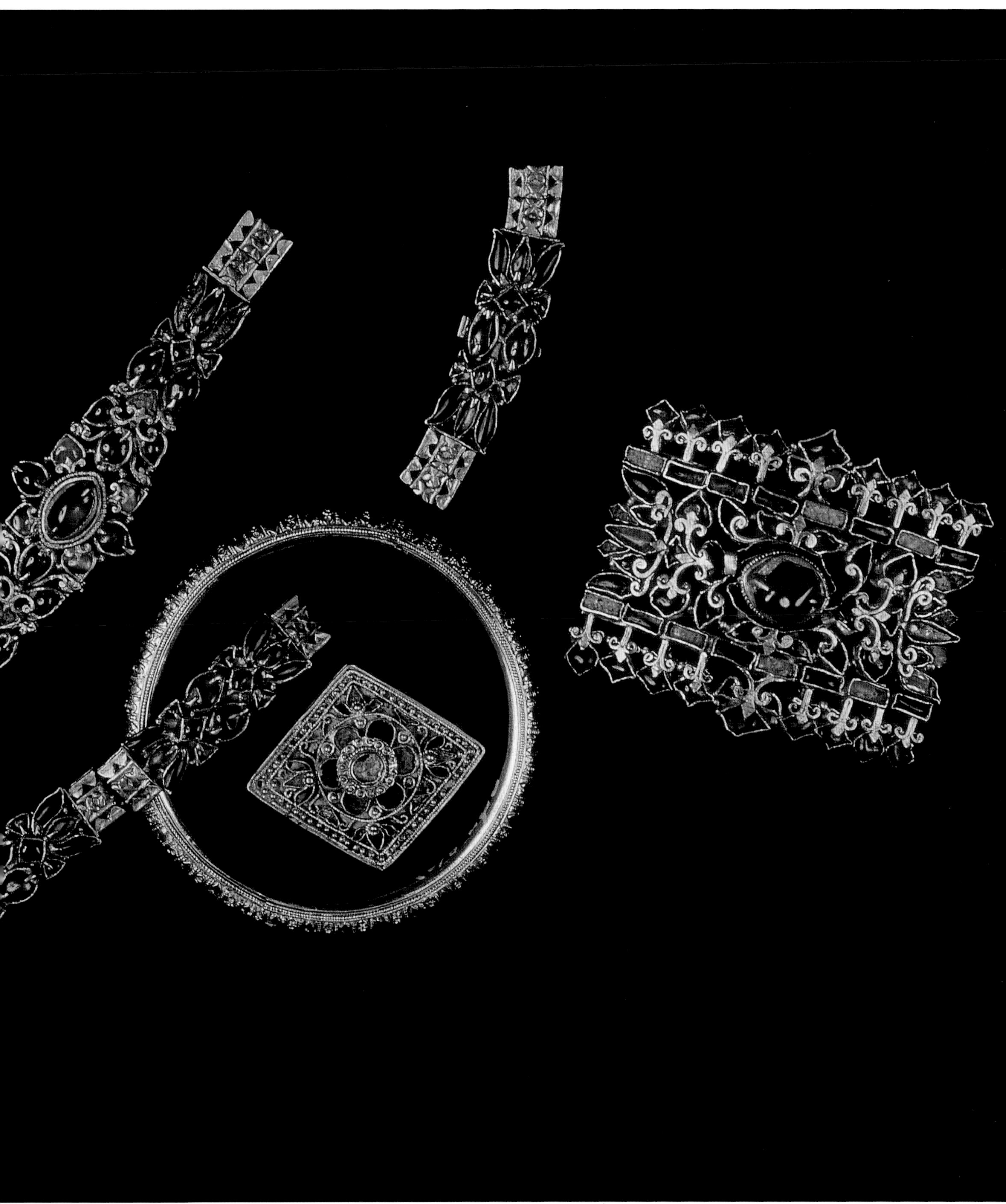

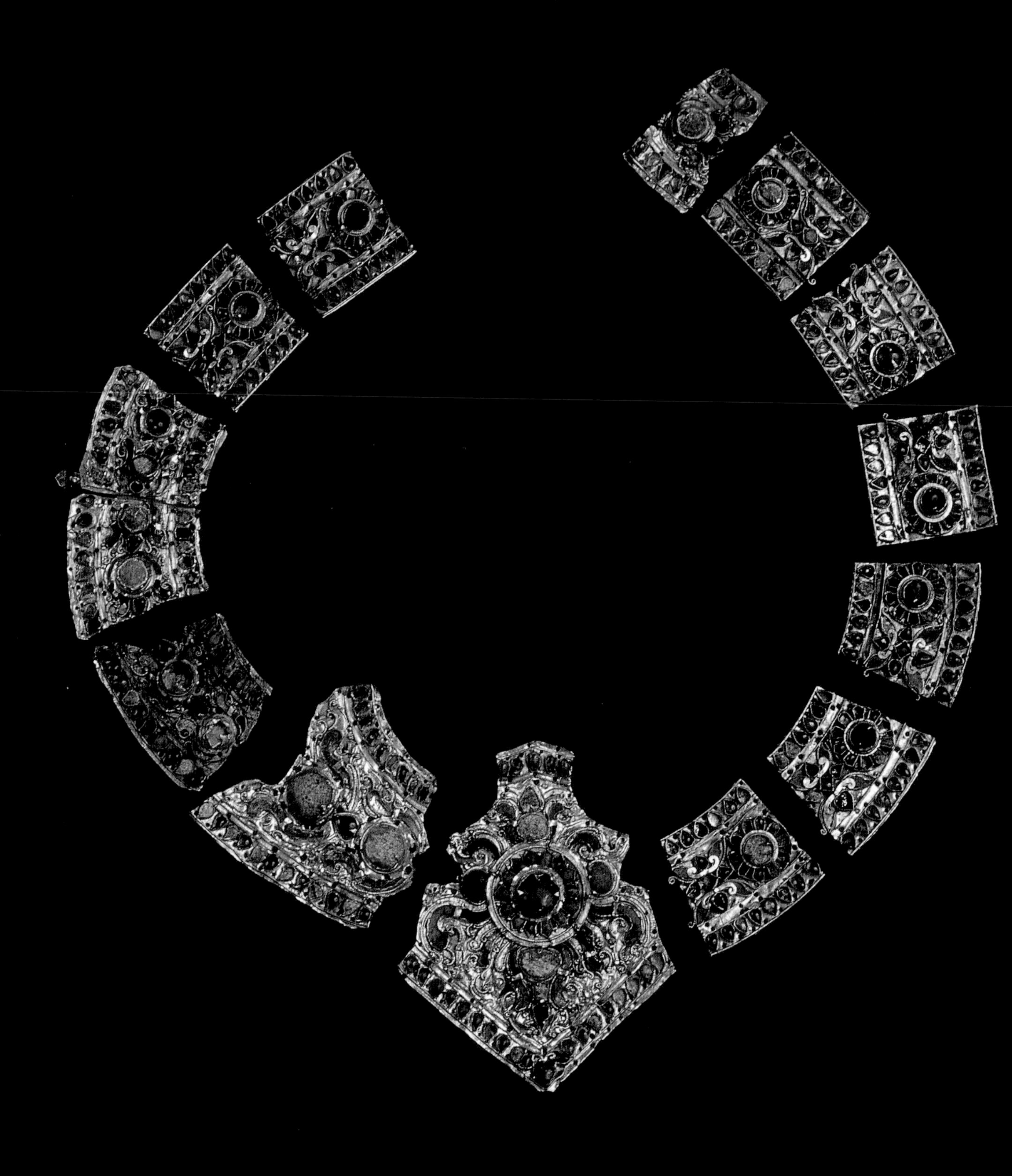

89

90

Thailand

These 15th-century royal ornaments were also hidden at Wat Ratchaburana, Ayutthaya (cf. Pls 86–88). They display the diversity of techniques and stylistic influences current at Ayutthaya.

89 Gold collar composed of separate elements. Again, the complex surface texture and the colour provided by gemstones are used to greatest effect.

90 Gold leafy pendant with a central stone, subtly embossed with vegetal motifs. It is an early example of the central pendant seen in later necklaces in Thailand, Indonesia (cf. Pls 194, 265, 270, 272) and the Malay Peninsula (Pls 293, 294).

91 Embossed openwork gold bracelet, set with gems. This shows some continuity with earlier Cambodian embossed jewelry decorated with bold curvilinear motifs and whorls.

91

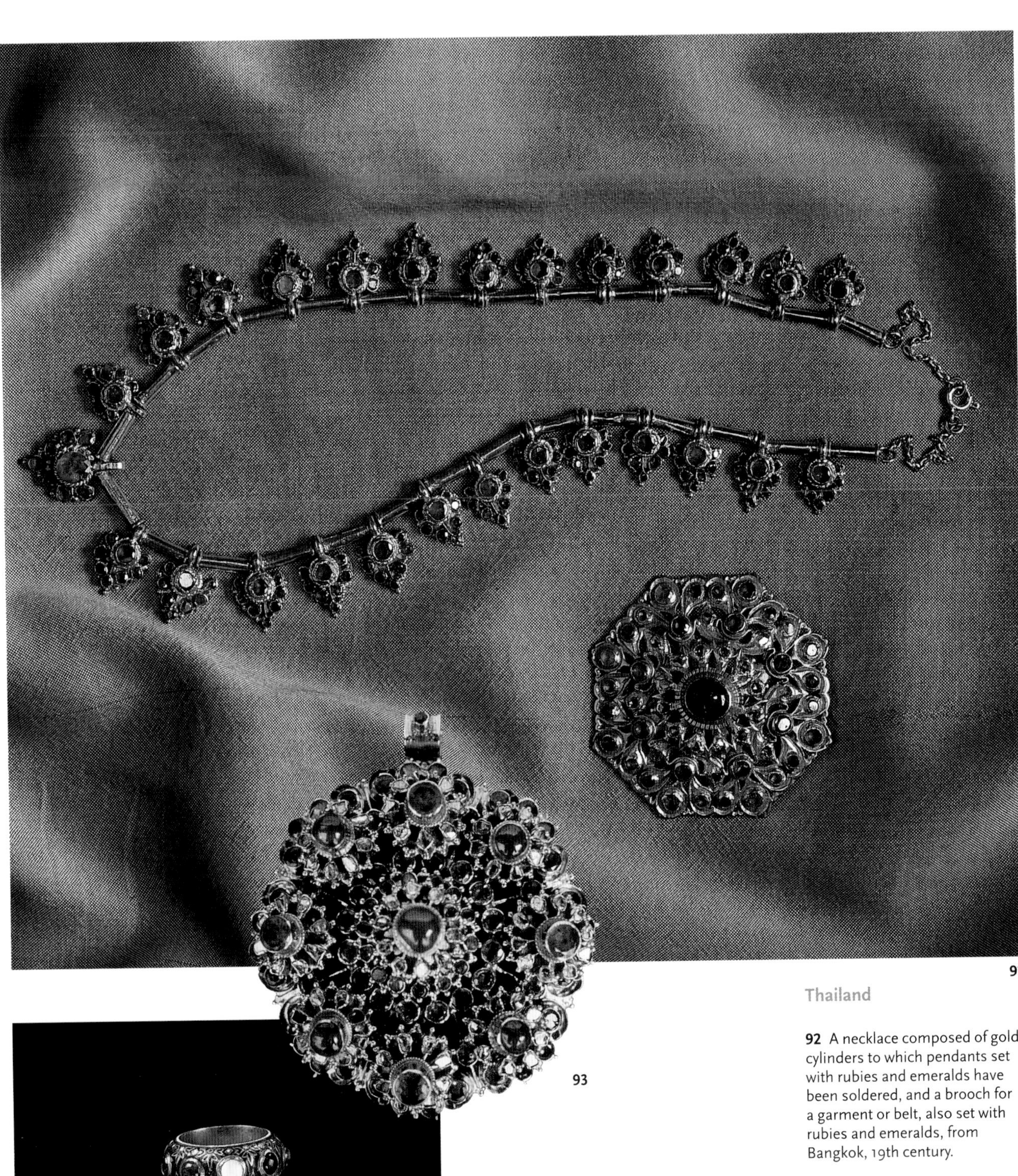

92

93

94

Thailand

92 A necklace composed of gold cylinders to which pendants set with rubies and emeralds have been soldered, and a brooch for a garment or belt, also set with rubies and emeralds, from Bangkok, 19th century.

93 Gold pendant of complex construction, richly ornamented with very fine rubies and emeralds and clear stones, which can also be worn as a brooch, 19th century.

94 The upper three rings, with fine gems, filigree and enamel, are outstanding examples of 19th-century Bangkok jewelry. The lower repoussé gold rings, set with large cabochon rubies, date from the 18th century.

95–97 Gold pendant and buckle ornamented with coloured enamels and rose-cut diamonds set in resin, from Bangkok, 19th century. The necklace is more recent. The back of the buckle (Pl. 97) shows the mechanism for attaching it to a belt and the engraved floral decoration which gave pleasure to the owner but was unseen by others.

98 Gold armlets set with rubies, which also display interior floral engraving, from Bangkok, 19th century. They were worn at the royal court.

99 A belt of finely woven gold mesh with a gem-set buckle, and two other buckles ornamented with precious stones that would have been worn with such a belt, from Bangkok, late 19th–early 20th century. Some influence of Western expatriate jewellers is apparent in the floral sprays on the two enamelled buckles.

100 Diamond-set buttons used to fasten the velvet and brocade jackets worn by wealthy men, from Bangkok, 19th century.

95

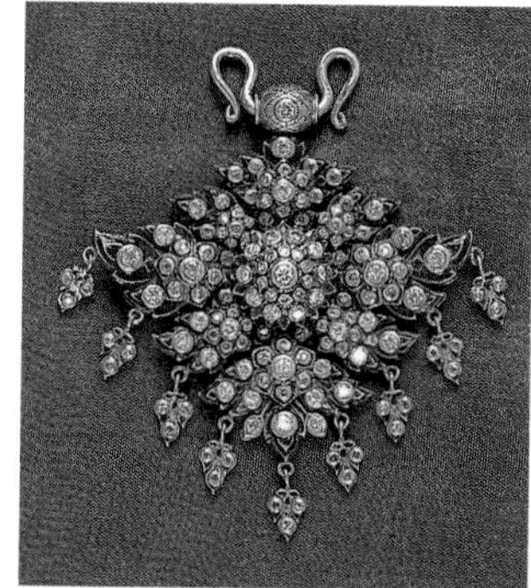

96

97

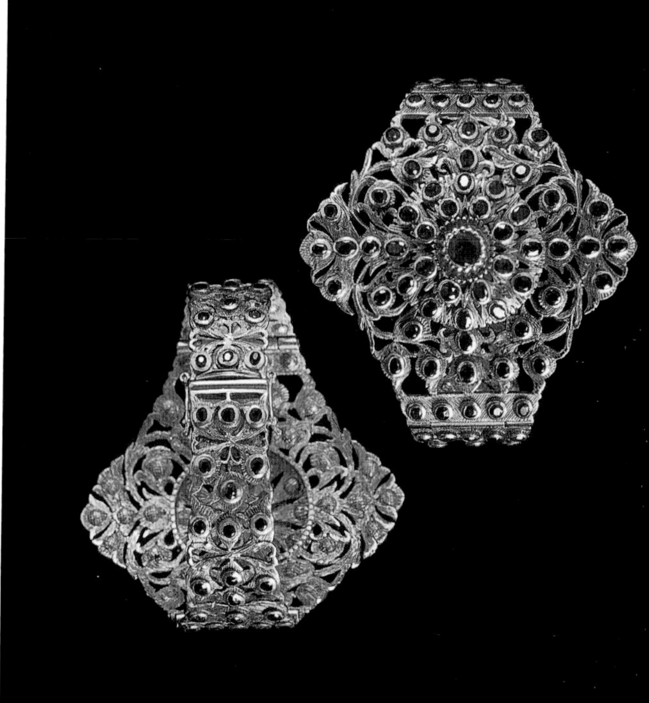

98

100

99

Thailand

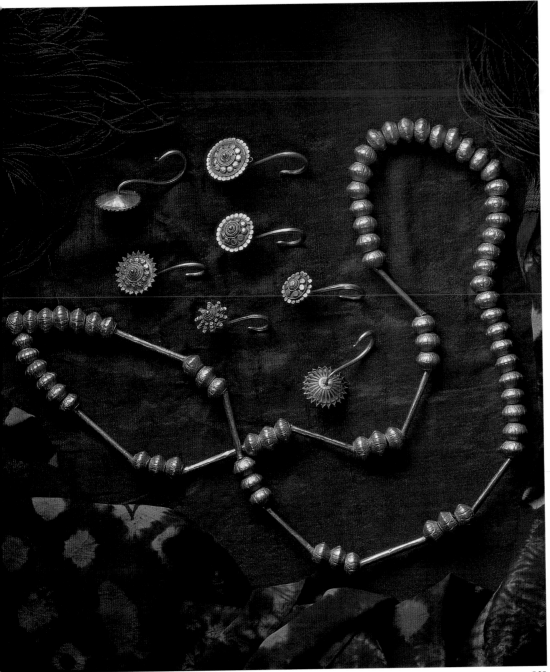

101 Gold ear-pendants, and a chain composed of gold *takrut* cylinders and resin beads covered with gold foil, 19th century. The ear-pendants, decorated with granulation and applied filigree, were secured by a long S-shaped hook passed through a hole in the lobe; ornaments of this type were worn in Thailand and Cambodia and resemble the *nata brongto* ear-pendants of Java (Pl. 185).

102 Hollow gold anklets with lotus-bud tips and delicate engraving in key fret patterns, from Bangkok, 19th century.

103 Gold hairpin stained red and ornamented with filigree and gems, from Bangkok, 19th century. Such hairpins were employed to secure the topknot of hair subsequently cut off at the tonsuring ceremony.

101

102

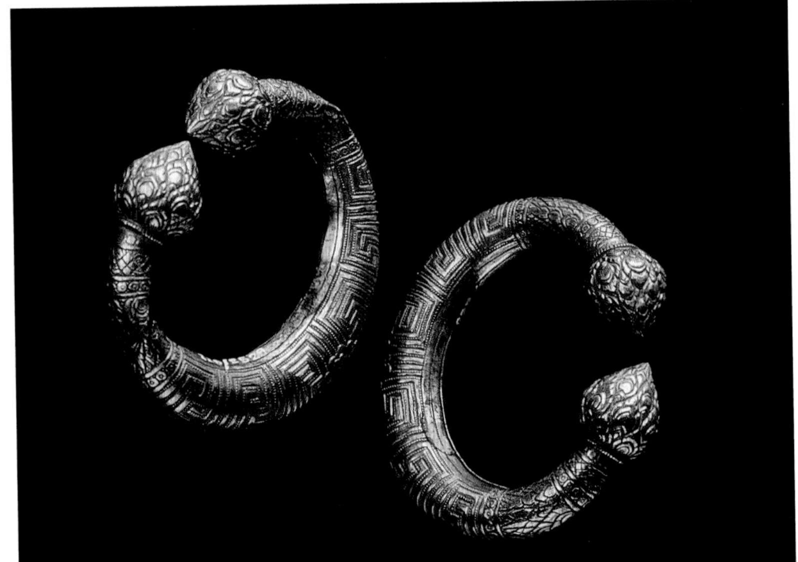

104 Gold ring in the form of a *naga*, set with rubies and richly decorated with enamels, 19th century or earlier. This and a similar well-known ring were acquired in Burma/Myanmar in the early 20th century by Western collectors; however, most known examples are owned by the Bangkok nobility and are regarded as family heirlooms.

105 A man's gold naga ring with a ruby tongue, from central Thailand, 18th century.

106 In this late 18th-century woman's ring from Ayutthaya, a lotus bloom set with a central garnet and rubies is supported by a pair of tiny serpents. The lotus is composed of a clay core covered with gold sheet. The faceted rubies were set at a later date into shallow depressions. This style of ring was popular in Java in the 19th century and probably before.

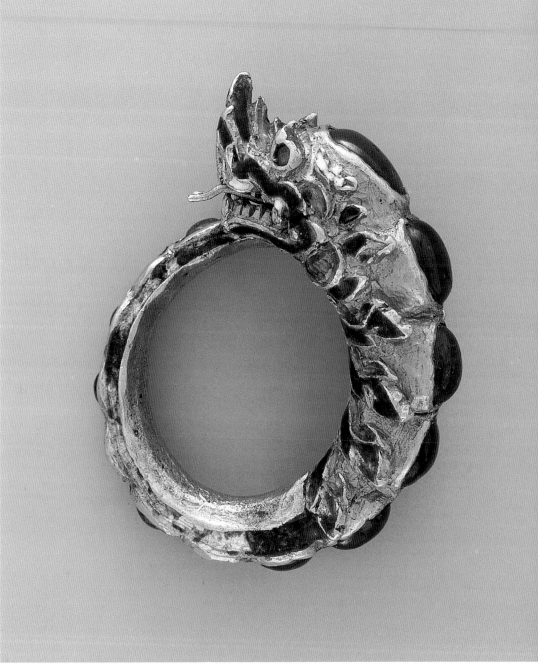

104

103

105

106

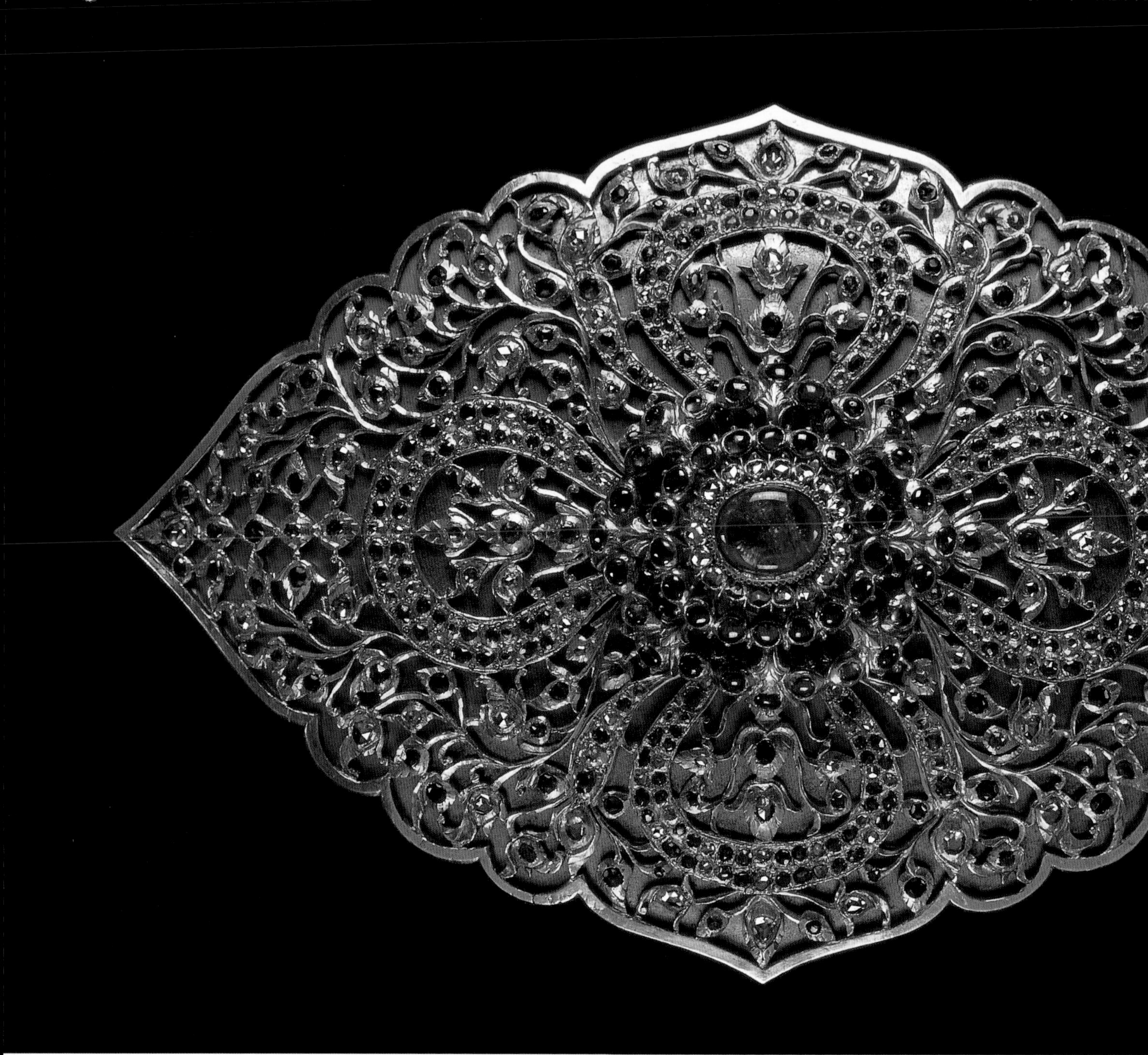

Thailand and Laos

107 A magnificently crafted buckle, of pink gold surmounted by a pierced plaque of yellow gold which is decorated with motifs of shoots and buds and set with cabochon emeralds and rubies and rose-cut diamonds, 19th century. The gently lobed ogival shape and piercing suggest Malay (cf. Pl. 283) and Malay–Chinese influences prevalent in southern Thailand.

108 These 19th-century gold rings from southern Thailand show Malay influence in the combination of red staining and granulated decoration.

109 A plaque of red-stained gold with embossed leafy patterns, from Shan state, on the Burma/Myanmar–northern Thailand–Laos border, 19th century. It was attached to the chignon with a broad pin soldered at the back.

108

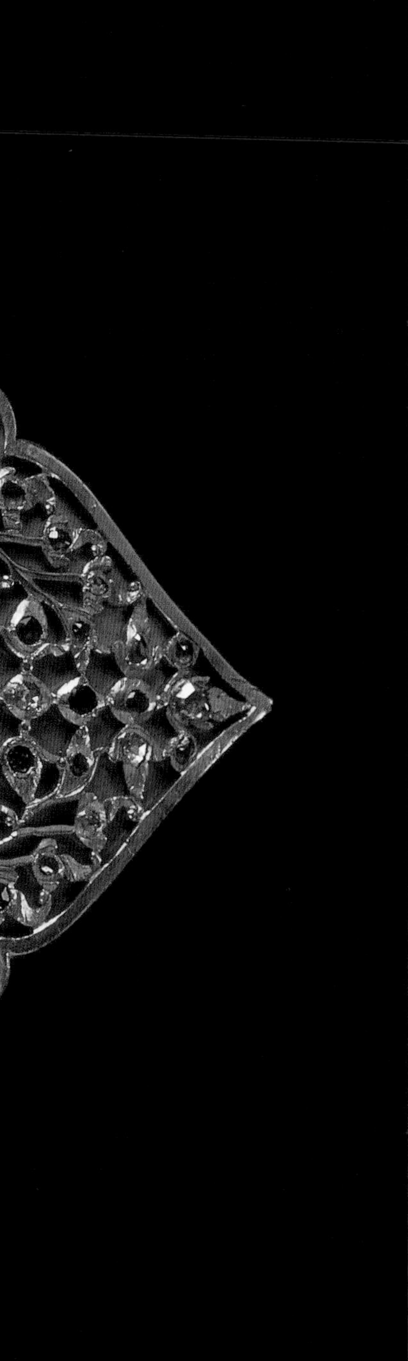

107

109

110 Gold ring embossed and engraved with floral motifs and set with a dark peridot, from Luang Prabang, Laos, late 18th century. It is likely to have been made from alluvial gold, traditionally panned in the Mekong river near Luang Prabang.

111 Traditional ear-studs, hair chain and hairpins of red-stained gold, made in Vientiane. Although these examples are recent, they are consistent with Lao jewelry shown in 19th-century murals and 19th- and early 20th-century photographs. The ear-stud attachments have been reduced considerably to accommodate small lobe-holes.

110

111

112

113

114

Thailand and Laos

112 Hollow silver bracelets from northern Thailand or Laos, engraved and embossed with unusually free-flowing vegetal motifs, 19th century.

113 A pair of bracelets of twisted hollow silver tubes and twisted solid silver cords, which may have originated in the borderlands of Yunnan–northern Vietnam–Laos.

114 Silver bracelets worn by Thai, Lao, and also immigrant ethnic Tai (Tai-speaking people from countries outside Thailand) and other minority groups such as the Akha and Lahu living in northern Thailand and Laos in the 19th and 20th centuries. The large hollow etched bracelets (centre) are of Shan manufacture. Solid silver bracelets with lotus tips (far right) were made by the Shan, and were worn by them and by other groups to whom they were sold. Another Shan solid silver bracelet appears far left. The bracelet with coiling (front left) is a similar but more rustic version of gold types which adorned Lao aristocracy in the 19th century and are worn today at traditional festivals in Luang Prabang. The bracelet of massive silver cords (rear centre) is of the kind worn in pairs by Princess Ubon of Chiang Mai in a photograph taken in 1867, and may have the same origin as the twisted silver pair (Pl. 113).

115 Lao daggers from Luang Prabang, Laos, 19th century or earlier. The silver hilts and scabbards are embossed and engraved with a typically dense arrangement of vegetal ornament and flowers in lozenges and with the three-headed elephant of Indra (the insignia of the royal family and the Lao state). One hilt is of ivory. Daggers of this type were employed in marriage ceremonies as symbols of protection.

116

116 Silver ring set with a black stone and ornamented with spirals of silver wire, from the Vientiane area of Laos, early 19th century.

117 Two silver belts with embossed panels that depict zodiacal and mythical animals and birds, from the Vientiane area, early 19th century. In one, the panels are separated by chains and decorative sections of spiral wire. Both fasten by means of a separate buckle that hooks into the belt terminals.

118 Silver buckles with chain or spiral wire belts. The embossed buckles with vegetal, lotus and bird motifs were made in the Lamphun, Chiang Mai and Lampang districts and are typical of northern Thailand in the 19th century. The arrangement of conical motifs on the buckle at the bottom resembles that on brooches worn by Shan women, which evoke a central Mount Meru surrounded by subsidiary mountains.

117

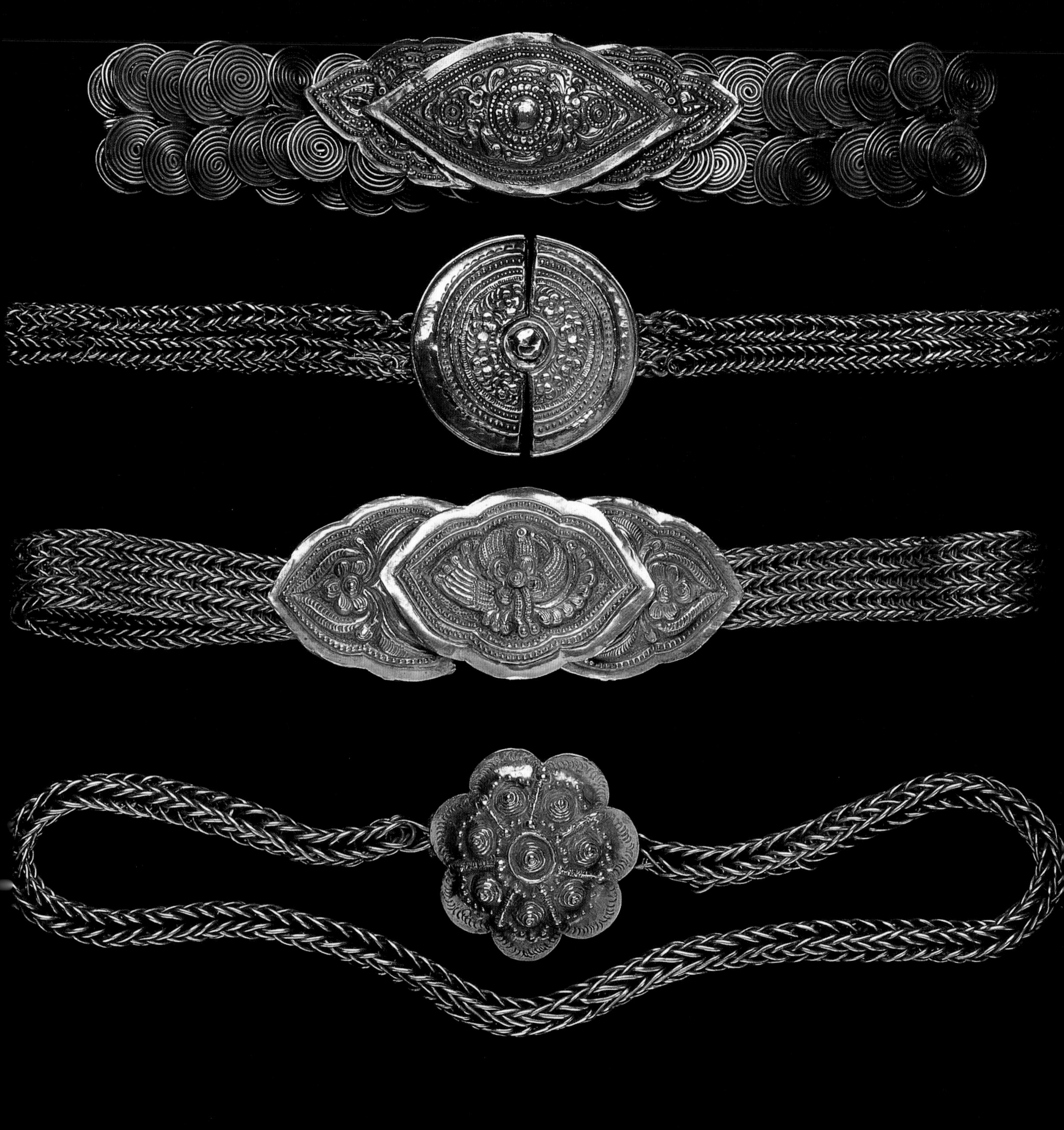

118

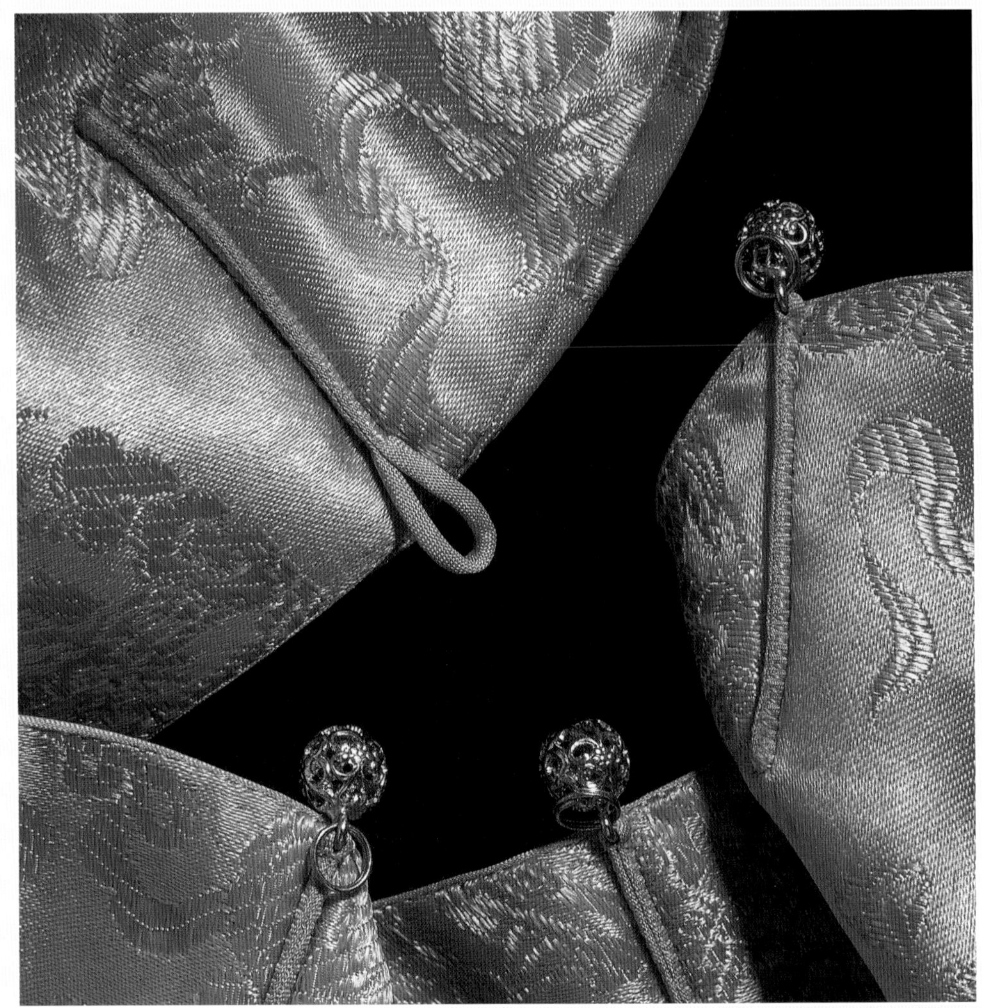

119

VIETNAM

119 Gold filigree buttons from Hue, central Vietnam, of the type that ornamented the sleeves of gowns worn on a daily basis by the Emperor Khai Dinh (1916–28).

120–122 Silver ceremonial sword of state from Hue, central Vietnam, used by the Emperor Tu Duc (1848–83). The details show the high quality of Vietnamese engraving, set off by fine ring-matting for the backgrounds. The animal motifs include the unicorn and the dragon, which together with the phoenix and the tortoise comprise the four creatures accorded supernatural powers. Each Nguyen emperor, commencing with Gia Long in 1802, commissioned a ceremonial sword.

120

121

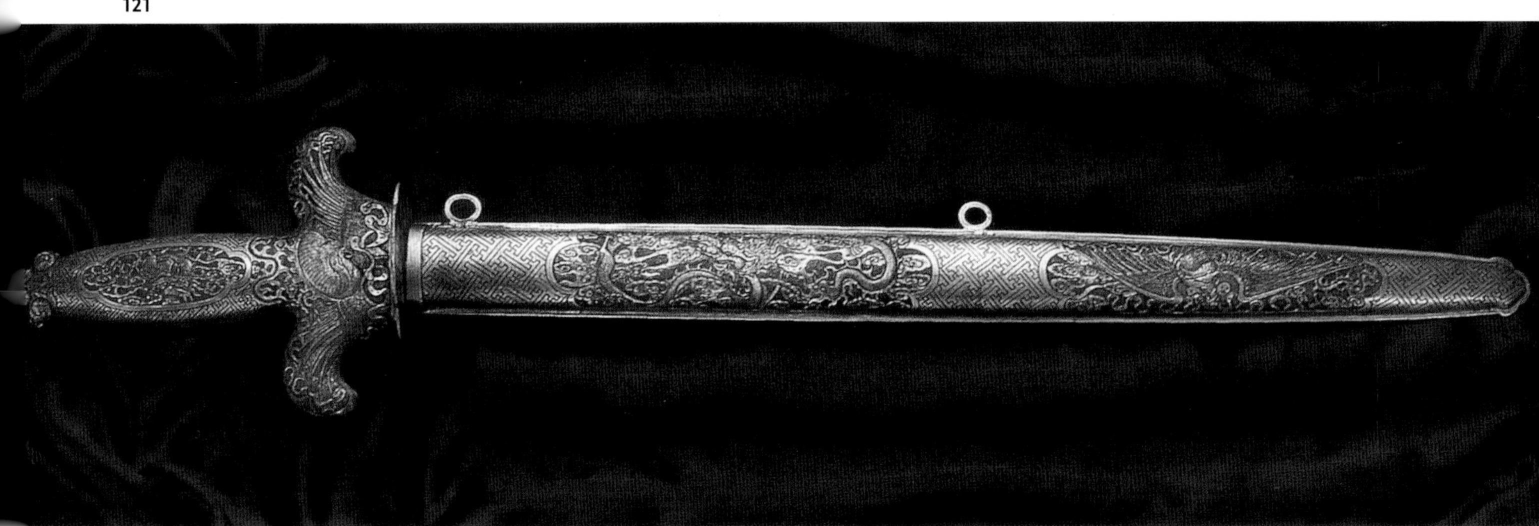

122

123 Portrait of a royal lady, painted by an unknown artist at the palace at Nah-trang, southern Vietnam, early 20th century. She wears the delicate filigree ear-pendants typical of the Hue court and her gown is fastened by a jade plaque. She may be Tu Cung, mother of the Emperor Bao Dai, in her later years, or Khai Dinh's last secondary queen, Ho Thi Chi.

124 Detail of a ceremonial gown of Tu Cung, from Hue, central Vietnam, early 20th century. It is fastened by a split and hinged red-stained gold plaque.

123

124

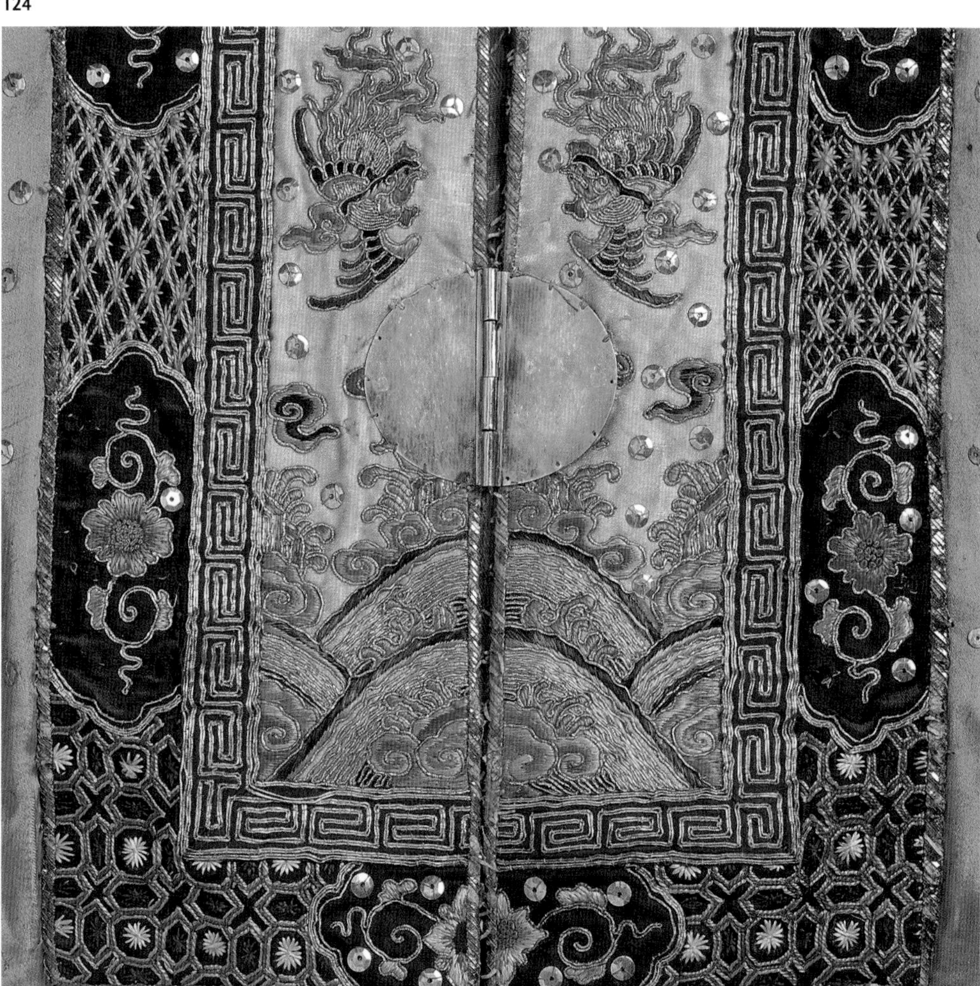

125 Gold openwork torque with the embossed dragon and phoenix motifs of the Nguyen dynasty; though recent, it is the same as those worn at the Hue court in the early 20th century. The gold ear-pendants of delicate filigree with flower vases, tiny phoenixes and dangling spangles, set with clear sapphires, are typical of those worn by female courtiers and the wives of mandarins. Today both types serve as wedding jewelry in Hue and are made by descendants of the royal artisans, who belong to the Hue Goldsmiths' Co-operative.

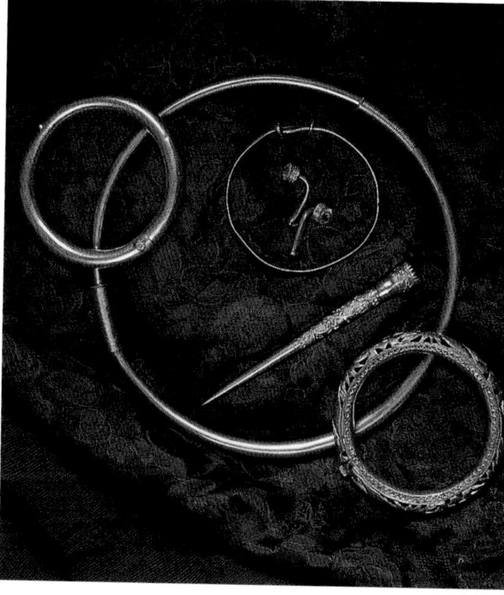

126

126 A plain gold torque, gold hairpin, ear ornaments set with diamonds or semi-precious stones, and bracelets, typical of those worn by upper-class women of northern Vietnam, early–mid-20th century.

125

127 A silver comb engraved with phoenix and dragon motifs and set with jade, silver hairpins, ivory beads carved to represent flower buds, a bracelet set with ivory, and an anklet set with jet, ornaments of the middle-class woman of southern Vietnam, early–mid-20th century.

128 Chatelaine worn suspended on a chain at the waist by Vietnamese women, early 20th century. It includes tools for personal grooming fixed to a French silver coin, and silver boxes for tobacco, lime and cosmetics decorated with repoussage and engraving. The dragon is the most common motif on the largest heart-shaped containers, while smaller ones are decorated with motifs of seasonal plants. To these ensembles made by Vietnamese silversmiths Muong and Red Tai women in rural areas in northern and central Vietnam added protective tiger-claw charms.

127

128

129

130

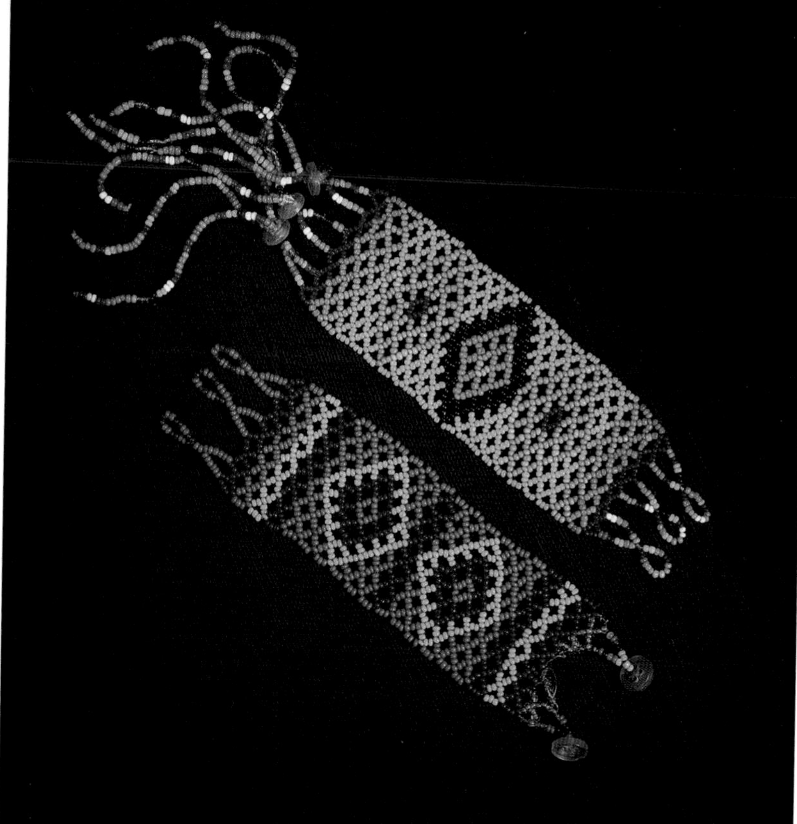

131

MINORITY PEOPLES OF BURMA/MYANMAR, THAILAND, LAOS, VIETNAM AND CAMBODIA

129 Bronze and silver bracelets, and necklaces of antique Chinese and modern beads, worn by the Mnong people of Dac Lac province, central Vietnam, 20th century. Bracelets record promises and obligations. The ivory ear-plugs, also 20th century, are worn by young Xtieng women of Song Be, central Vietnam. Both groups speak a Mon-Khmer dialect – as do the other peoples considered here, apart from the Chu Ru [**133**].

130 Bronze bracelets filled with rattling grains, used as musical instruments by the Brau people of Kon Tum province in central Vietnam and Ratanakiri province in Cambodia, 20th century. Their spiral and lozenge motifs recall Dong Son ornament.

131 Bracelets with bells and coloured beads woven in lozenge patterns by the Co Ho (Chil) people of Lam Dong, central Vietnam, 20th century.

132 Glass and amber beads, a torque with an attached bell, and a Vietnamese silver plaque with the character *tho* for longevity, seen on a Hre woman's cotton jacket with double spiral embroidery, from Quang Ngai province, central Vietnam, mid–late 20th century.

132

134

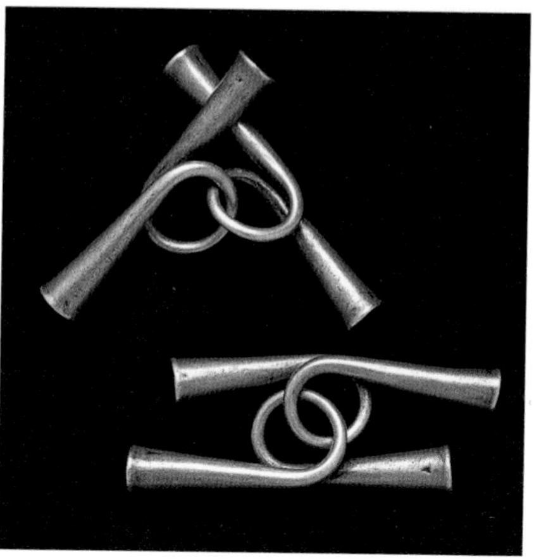

133

133 Silver ear ornaments worn by the Chu Ru people of central Vietnam, who speak a Cham language of the Austronesian (Indonesian) family. The form may be very ancient: they resemble some Javanese gold jewels of the first millennium (Pl. 161).

134 Jewelry of the Ta Oy people, of Quang Tri province in central Vietnam and Salavan and Xekong provinces in south-eastern Laos, 20th century and possibly earlier. Ancient traditions survive in the beads and in the heavy copper alloy spiral ear ornaments and bracelet with flaring terminals. The aluminium alloy bracelet and chain are of more recent manufacture and style.

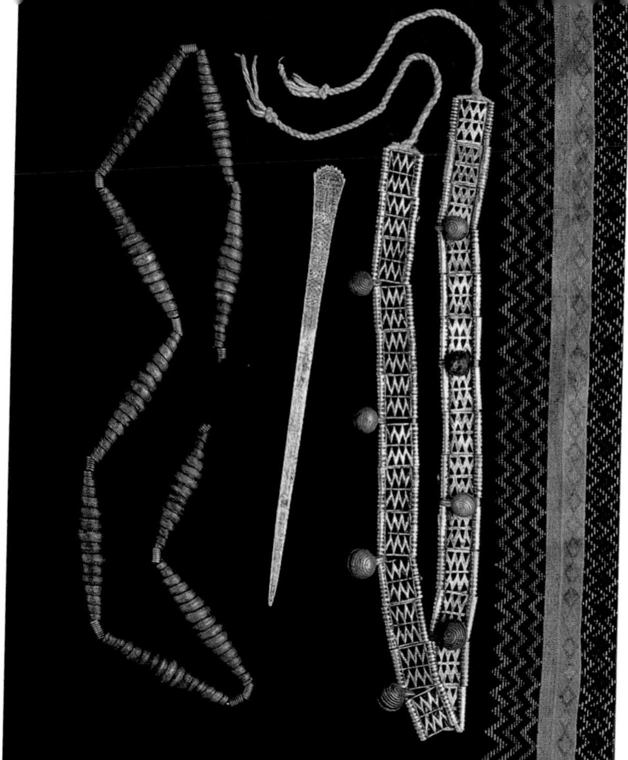

138

136

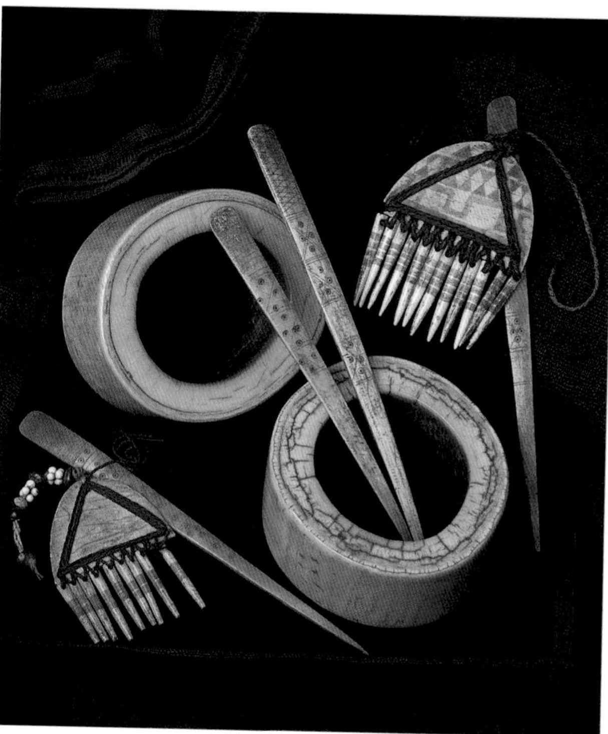

137

135

135 Tasselled belt embellished with cowrie shells, worn by the Chin people of Chin state, western Burma/Myanmar, early 20th century. In Southeast Asia shells, especially cowries, were thought of not only as beautiful and prestigious ornaments for clothing and jewelry but also as a form of currency.

136 Necklace of conch shells, cut and set with carnelian beads, from the Chin's north-western neighbours, the Naga people, early 20th century.

137 Ivory armlets, combs and hairpins. Among several Naga groups broad armlets of ivory were associated with varying degrees of high status and worn almost exclusively by men with a hereditary right to do so; this right could, however, be won by sponsoring important feasts.

138 Ornaments of the Chin people, 20th century. A brass belt composed of geometrical panels with jingling bell ornaments and a necklace of flat alloy wire twisted into spools show the pleasure taken in the varying hues of different metals. The delicately engraved hairpin is of silver.

139 Ornaments worn by the Tai people of northern Vietnam in the mid-20th century include a hairpin, bracelets, and a chain with a protective amulet engraved with tiger motifs (the attached heart-shaped box is of Vietnamese manufacture).

140 Woman's costume of the Tu Di subgroup of the Bo Y people of Lai Cau, northern Vietnam, mid–late 20th century. The Tu Di are ethnically Tai, but they speak Chinese and their costume shows clear Chinese influence. The apron is supported by silver chains with butterflies, fish and charms called *vui xeo xo* and *gia xe*.

141 Small silver buttons in butterfly shape used to fasten upper garments by Black Tai women and children of north-western Vietnam and Laos, early–mid-20th century.

142 Silver container for tobacco with attachments for a belt or bag, from Shan state, Burma/Myanmar, 19th century. It displays greater affinity with the restrained embossing of northern Thailand than the bolder style of Burmese silver work. Containers of this type were traded in Shan state, Laos and northern Thailand.

143 Hollow silver hairpins with lids, also used as containers by Red Tai women of Laos, Muong women of Vietnam, and Mon-Khmer-speaking minorities in northern Vietnam, 19th–early 20th century.

139

140

141

142

143

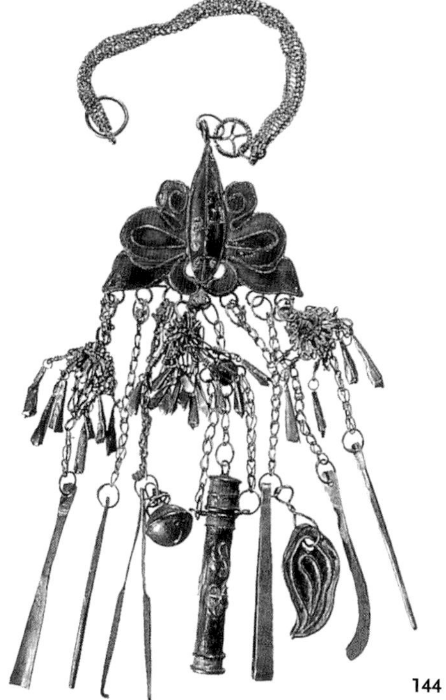

144

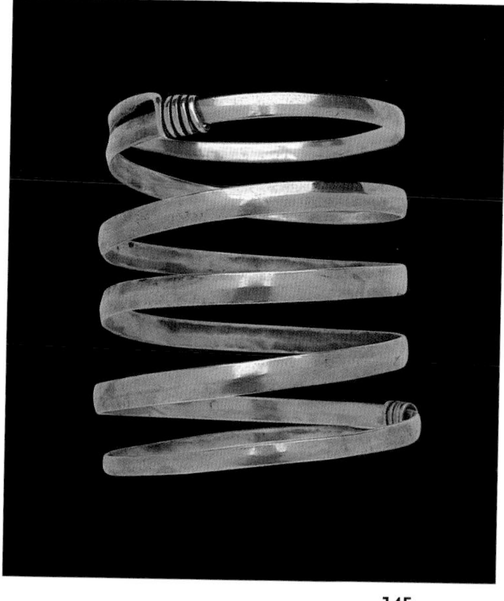

145

146

144 Shan butterfly chatelaine decorated with coloured enamel, 19th century. By around 1900 enamel work was created by Shan artisans from China.

145 A spiral silver bracelet of the type worn by the Wa people of southern China and Burma/Myanmar and various minorities including the Akha in Thailand.

146 A massive silver bracelet of Shan manufacture decorated with applied filigree and bosses, 19th century. Such pieces were worn by married Shan women in Kachin state, Burma/Myanmar, and were also sold to Kachin women.

147 Delicate Shan silver bracelets decorated with applied filigree and coloured enamel, typical of Shan state and the borders with Laos, northern Thailand and southern China, 19th century.

147

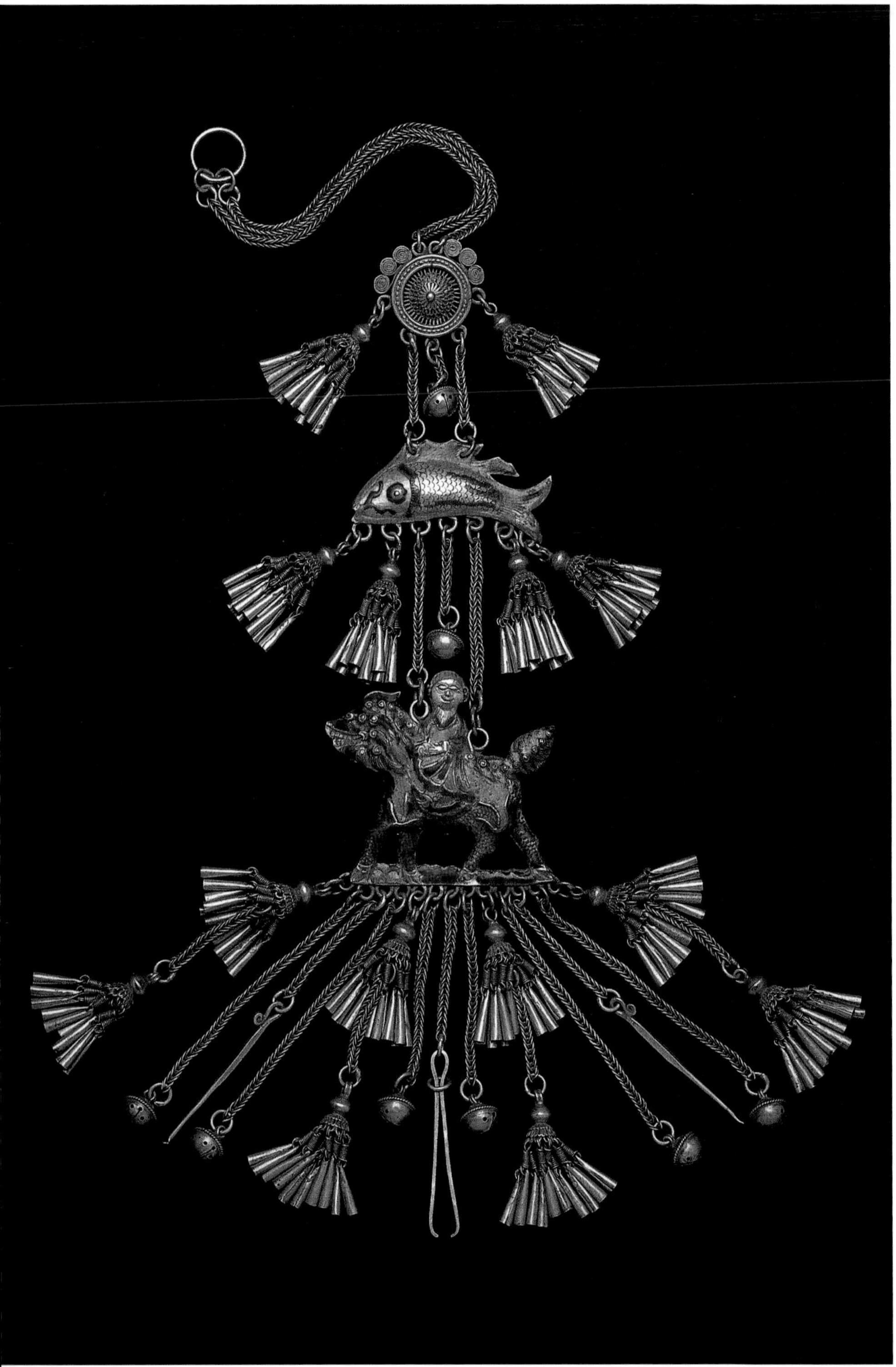

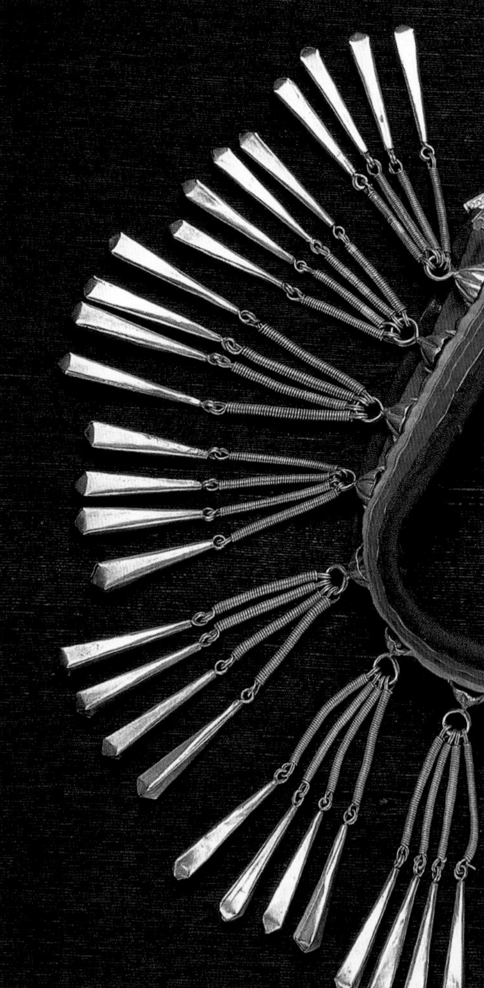

148

149

150

151

152

148 Yao silver pendant elaborated with embossed and enamelled ornaments, 19th century or earlier. Usually worn at the back, on ritual and festive occasions, it is a variant on a traditional Chinese type in which the unicorn associated with longevity, harmony and fertility is ridden by the Goddess of Fecundity or a young male scholar, invoking the birth of intelligent and industrious sons.

149 Yao torque and bracelet with dragon motifs enriched with coloured enamels and fine engraving, 18th–19th century. These masterly ornaments were probably made by Yao Ta Pan silversmiths in southern China or northern Vietnam. The dragons recall the primordial ancestor of the Yao people, Pan Hu, the multicoloured dragon-dog man.

150 Lisu collar of woven cloth with silver bud pendants, from northern Thailand or Burma/Myanmar, late 19th–early 20th century.

151 Akha torque of beaten and engraved silver, from northern Thailand or Burma/Myanmar, late 19th–early 20th century.

152 The sombre indigo-dyed jacket and blue-and-white patterned batik skirt worn by Yao Tien women of northern Vietnam are set off by large semicircular silver buttons which reflect in number the multiple souls of the wearer. These are from Chiem Hoa, Tuyen Quang province, north-eastern Vietnam, early 20th century.

153

154

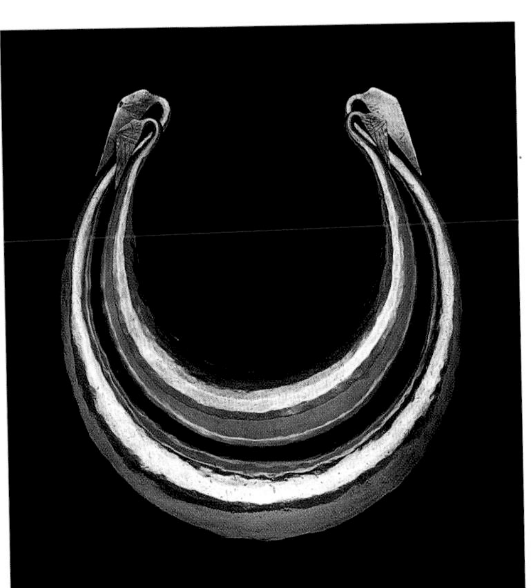

155

153 Hmong or Yao silver torques, 19th century or possibly earlier. The hook terminals served for the attachment of chains; in these especially fine examples they are engraved with characteristic geometric, bird and floral ornament.

154 Hollow silver bracelets of plain, twisted and ribbed silver tubes, of Shan manufacture, often worn by Lahu and Akha men in the Thailand–Burma/Myanmar border area.

155 Massive but hollow 19th-century silver torques, of Hmong or Yao manufacture and use.

156 A variety of silver earrings worn by Hmong and Yao women. The flat broader ones engraved with shallow geometrical and vegetal patterns are typical of Hmong workmanship. The earring with an arrow tip is of Yao origin, worn by both Yao and Hmong. The torque with curled loops is favoured by the Lahu, who often wear Hmong and Yao ear ornaments.

157 Silver padlock ornaments with coloured enamels, 19th century or earlier. These were employed in healing ceremonies in which the wandering souls of the sick were called back and secured to the body. Hmong people attached them to the ends of torques by chains.

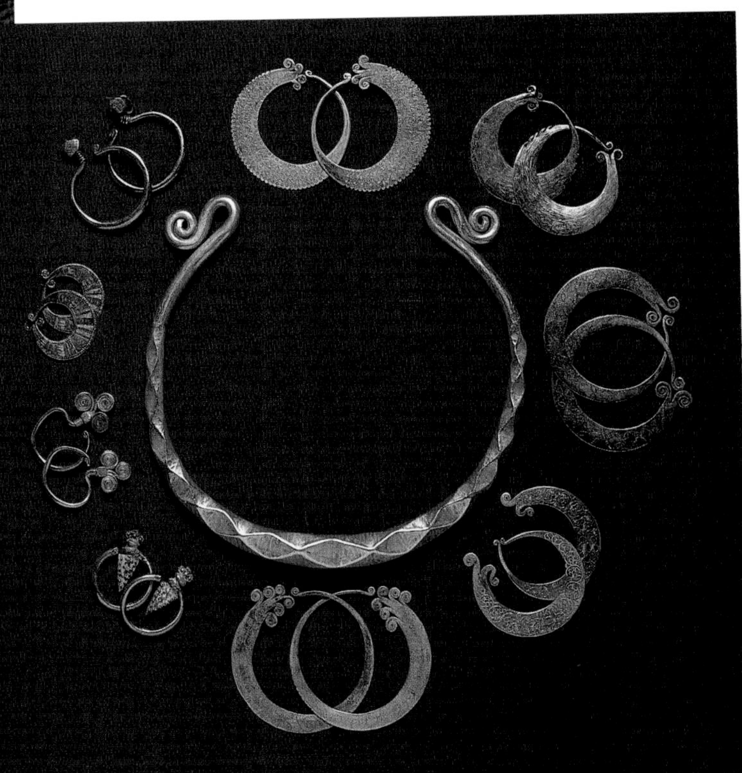

156

157

INDONESIA

158 Repoussé gold plaque or pendant from Kediri, east Java, 14th–15th century. The subject, from the *Ramayana*, shows the monkey warriors assisting Rama in rescuing his wife Sita from her abductor, the demon king Ravana of Lanka, by building a causeway to his realm. As they throw large rocks into the sea, they are surprised by a crab who attempts to frustrate their project.

159 Gold necklace incorporating sweet-water mollusc shells, from Gegerbitung, Sukabumi, west Java, 9th century. The long spiral shells may allude to the conch attribute of Vishnu, while the central phallus pendant evokes the *linga* of Shiva. The oval elements may represent mangoes and thus the feminine life-giving power of the *yoni*. The overall intention of the ornament may be to represent and invoke fertility; however, the oval pendants are often interpreted as stylized tiger claws like those worn by the youthful Krishna and the Buddhist Bodhisattva Manjusri. Tiger-claw amulets were traditionally worn by boys. Similar gold necklaces from about the same period, but with finer shells and also delicate stylized dragonflies, have been found in the Philippines.

158

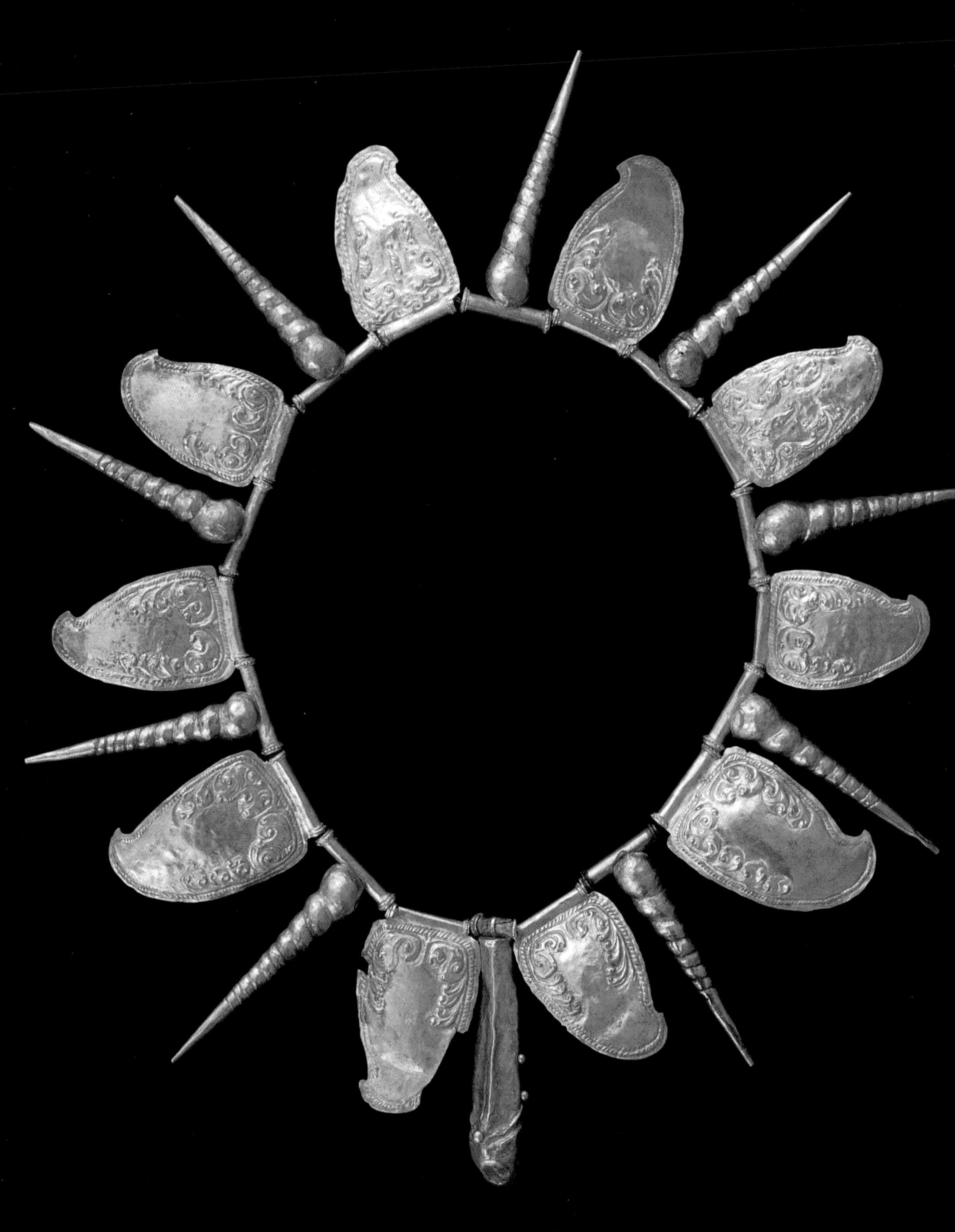

160

160 Gold ear ornaments formed as double spirals were manufactured and traded throughout Southeast Asia. Those in this collection of pieces found in Samar in the Philippines, of 500–1000 CE, are very similar to examples from Java in Indonesia, as well as Oc Eo in southern Vietnam and Champa in central Vietnam, and show the continuing influence of Bronze Age aesthetic ideals during the 1st millennium. Earrings in star form occur in stone much earlier in Thailand, and, in gold, are found throughout the region in the 1st millennium.

161 Gold ear ornaments formed as looped bars, Proto-Classic period (200–700). These were found in the Philippines, and may have been made there or traded from Java. They are similar to those of the Cham-speaking Chu Ru people of central Vietnam (Pl. 133).

162 Small split-ring ear ornaments from the Proto-Classic period, and an elaborate earring with granulated decoration and a tiny figurine of a *kinnara* (Hindu celestial musician in which bird and human elements are combined) from the Early Classic period (700–1000).

161

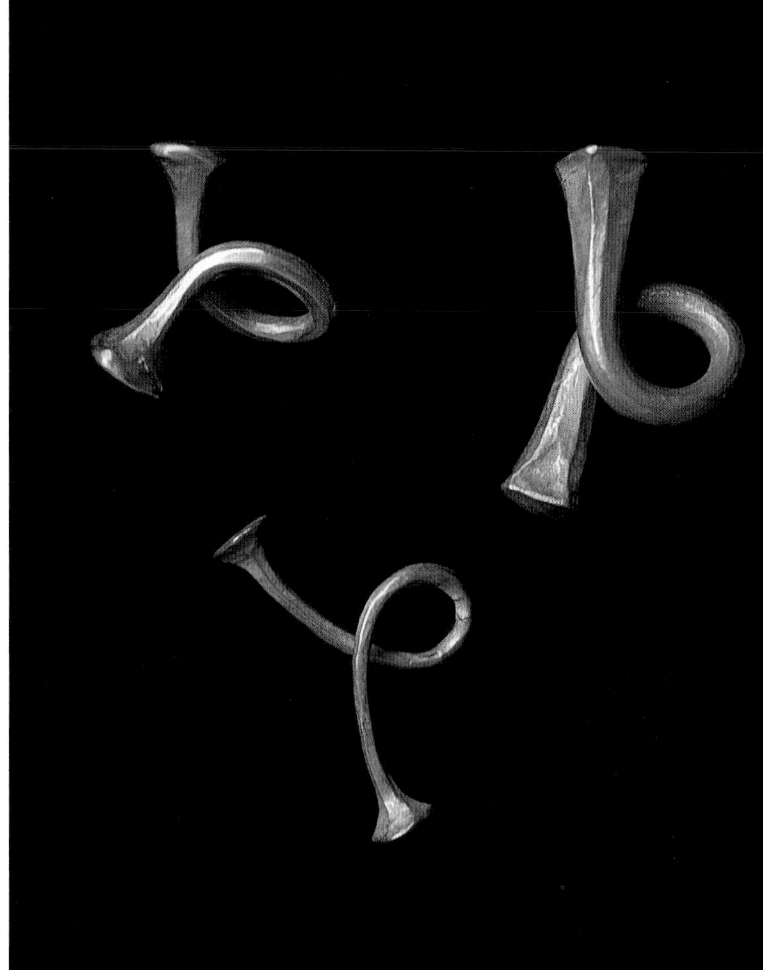

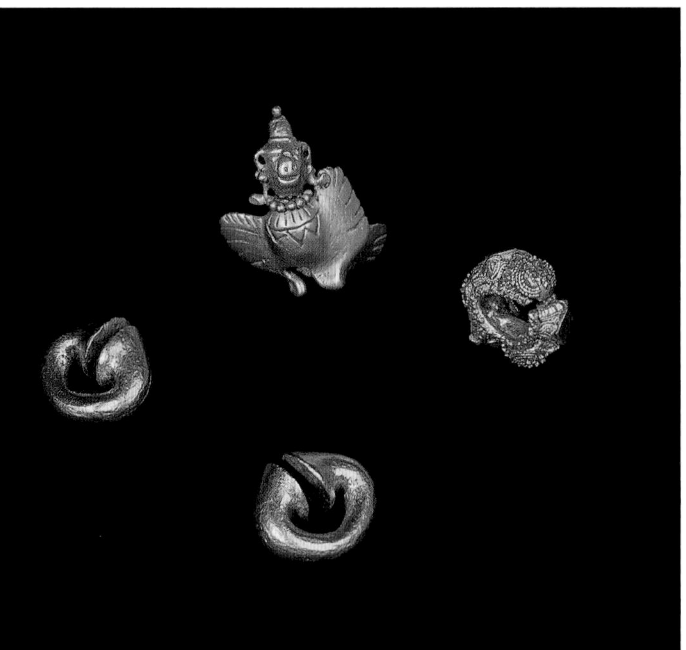

162

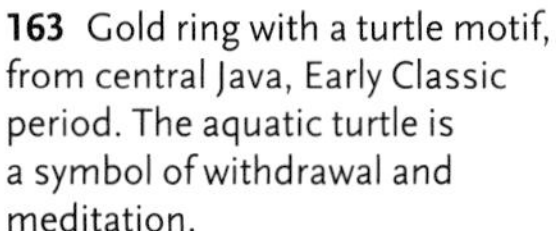

163 Gold ring with a turtle motif, from central Java, Early Classic period. The aquatic turtle is a symbol of withdrawal and meditation.

164 Small gold jewels found in central Java. The ring of twisted gold wire derives its form from the sacred Indian ring of woven kushu grass. The ear ornament composed of gold discs soldered into a circlet is of a type common in the Proto-Classic period in Java and also in Thailand (Pl. 80). The other ear ornaments are typical of the Early Classic period. The two tall gem-set earrings may represent the *vajra* (thunderbolt) of Indra; they too occur in Thailand (cf. Pl. 83). Most complex is the gold cord clasp formed to represent the conch shell of Vishnu; it dates from the Late Classic period (1000–1400).

163

164

165 Glass beads from east Java, probably made from segments of imported and/or locally produced beads. The type is sometimes called 'Majapahit beads' after the great Javanese empire, but is much older, of the 9th century or earlier.

166 Heavy gold clasp, found at Gemblung, central Java, 9th–10th century. It was attached to the *upavita* cord worn diagonally across the upper body by high-caste participants in Brahman ceremony. The massive leafy scrolls show a resemblance to gold ornaments found at Oc Eo and in Cambodia.

167, **168** Gold seal rings, one with *kawi* script on its oval bezel and the other with a pointed bezel inscribed with ornamental *nagari* script, from east Java, *c.* 10th century. Many inscriptions invoke good fortune.

165

166

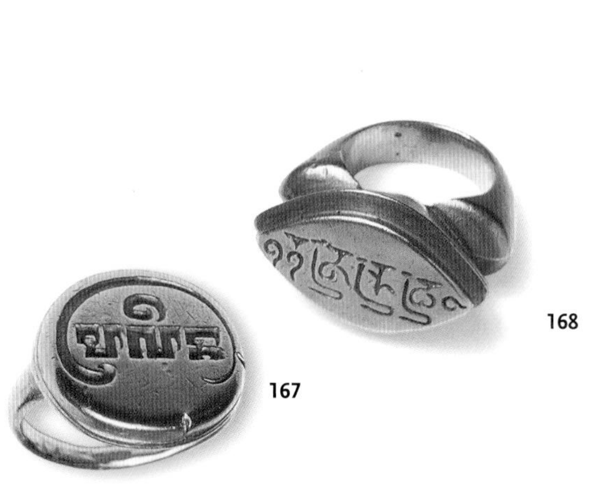

168

167

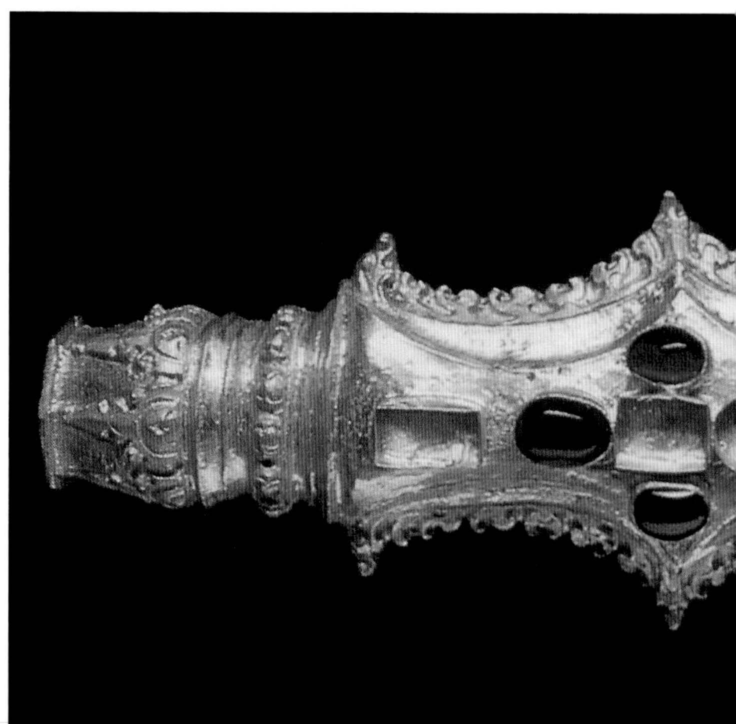

169 Gold royal armlet of *gunungan* (mountain) form, from a hoard of 10th-century royal ornaments found at Wonoboyo, central Java. The mask of the fierce *kala* averts evil and affords protection. The *kala* is also associated with Shiva and with Rahu, who causes eclipses by swallowing the sun and moon and then regurgitates them to restore light. Bold vegetal motifs rise on either side to form wings surmounted by heads of *makaras*. The combination of sunlight and water imagery invokes fertility and cosmic equilibrium.

170 Gold clasp for the *upavita* cord (cf. Pl. 166), set with coloured rock crystal and obsidian, from the 10th-century Wonoboyo treasure. Its decorative style suggests the emergence of a preference for more delicate vegetal ornament. The ends are decorated with triangular petals and a border of coconuts.

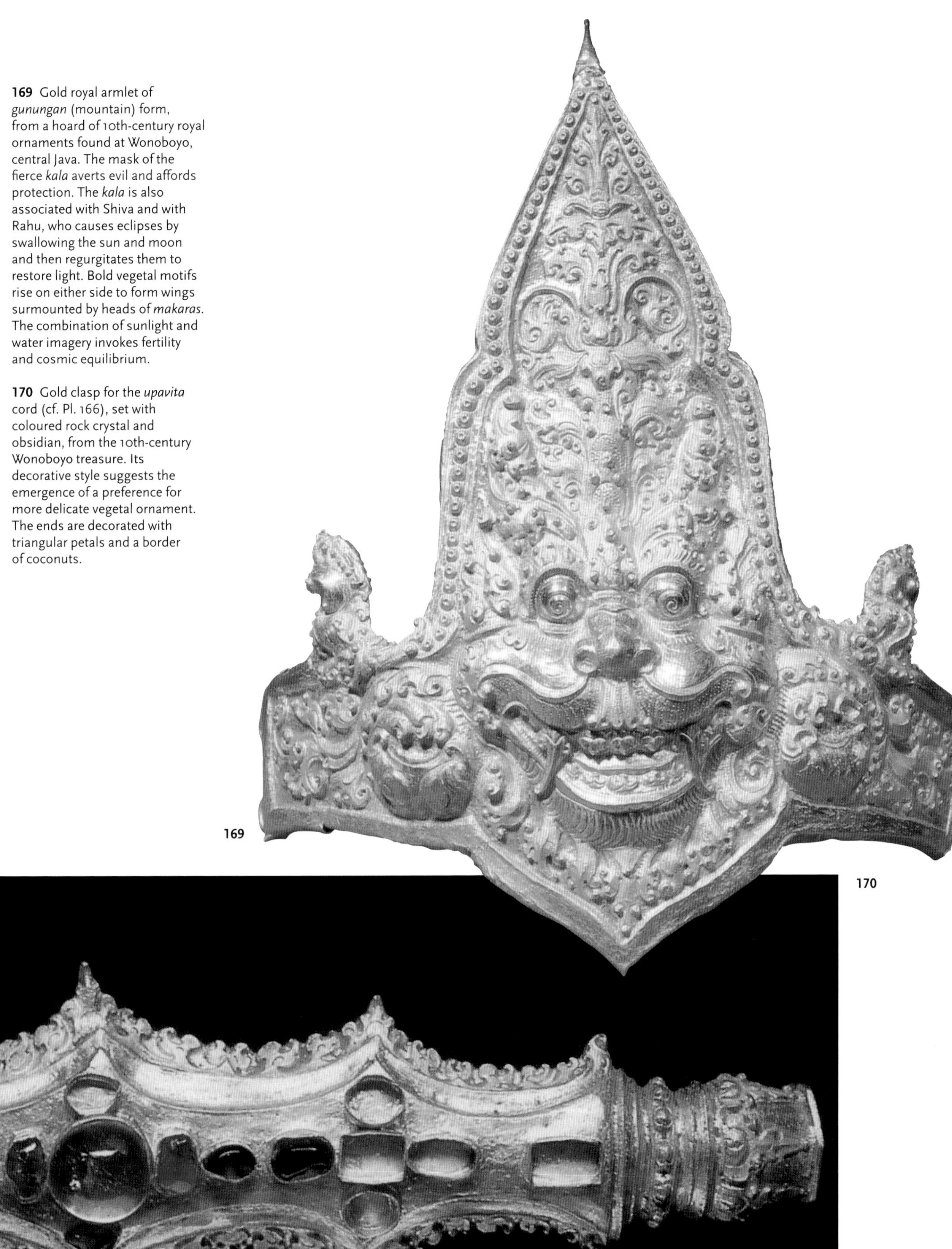

169

170

171

172

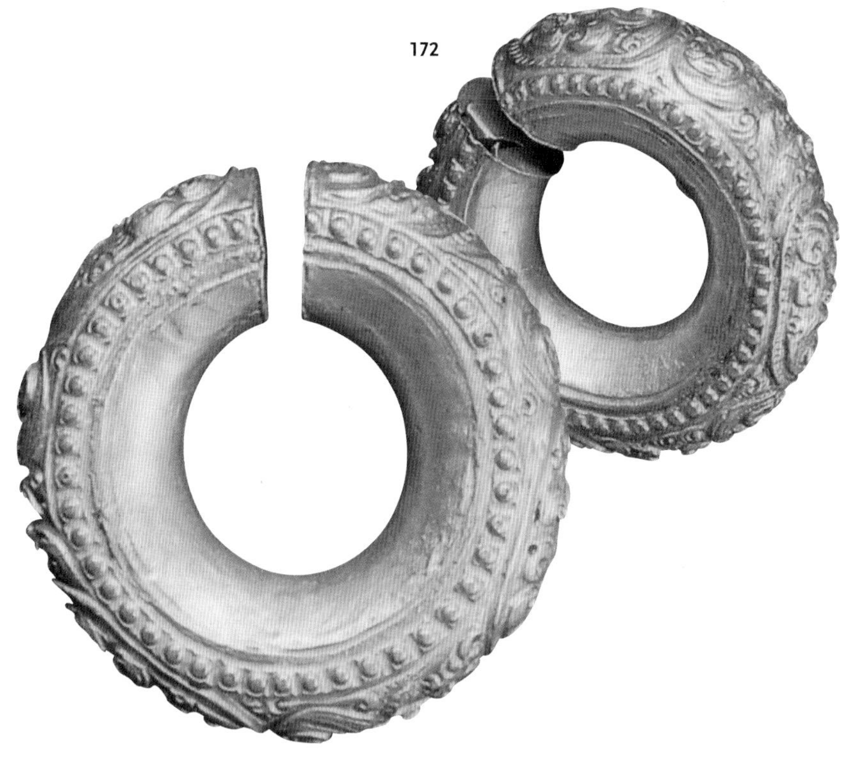

173

174

175

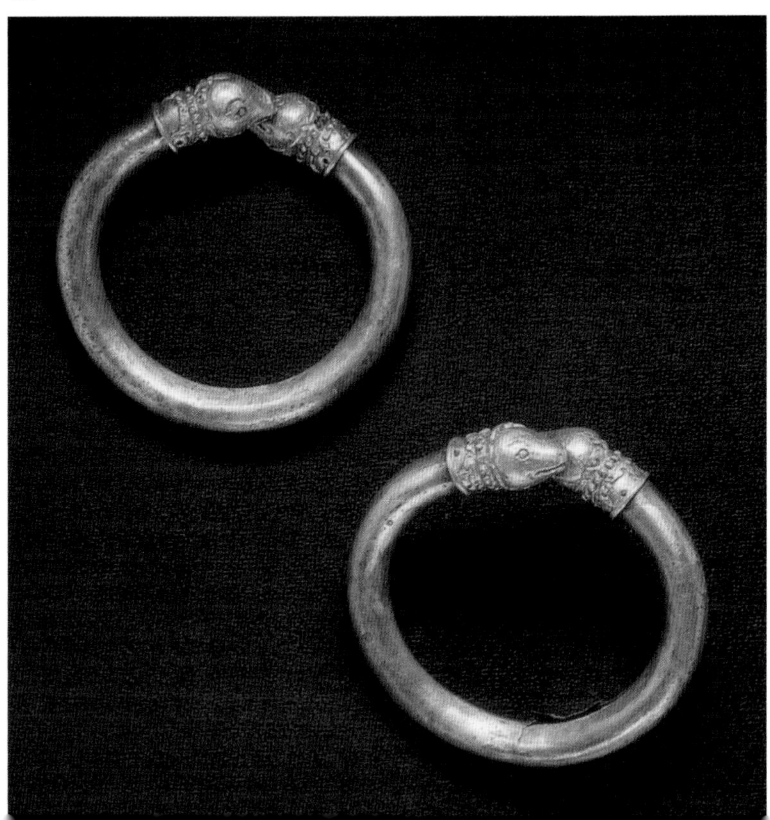

Java

171 Gold ear ornaments of elongated S-form, from east Java, 14th–15th century. The motifs suggest stylized birds surmounted by curling tendrils, rising shoots and flames.

172 Gold earrings with vegetal designs and a border of beads, from east Java, 12th century. They were formed in clay and covered by successive layers of gold leaf.

173 Gold ear ornament formed as a *makara* head, from east Java, 14th century.

174 Gold U-form ear ornaments set with rubies, from east Java, 14th century.

175 A pair of silver bracelets with ornamental tips in the form of serpents' heads surrounded by floral garlands, from Semarang, central Java, 10th–11th century. The hollow tubes contain small tinkling bronze balls. The heads are solid, cast by the lost-wax method.

176 An armlet (*kelat bahu*) worked in repoussage in *gunungan* or mountain form, from Mojokerto, east Java, 14th–15th century. The decorative bosses resemble jewels, surrounded by curling vegetation. Similar armlets are depicted in 8th–9th century sculpture of central Java, and some pieces in the 10th-century Wonoboyo treasure have similar vegetal ornament (Pl. 169).

177 Gold repoussé plaque with profuse vegetal ornament which almost obscures a central *kala*, from east Java, 15th–16th century. The masking of Hindu motifs by decorative vegetation is typical of some early Islamic art in east Java. The original purpose of the plaque is uncertain, but it appears to have been attached at some stage to a garment, sash or other cloth.

178 Gold repoussé bracelet with a border of coconuts, from Mojokerto, east Java, Late Classic period (1000–1400). It was filled with clay and strengthened by an interior bronze plate, which is now missing. Similar bracelets appear on the 9th–10th-century gold statuettes of Shiva and Parvati found in a mountain grotto at Seplawan, central Java, and in an illustration of a Javanese bridegroom in T. S. Raffles' *History of Java*, of 1817.

179 Large gold repoussé ornament from Madiun, east Java, 14th century. This may have been suspended on a string and worn as a modesty plaque. The scene shows Sri Tanjung, who, murdered for her infidelity by a tragically mistaken husband, rides a *makara* through the waves of the underworld to the gates of heaven where she is brought back to life.

176

177

178

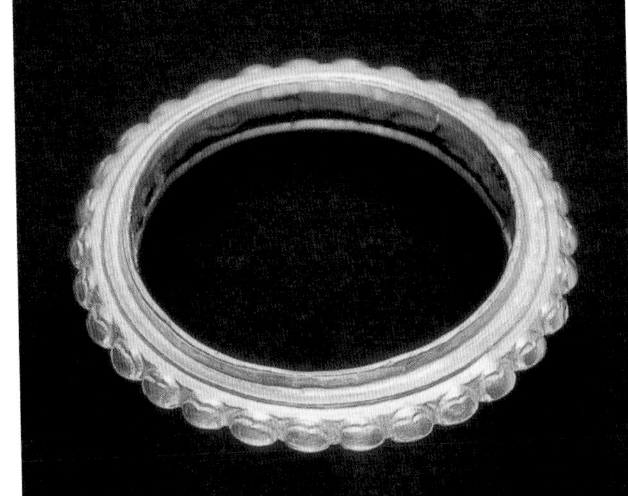

179

184

180

181

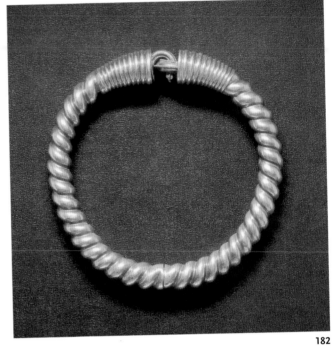

182

Java

180 The fez-like gold crown of Demak, the first Javanese Islamic state, *c.* 16th century. Its form shows Ottoman influence, and the engraved patterns reflect Islamic aesthetic traditions.

181 The 18th-century crown of Banten, of gold with rubies, emeralds, pearls and enamel, shows Islamic decorative influence, while its form recalls Hindu-Buddhist crowns (cf. Pls 35, 251).

182 Gold collar for a woman, from east Java, 16th century, of two twisted hollow cylinders.

183 A pair of gilded armlets worn by the groom at a wedding, from central Java, 19th–20th century, in the form of sharp-toothed *nagas* made of flexible gilded wire wound around a copper band, their heads set with clear stones.

184 Gilded silver wedding necklace from central Java, late 19th–early 20th century. The pendant has applied filigree and is set with Borneo diamonds.

185 Gold and silver ear pendants of the *nata brongto* ('the king pining for love') style, late 19th or early 20th century.

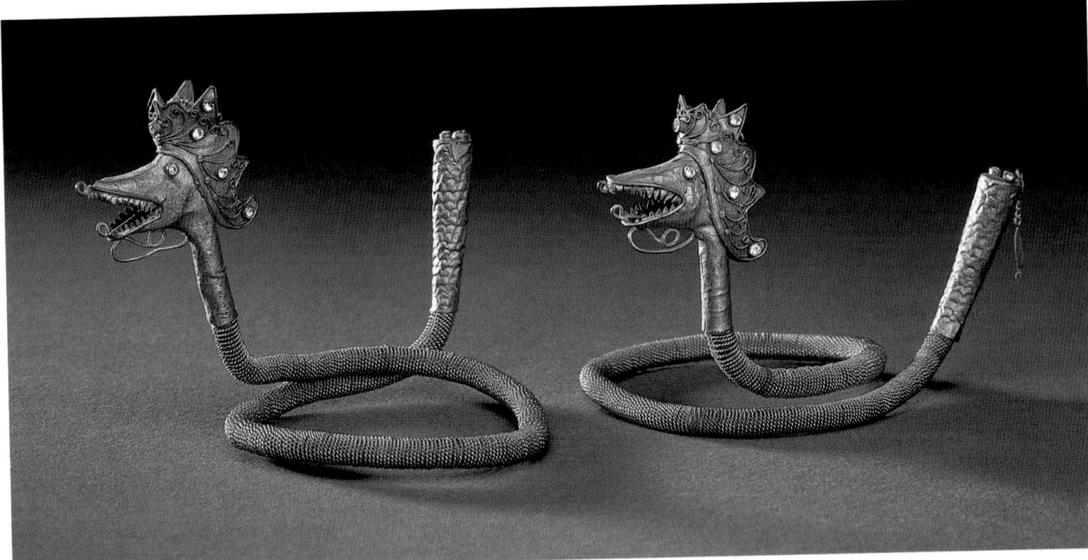

183

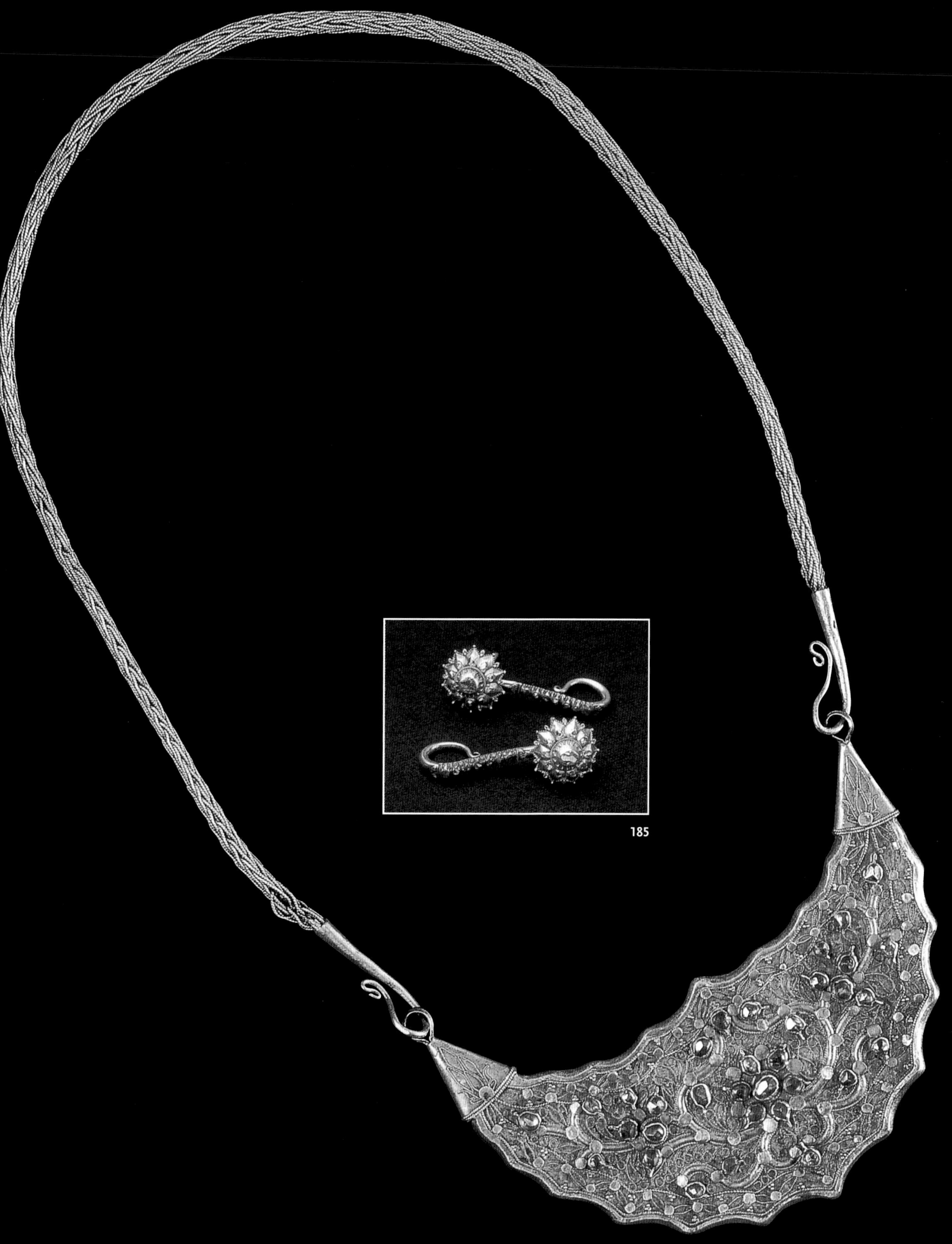

185

186

186 Two gilded silver belt buckles (*timang*) with matching attachments (*lerep*), worn by men, from central Java, late 19th–early 20th century. They are set with small Borneo diamonds, rubies and glass.

187 Gilded silver comb (*sisir ronjok*), two single hairpins (*kucuk kembang intan*), and a curved double pin (*toesek konde lintringan*), late 19th–early 20th century. They are shown with a Javanese hairpiece (still popular on celebratory occasions) and *cempaka* flowers, worn in the hair.

188 Iron belt buckle (*olan-olan*) and attachment formed as twining serpents and inlaid with gold leaf, of a type widely worn in central Java in the 19th century, usually fixed to a cloth sash or a belt woven from human hair.

189 Gold ear studs (*suweng*) of very fine filigree; a separate diamond-set disc fits on to the front and is held by a connecting shaft.

190 Typical late 19th–early 20th-century Javanese women's ornaments. The European crown became a common motif in Southeast Asian jewelry, as exemplified in this gilded brooch. The silver floral ring set with Borneo diamonds is of the *tamengan* style. Lozenge-shaped diamond rings were worn in the early–mid-20th century in Java and Bali and also in Malaysia. The grey diamond ear-studs are of the same date.

187

188

189

190

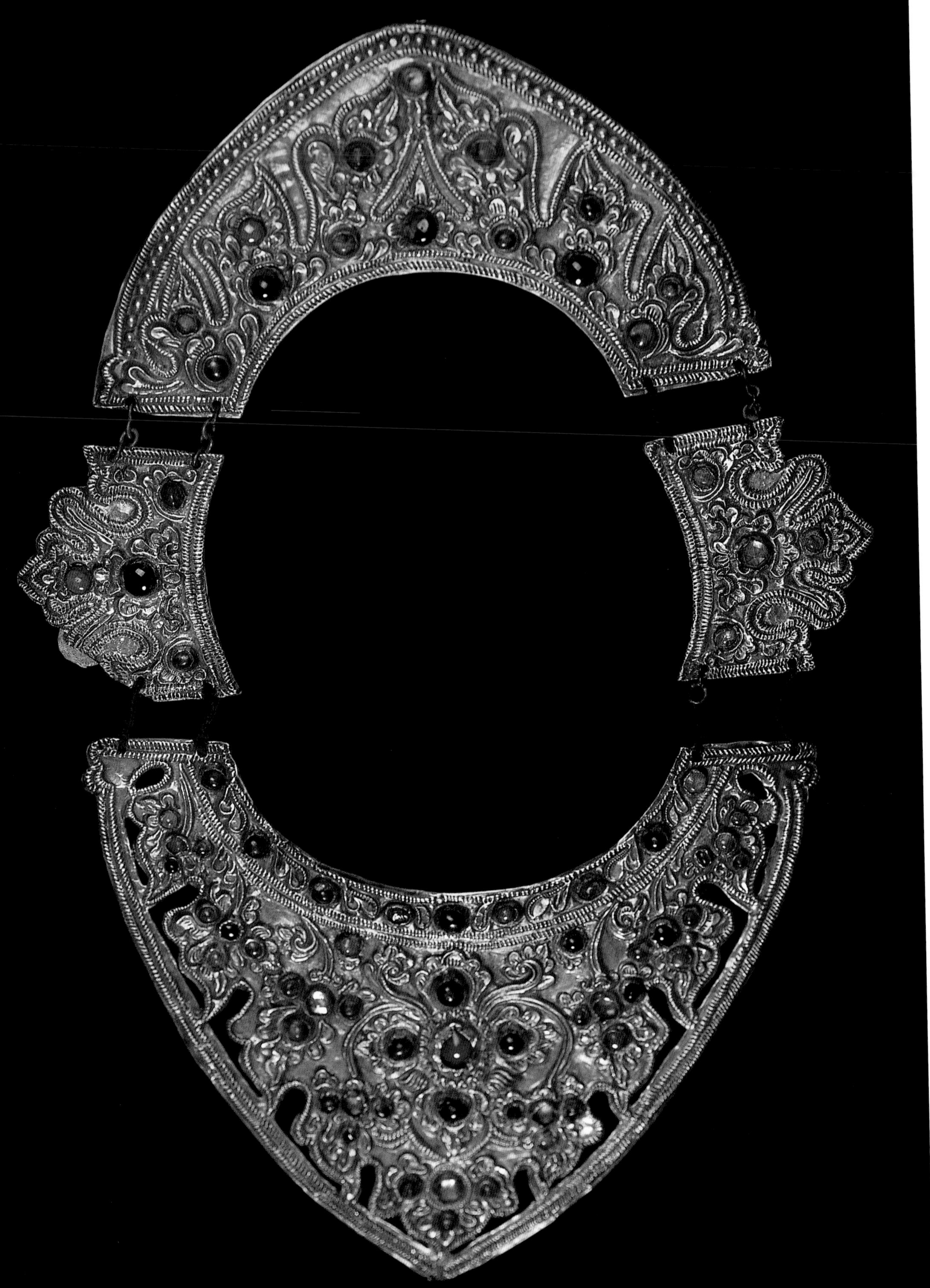

192

193

Bali

191 Dancer's collar, 19th century. Embossed gold alloy is mounted on a copper backing and set with rubies, garnets, amethysts and crystals. The larger and finer precious stones have been replaced by coloured glass.

192 Two gold rings, 19th–early 20th century. The smaller one, for a woman, from the south, has granular decoration that suggests the influence of Islamic goldsmiths. The man's ring, from the north, is worked in repoussage and engraving.

193 Gold ring in the form of a *naga*, exquisitely embellished with filigree and granulation at which Balinese goldsmiths excel, early–mid-20th century.

194 A ruby- and diamond-set gold necklace believed to have come from the palace at Klungkung, 19th century. Necklaces of this type were worn by aristocratic participants in important life-cycle celebrations; babies and very small children wore them at ceremonies such as the *odalan* (first birthday).

195 A pair of silver boxes (*klopok*) used to store tobacco and *gambir* resin for the betel plug, late 19th–early 20th century. Each has a lotus motif on one side and a local flower (*karang kaketosen*) on the other.

195

196 Part of a gold dagger (*kris*) of royal type, richly ornamented and set with gemstones, from the Klungkung palace, 19th century. The demon (*raksasa*) form of the hilt and the monstrous *kala* face on the grip provide protection.

197–199 Three unusual large gold repoussé thumb rings, 19th and 20th centuries. That on the left displays a princely character from epic literature and dramatic dance. The central ring depicts a male figure – perhaps one of the wise clowns of epic drama – wearing a sarong and armlets. The ring with a black cabochon bears the protective mask of a demon (*raksasa*) on the shoulders.

197

198

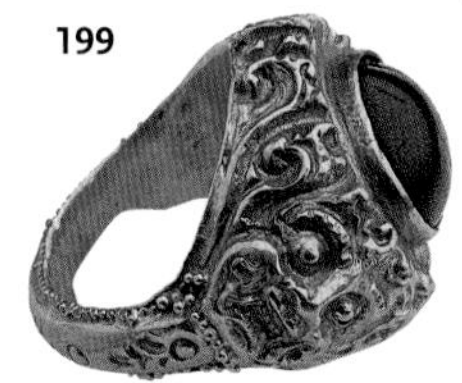

199

194

196

200

203

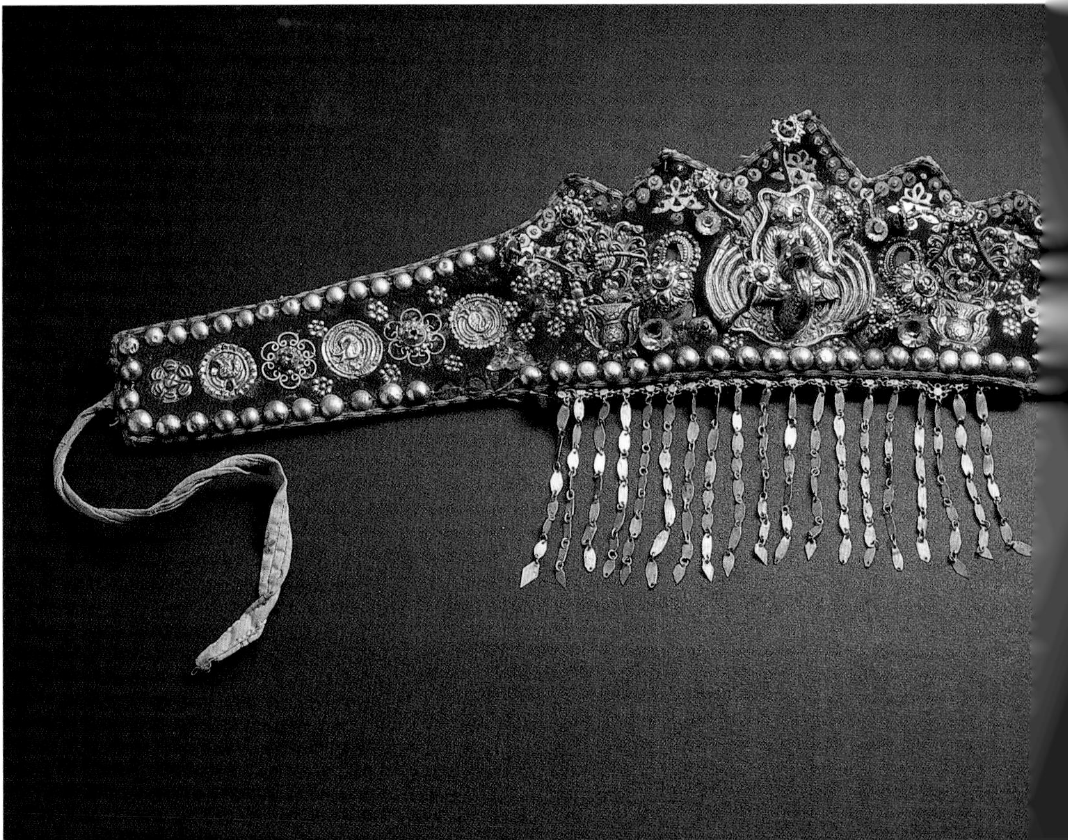

204

201

202

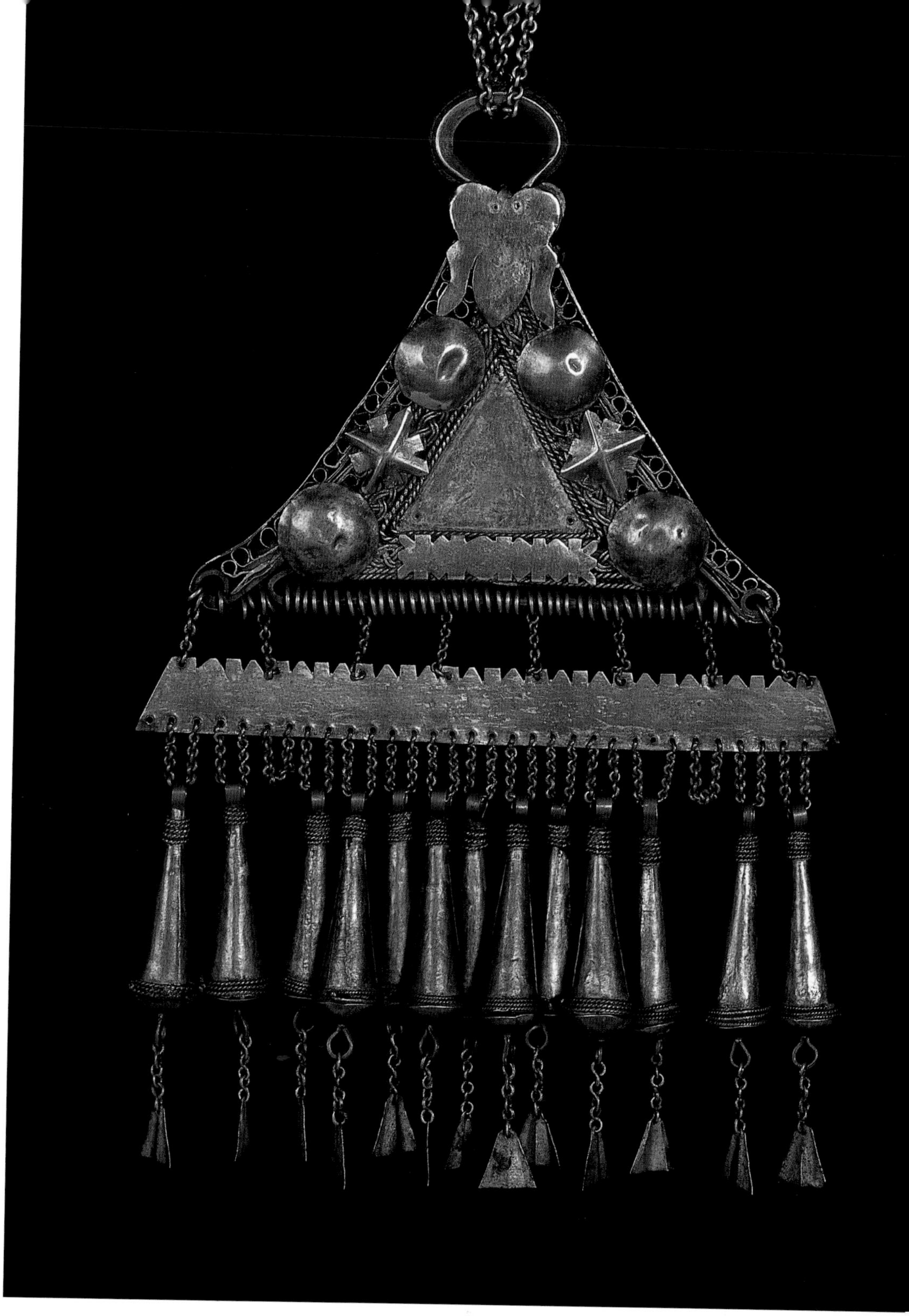

205

Sumatra

200 Comb (*sugu*) of buffalo horn and gilded copper from Palembang, south-east Sumatra.

201, 202 Painted wooden combs from Lampung, south Sumatra, 19th–early 20th century. Their form evokes buffalo horns, boats and trees. One is embellished with mother-of-pearl, rock crystal and beads.

203 *Naga* anklet of gilded silver, from Palembang, 19th century.

204 Red cotton ceremonial diadem with gilded copper ornaments, worn by Chinese and Malay brides and courtiers in Palembang, 19th–early 20th century. It is based on the Chinese *Ba Xian* (Eight Immortals) headband; in Indonesian versions, the central figure of the God of Longevity may resemble Vishnu astride Garuda.

205 Gayo-Alas woman's hair ornament (*lelayang cemera*), of silver and *suasa* (an alloy of copper, gold and silver) with filigree and dangling pendants, from central Aceh, north Sumatra, late 19th–early 20th century.

206 Silver and *suasa* beads, and silver and steel implements for personal grooming, attached to a kerchief folded into a loose bag and worn over the shoulder by men. From Aceh, north Sumatra, late 19th–early 20th century.

207 The gold chains and star-like medallions of the *simpleh* ornament were displayed on the chest and back of an Acehnese bride. These very fine 19th-century medallions display gems and cloisonné enamel.

208 Jewelry from Aceh: a gilded silver filigree bracelet of gold chains linked by tiny gem-set mimosa flowers, late 19th–early 20th century, and a gold pendant of the *Pintu Aceh* type, based on the gates of the Gunungan building at Banda Aceh, *c.* 1935.

209 A magnificent hat ornament, worn on top of the tall hat of bridegrooms and noblemen, of gold enriched with precious stones and cloisonné enamel, from Aceh, 19th century. Islamic and Hindu motifs are combined: the two lower tiers are formed as stars, while the layered pinnacles above evoke Mount Meru, and possibly the Gunungan building.

206

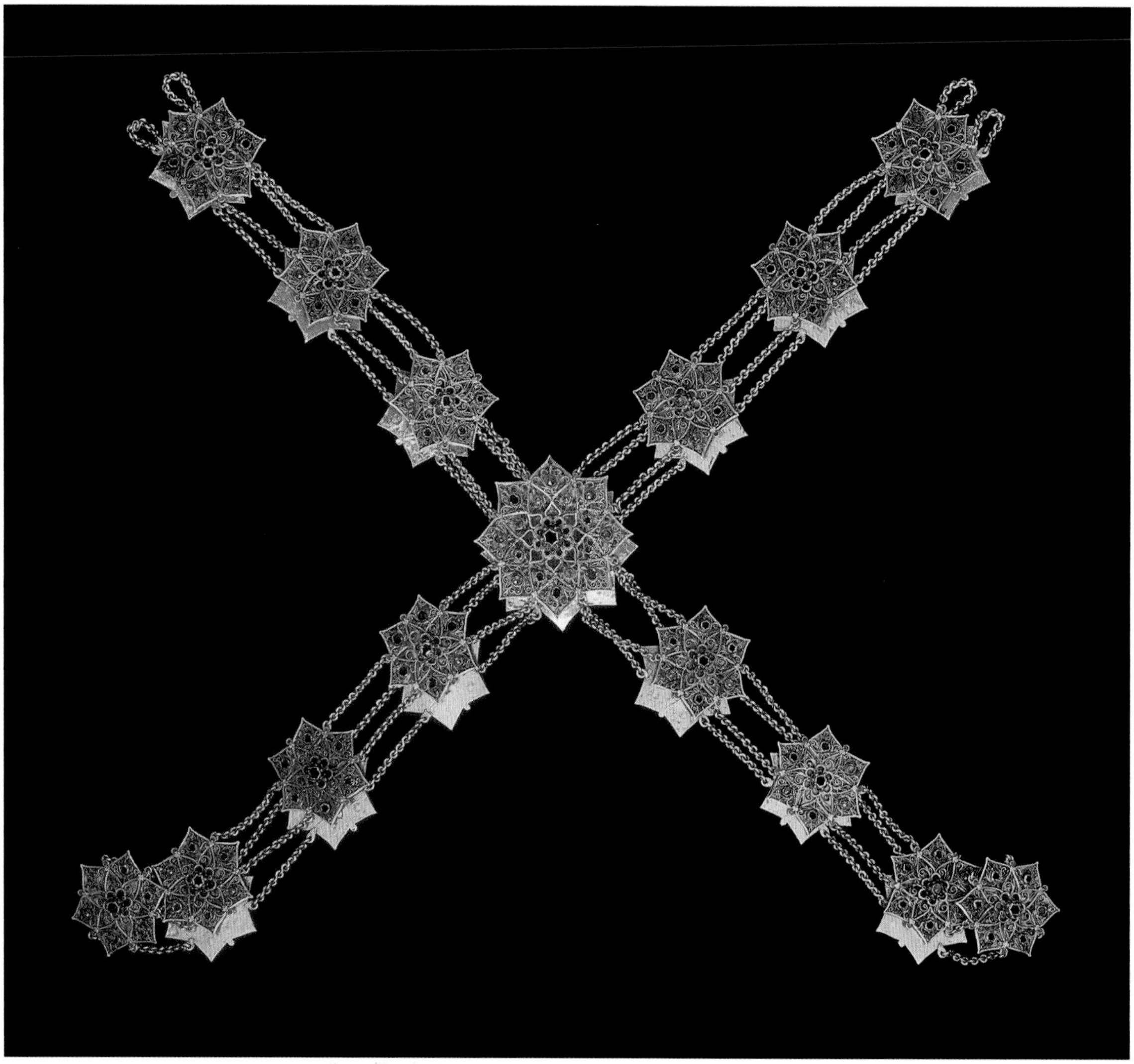

207

208

209

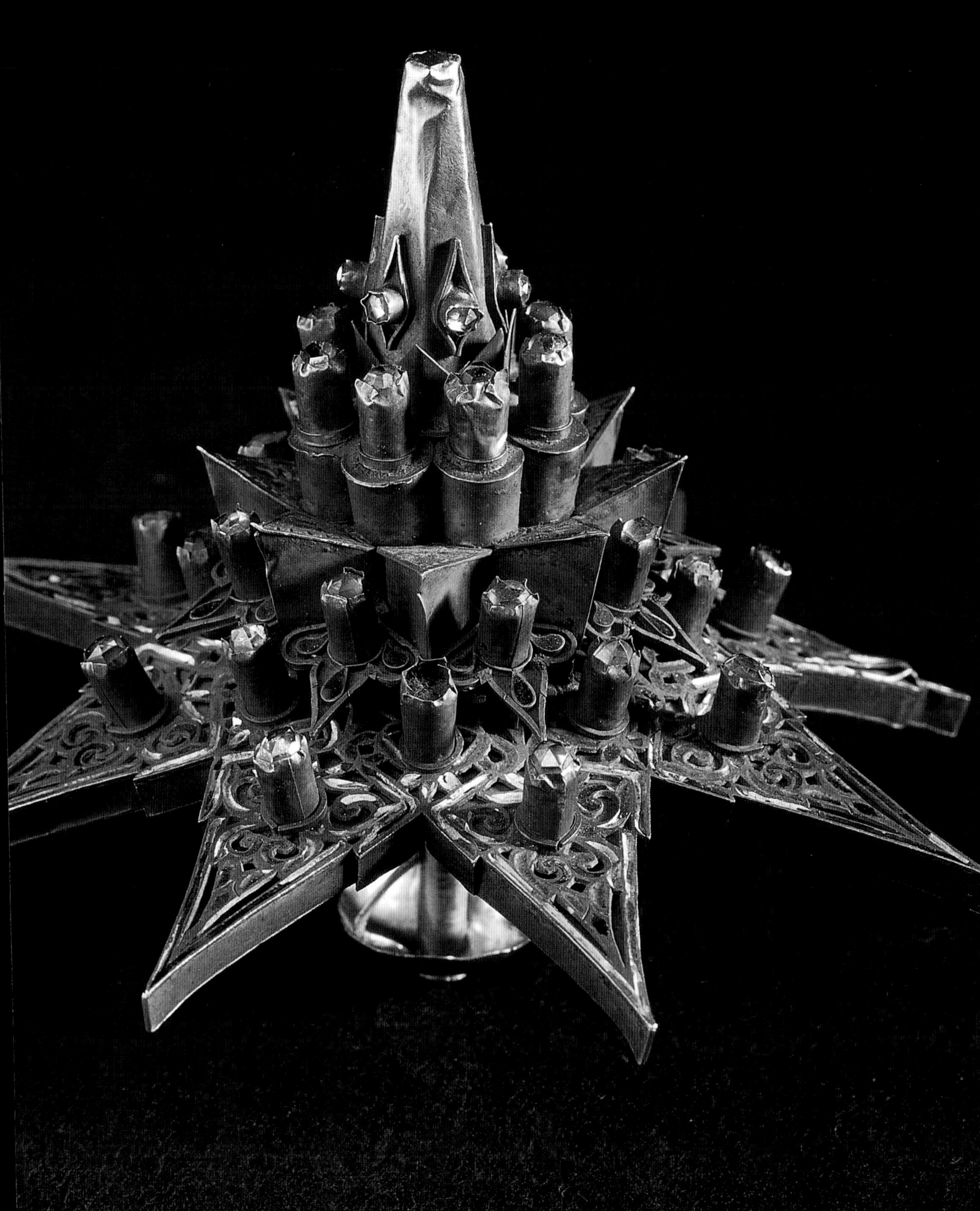

210

211

212

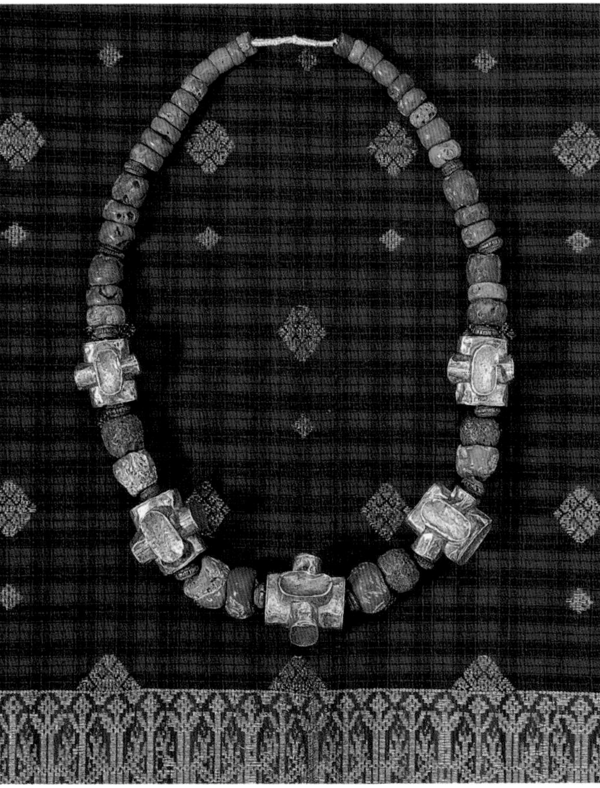

213

Sumatra

210 Royal gold necklace ornamented with granulation and applied filigree, made by the Minangkabau people of west Sumatra in 1872. The central plaque depicts a composite *makara*-like creature (*gajah minong*) which includes elephant, plant and crocodile elements.

211 One of a pair of Minangkabau woman's bracelets of gold alloy set with rubies in resin, from Payakumbuh district, west Sumatra, early 20th century. The vegetal scrolls between the gem-set latticework and plain metal represent banana shoots.

212 One of a pair of large bridal bracelets of embossed red-stained gold set with a red stone, from Padang district, west Sumatra, early–mid-19th century.

213 Minangkabau necklace of coral beads and hollow gold boxes, from Payakumbuh district, west Sumatra, 19th–early 20th century. Such necklaces are worn by married women with bracelets like the one seen in Pl. 211.

Sumatra

214 Minangkabau silver and niello man's belt buckle with foliate patterns, from the Padang hills, west Sumatra, 19th century. One or more layered central plaques mark the social status of the owner.

215 Minangkabau brass and niello buckle decorated with lotus flowers and vegetal scrolls, from the Padang hills, west Sumatra, 19th century.

216 Minangkabau buckle of red-stained gold embossed with foliate patterns, mounted on a copper alloy backing plate, from Padang, west Sumatra, 19th century. The central stone (perhaps a replacement) is hematite, commonly employed in rings for men in coastal Sumatra.

214

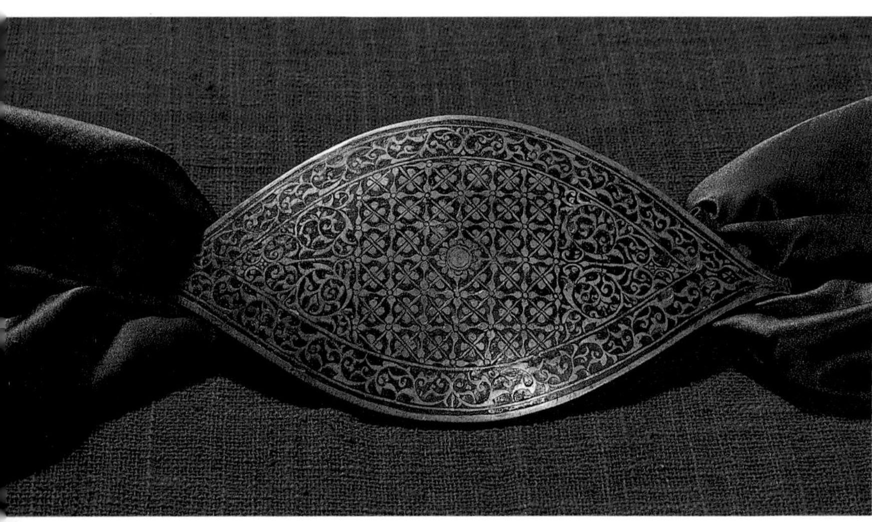

215

21

217 A small Minangkabau gold turban (*deta gadang*) with red staining, geometric ornament, and subtle embossing to simulate cloth folds and floral ear posies, from west Sumatra, 19th century or earlier. The metal sheeting covers a wooden form which was probably worn in combination with a supporting headcloth. Courtiers at Aceh in the 17th century wore gold turbans; the custom spread to west Sumatra, where silver turbans formed part of the ceremonial costume among the nobility in the 19th century. They are worn today, but rarely.

217

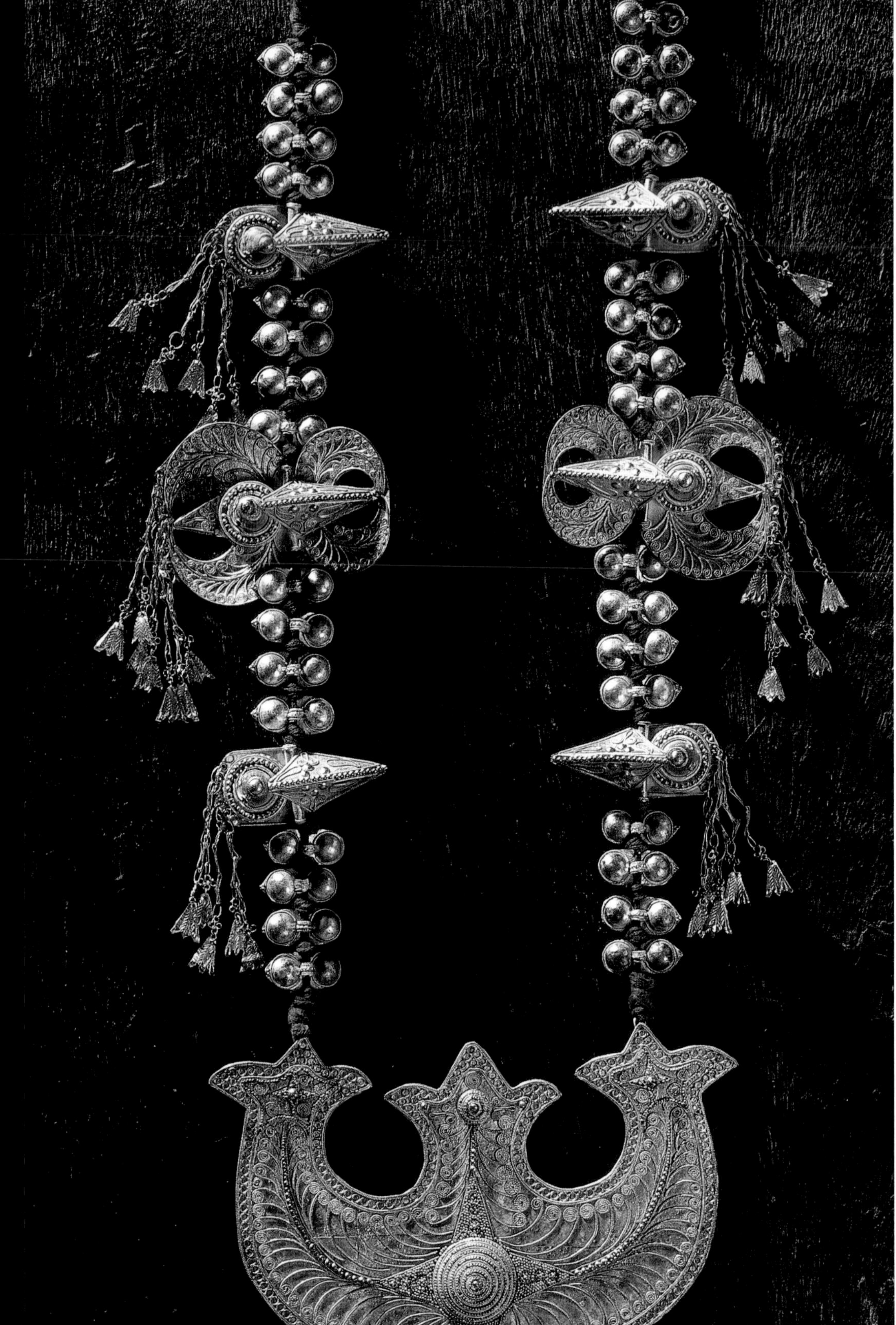

Sumatra

218 An unusual Karo Batak necklace of gilded silver with applied filigree, from north Sumatra, early 20th century. It is composed of the pendant from a bridegroom's necklace (*bura layang-layang*) representing a bird, and a chain (*sertali*) of the type worn on the bride's headdress, which includes buffalo horn and house roof motifs. These symbolize the traditional clan house and its inhabitants – the ancestral dead and their living descendants. Such composite necklaces were employed by shamans to call back the souls of the sick.

219, 220 Two gilded silver Karo Batak ear pendants, the upper known as *rajah mahoeli* and the lower as *karabu kudung-kudung*, from north Sumatra, late 19th–early 20th century. They are worn by brides in pairs with the *bura-bura* wedding necklace, and at other major life-cycle celebrations.

221 Necklace of ribbed gold sheet with spiral decoration, from Nias island, north Sumatra, 19th–early 20th century. Such necklaces were worn in the north (as *nifato-fato*) by men of high status; in the south (as *kalambagi*) they were worn by both sexes.

222 A pair of double-spiral ear ornaments of finely ridged gold sheet, from Nias island. They are called *gaule* when worn by men singly, *saru dalinga* when worn by women in pairs.

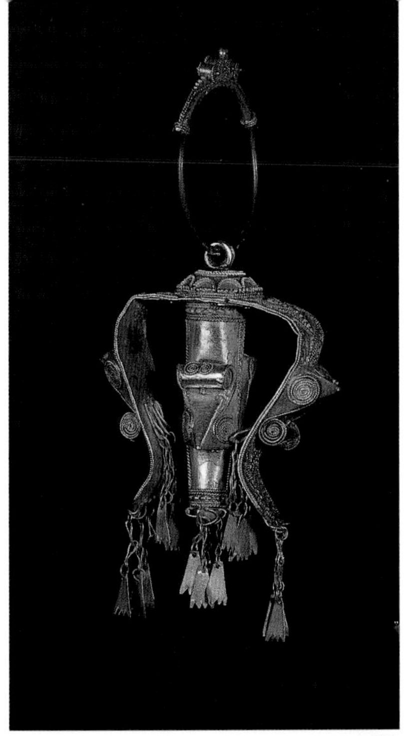

219

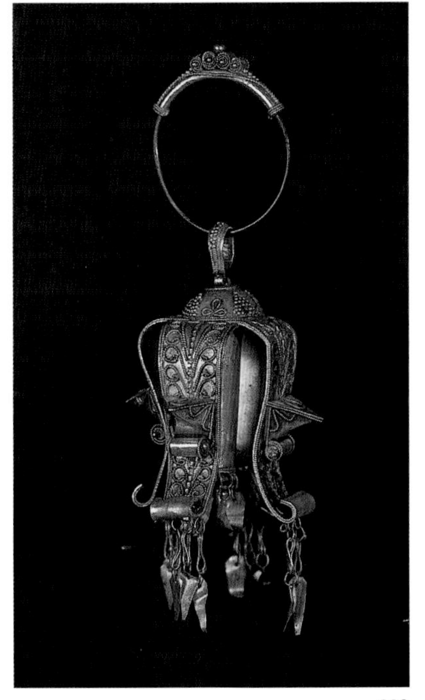

220

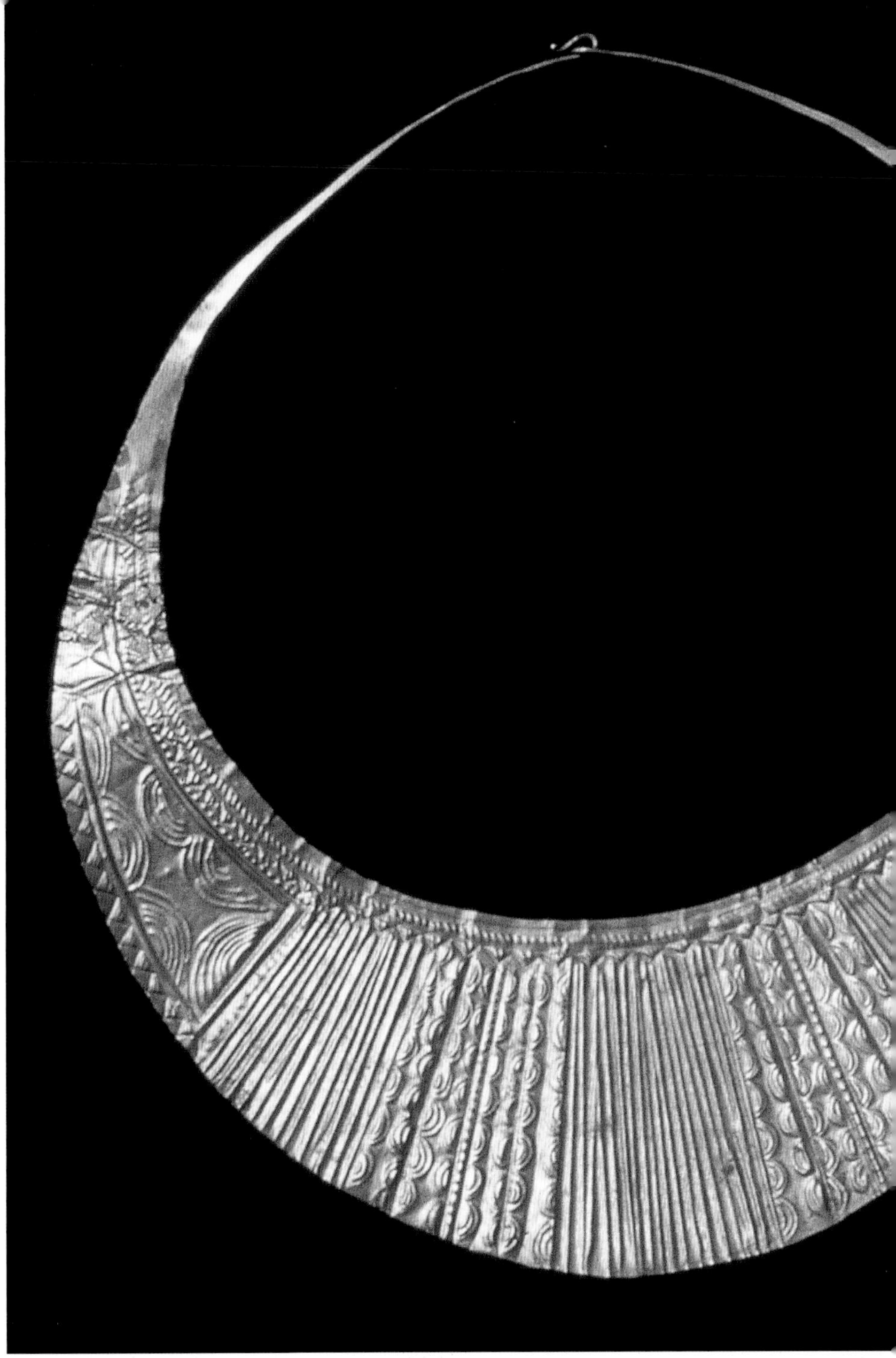

221

222

223

224

225

Sumatra

223 Toba Batak brass *sitepal* earring with projecting knobs, from north Sumatra, 19th century or earlier. Men wore the asymmetrical *sitepal* in the right lobe. The symmetrical *duri-duri* was worn in the left. These earrings may be local versions of the spiky pendants from Oc Eo and Java, and the knobbed Dvaravati ear ornaments from Thailand, Maluku and the Philippines, which may represent stylized *nagas* (Pls 33, 78, 243, 324). It is also possible that, like similar ear ornaments in Indonesia and the Philippines, the form is based on female genitalia.

224 Gilded silver earrings (*padung curu-curu*) worn by aristocratic Karo Batak women, early 20th century. The pendants represent a bird's nest which, like the homes of wealthy women, is filled with accumulated treasures.

225 Gold and gilded silver Karo Batak bracelet for a nobleman (*gelang sarung*), late 19th–early 20th century.

226 A collection of Karo Batak pieces, late 19th–early 20th century, shown on a ceremonial mantle (*ulos*). The woman's ear-pendants are of gilded silver. The ceremonial bracelet for a man (*gelang sarung*) is of a simpler type than that seen in Pl. 225; of gilded silver and *suasa* alloy, it is decorated with house-roof/horn motifs and applied filigree and granulation. The beaded bag displays the characteristic colours of red, white and black or indigo, which symbolize the Batak marriage alliance system and the three realms of the ancestors, human beings, and the underworld.

226

The eastern islands

227 Gold *mamuli* ear ornament from east Sumba, 19th century or earlier. Like other ornaments of this type found in the eastern islands (Pls 13, 228) and in the Philippines, the form is thought to invoke the life-giving power of female genitalia. The rigged boat, sun and sailor motifs in this example are very unusual. They may be intended to represent the primordial journey of the founding ancestors who came from far away at a time when the space between earth and sky was narrow. The boat may also evoke the wealth and status generated for the aristocracy by inter-island trade in horses and slaves, which were exchanged for exotic goods.

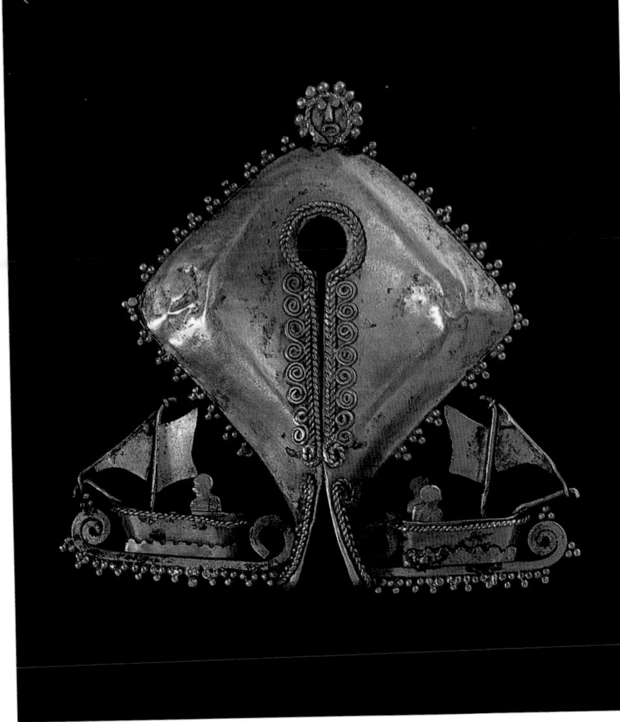

227

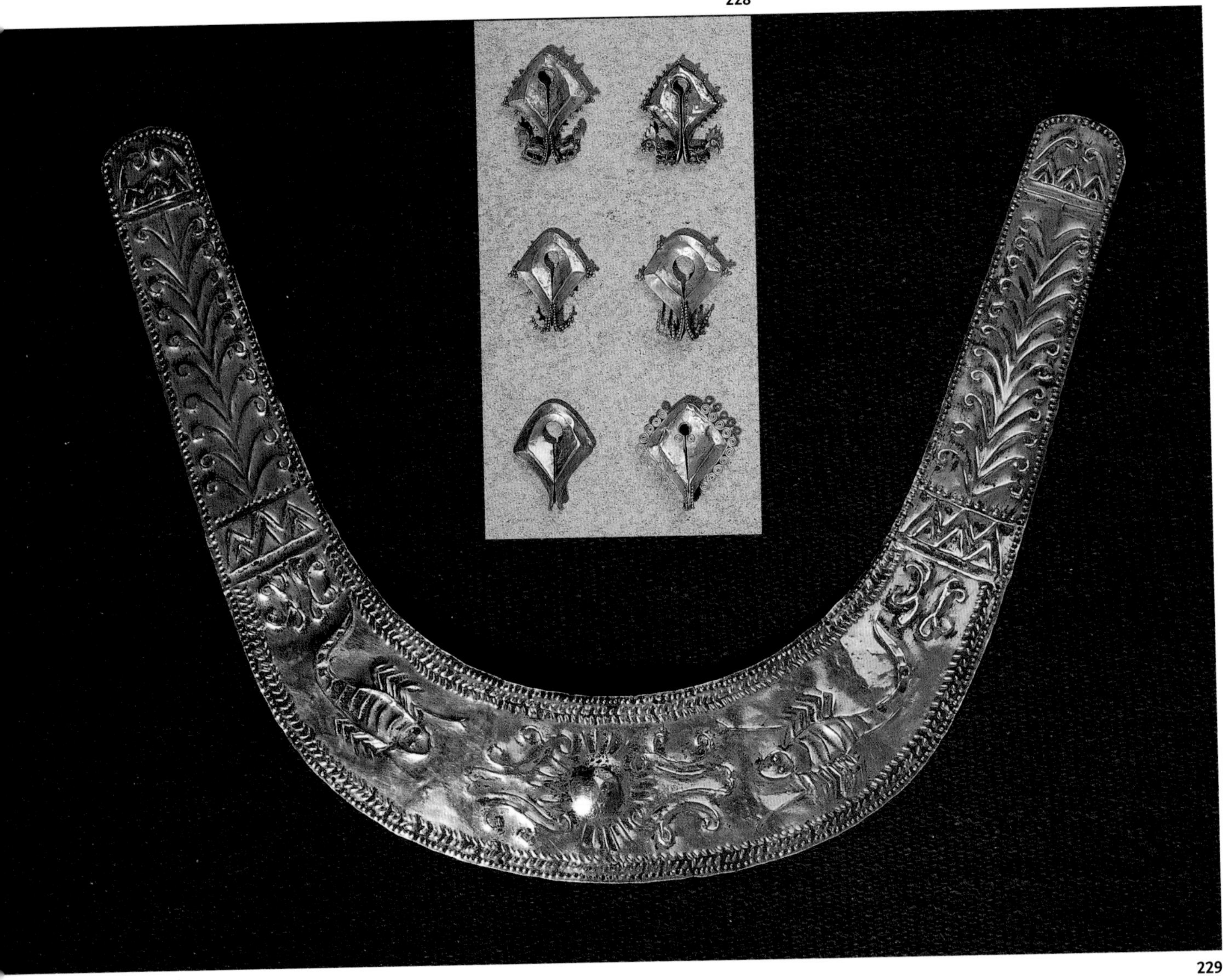

228 Gold *mamuli* ornaments with applied filigree spirals and granulation, from east Sumba, 19th century or earlier. Complex *mamuli* with animal, bird and human figures were usually regarded as house or lineage treasures and were not worn or given in marriage gift exchanges. Simpler ones were suspended from the ears or neck by strings or chains and worn at important festivities.

229 Gold repoussé frontal (*lamba*) worn on the forehead by aristocratic men at ritual celebrations and dances, from east Sumba, 19th century or earlier. The shrimp, which sheds its outer shells as it grows, symbolizes the endless renewal of royal power.

228

229

230

231

232

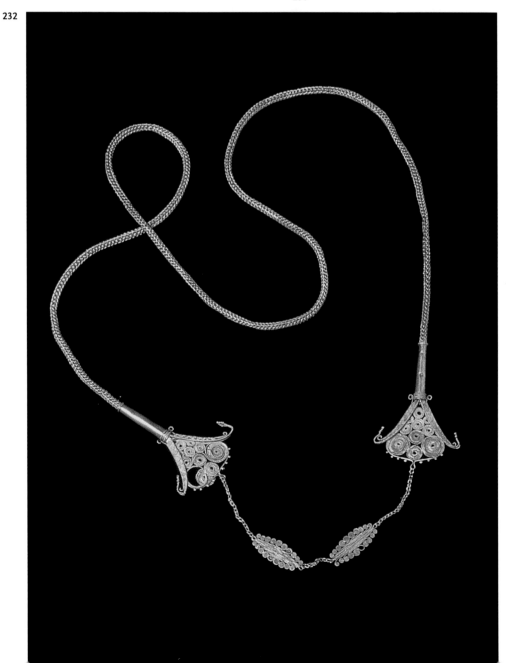

230 Gold pectoral ornament (*marangga*) from west Sumba, 19th century or earlier. Such ornaments are regarded as house treasures of immense magical power and are only used on especially important and sacred occasions. They may be related to first-millennium Javanese ornaments of the same shape but narrower (Pl. 161); they also resemble brass pendants found in central Sulawesi and ear ornaments worn by minority peoples in Vietnam (Pl. 133).

231 Gold repoussé Nage frontal in three tiers with applied filigree and motifs of bird heads, stars and suns, from central Flores, 19th century or earlier. The crescent forms evoke the moon, boats, and buffalo horns.

232 Royal chain (*kanatar*) of finely woven gold wire, from east Sumba, 19th century or earlier. The delicate terminals are formed as stylized *nagas* from whose open mouths, filled with complex spirals, the lower chains and filigree ornaments descend.
In the past the *kanatar* was worn not by the ruler but by his personal slave, who mediated in trance on his behalf between the mundane and spirit worlds. Gold ornaments with fine chains and spiral ornament were a speciality of the itinerant jewellers of Roti and Ndao islands.

233

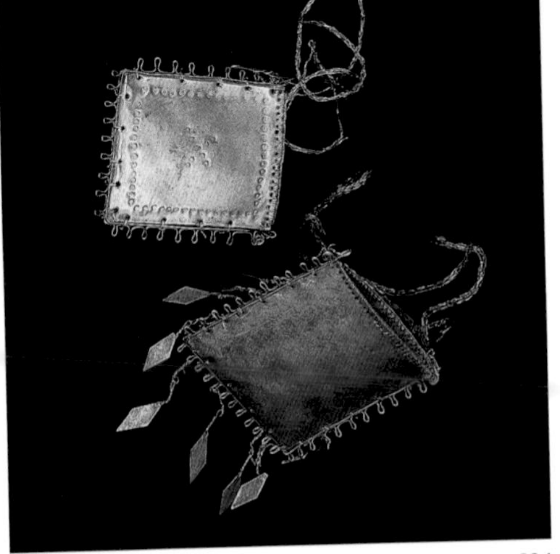

234

The eastern islands

233 Gold crown from eastern Flores, 19th century. The very unusual form seems to reflect Portuguese influence, which was absorbed into the repertoire of ornaments worn by noblemen. The repoussé bands may be of local origin; the stars appear to have been adapted from ear-studs common in Islamic trading communities of Indonesia or Malaysia.

234 Ngada pendant bags of gold and an alloy of copper, gold and silver, with decorative filigree borders, dangling leaves and chains, from central Flores, 19th century or earlier. Similar bags of pre-Islamic Javanese origin are in the National Museum in Jakarta: some may have been traded to the eastern islands, or subsequently copied.

235 Gold frontal with repoussé fertility motifs of ripe heads of grain, from central Flores, 19th century or earlier. The filigree balls suggest the influence of the Muslim goldsmiths of the nearby island of Sumbawa. Similar crescents were suspended on chains as pectorals.

236 Gold alloy Nage pectoral discs and an aristocratic warrior's necklace of gold pendants, perhaps intended to resemble the gold shells in royal necklaces (Pl. 159), from central Flores, 19th century or earlier.

237 Gold head ornament mounted on a comb, from central Flores, 19th century or earlier. Its tree-like form suggests the structure of the tiered cosmos, while the upper section also suggests the spreading horns of the buffalo.

235

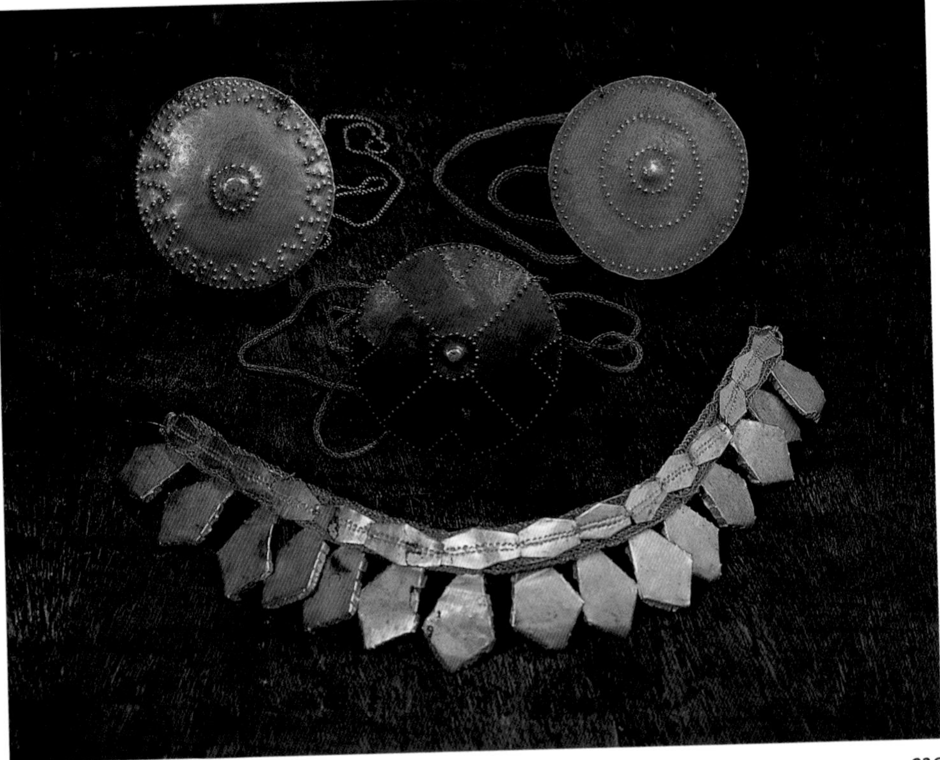

236

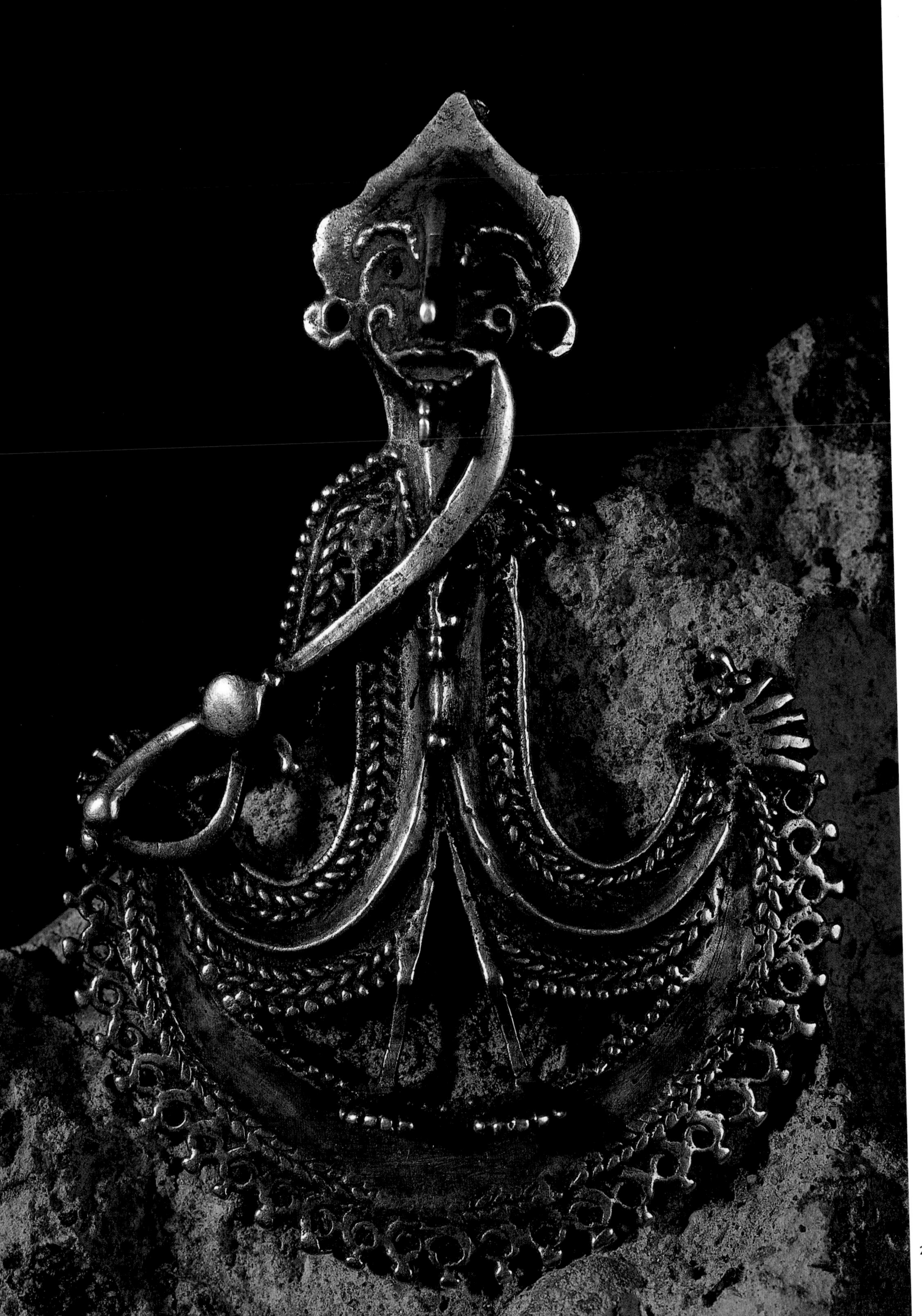

The eastern islands

238 A very rare stained silver and gold alloy ornament from central or eastern Flores, 16th–19th century. The figure appears to be wearing a helmet of Portuguese style and a long buttoned European jacket, and to wield a European cutlass. It may have been intended to invest an ancestor with the magical protective powers of Portuguese weaponry and costume.

239 Gold aristocratic Lio ear pendants (*tebe* or *ate saga*) with complex filigree decoration, from central Flores, 19th century or earlier. These are given as engagement presents to prospective brides; however, they are essentially the property of the ancestors and may embody magic powers. They have been known to move about and make tiny noises to indicate that the ancestors wish to communicate with their descendants.

240 Ngada and Nage ornaments from central Flores, 19th century or earlier. The gold pendant or *taka* (top), similar to the *marangga* (Pl. 230), is worn by Ngada men and women on a chain or suspended from a headband; the removal of a *taka* from its hiding place in the house roof requires the sacrifice of a small animal, and a blood libation is sprinkled on the ornament before it may be worn. The central ear pendants (*iti bholo*) have ridged decoration and filigree. The oval split-ring ear ornaments (*bela*) may be worn with a *taka*.

241, 242 Silver bracelets owned by aristocrats, cast by the lost-wax method by the Tetum-speaking people of the Belu area in central Timor, 19th century. They represent the house as a microcosm of the universe and the social world and its inhabitants.

239

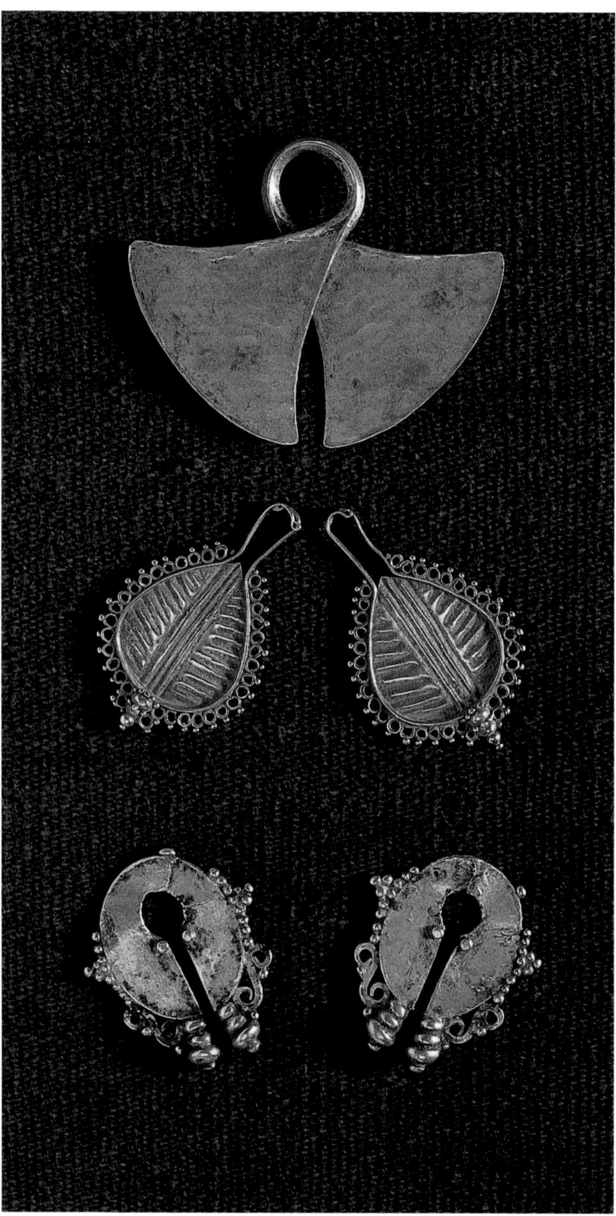

240

241

242

245

243

The eastern islands

243 Electrum pectoral disc and gold ear ornaments from Tanimbar in Maluku, eastern Indonesia, 19th century or earlier. Many of the ear ornaments resemble 1st-millennium ornaments of the mainland, Java and Sumatra; the one lower left recalls pieces from Oc Eo, early Thailand, Sumatra and the Philippines (cf. Pl. 223).

244 Gold alloy pectoral disc and bracelet from west Timor, 19th century or earlier. The 'moon' disc with 'eyes' signifies the heroism of the successful head hunter. It shows signs of red staining that has interacted with the silver content to form a brownish coating.

245 Pieces from island Indonesia, 19th century or earlier. The ivory bracelet is from Sumba. The silver pendant, worn by the Atoni people of west Timor, shows continuity of spiral decoration. Three heavy silver bracelets with spiral decoration and bold bosses were made by the Tetum-speaking people of Belu, central Timor. The woman's bracelet with a star-fruit bud flanked by birds symbolizes female fertility. The textile is an Atoni mantle (*selimut*), which incorporates typical Dong Son motifs. Baskets of woven pandanus leaves are often used to store jewelry.

244

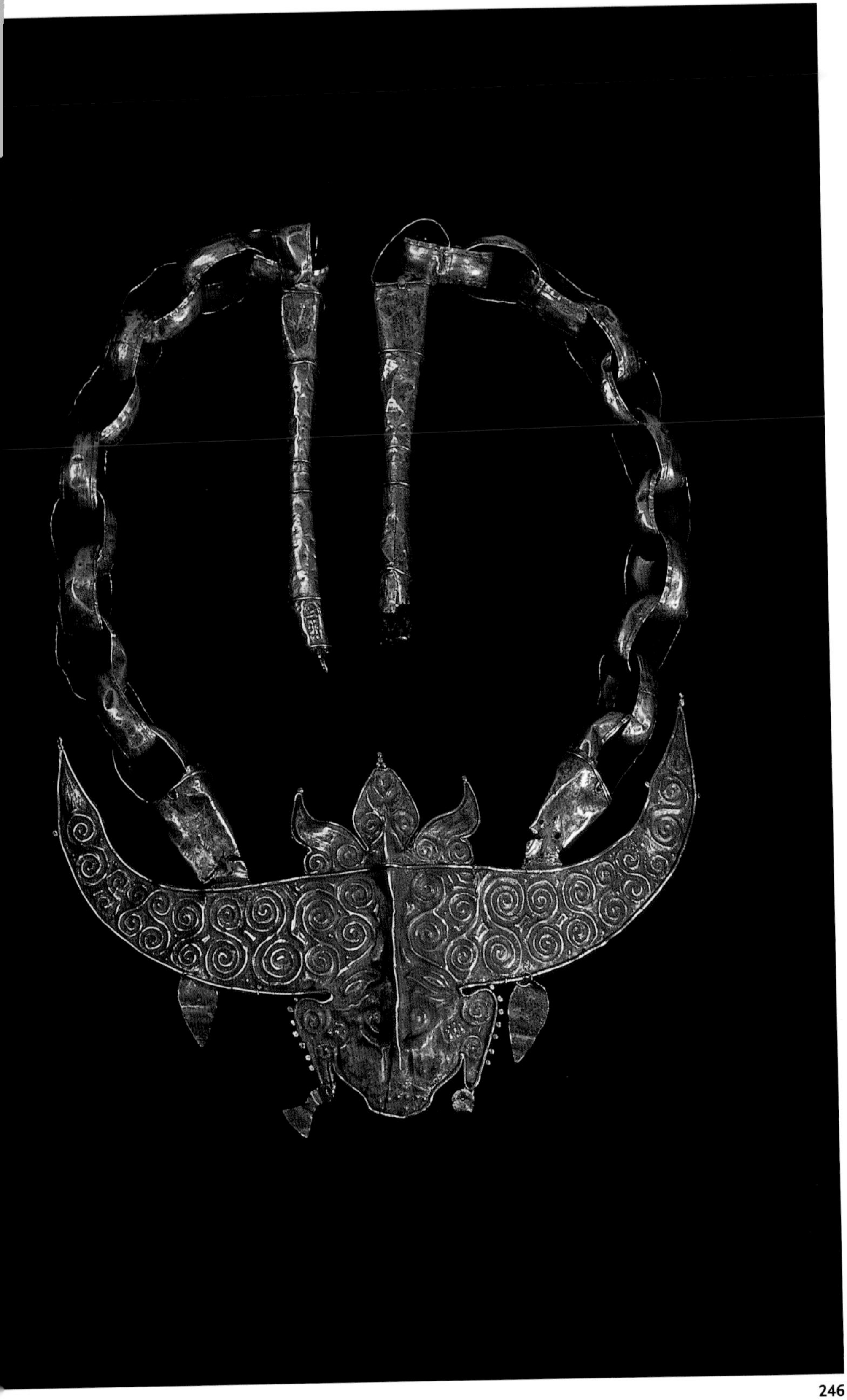

The eastern islands

246 Pectoral or frontal ornament of gold with red staining from Yamdena island, Tanimbar, Maluku, 19th–early 20th century or earlier. It depicts a human face surmounted by a wide crescent evoking buffalo horns. Ornaments of this type are the insignia of triumph in warfare and hunting.

247 Turtle-shell comb (*hai kara jangga*) worn by women and girls of east Sumba, 19th–early 20th century. Antlered deer symbolize royalty. The confronting fighting cocks or male parrots represent the upper world of spirits, ancestors and the nobility, but also the aggression of aristocratic warriors.

246

247

248 Pectoral ornament depicting a smiling human figure, from Tanimbar, Maluku, 19th century or earlier. Such pieces, not necessarily of religious significance, were probably acquired by trade from Bali or Java, or made by visiting goldsmiths from those islands.

248

249

249 Women's imported ear ornaments from Tanimbar, Maluku, 19th–early 20th century or earlier. Although composed of 'hot' gold, they are regarded as 'cool' because of their femininity and open lacy structure. They are employed in ceremonies for cooling the earth prior to the erection of a new house.

250 A gold bowl from Kisar, Maluku, 19th–20th century or earlier. These prestigious bowls might be worn upturned on the head or, suspended on string, as pectoral ornaments. While gold bowls were employed as trade items and diplomatic gifts in Java and on the mainland, they are also manufactured on Kisar island; however, the form may have been adapted from imported models.

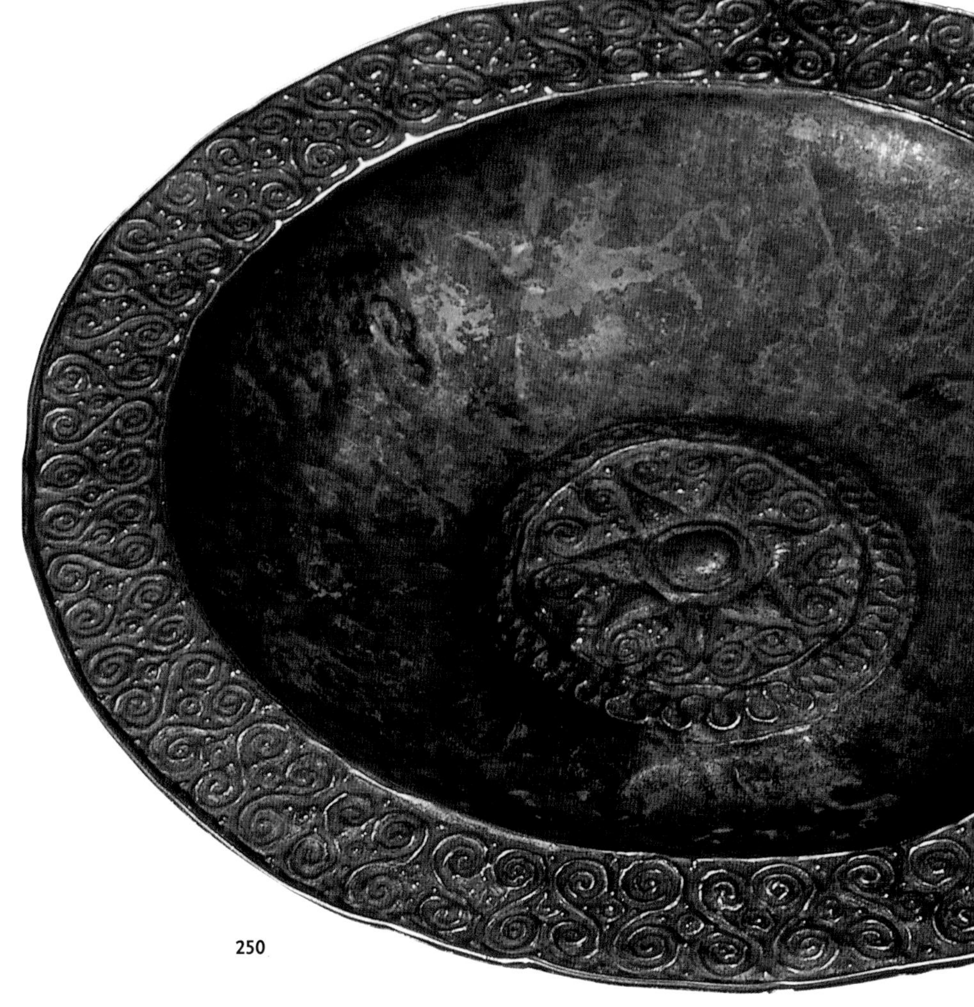
250

Sulawesi

251, 252 Royal regalia of the kingdom of Gowa, based at Makassar in south Sulawesi, *c.* 14th–15th century. The crown, *Salokoa*, of gold, diamonds and coloured stones, is believed to have been worn by the ancestral foundress of Gowa as she descended from the heavens. Its form resembles that of other Southeast Asian Buddhist crowns and helmets (Pls 35, 42, 87, 181). Bracelets in *naga* form – these are the royal *Ponto Janga Jangaya*, of gold with sapphire eyes – are still worn by bridegrooms in Java (Pl. 183) and south Sulawesi.

251

252

253

254

255

256

253 Silver amulet boxes (*jima boelaeng*) of the Bugis people, south Sulawesi, 19th century.

254 Modesty plaques (*jempang*) and pendant discs (*kawari*) from south Sulawesi, late 19th–early 20th century. Small girls from noble and well-to-do families wore these and often little else. *Kawari* were suspended on chains, usually one at the back and the other on the chest.

255 Gold ear-studs (*toge*) of the Bugis people of south Sulawesi and south Kalimantan, 19th–early 20th century. The stylized hornbill and plant motifs are an elaboration of a simpler dangling S-tail type (Pl. 171).

256 'The king's golden headdress', *Songko Mas Sangajikai*, of the Bima sultanate, Sumbawa, of red-stained gold set with diamonds, late 18th century or earlier. Buginese and Makassan influence was strong in west Sumbawa, and its shape resembles the *songkok* of finely woven vegetable fibre or precious metal worn in south Sulawesi. The Chinese character of the vegetal motifs, however, suggests the influence of Balinese goldsmiths.

257 Bugis gold cuff bracelet (*tigero tedong*) ribbed to represent the cervical vertebrae of the buffalo, with applied filigree and granulation, from south Sulawesi, 19th century. This type was thought of as a substitute for the numerous slim gold bracelets worn by royal women.

Sulawesi

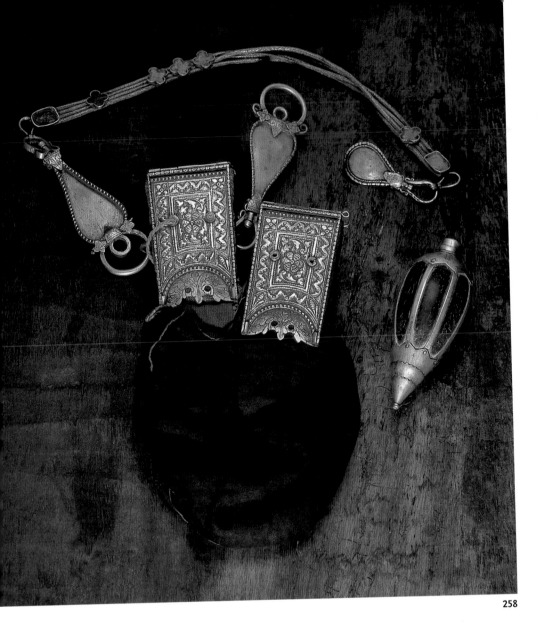

258 Bag of black cotton with silver fittings and chain attachments used to hold betel equipment and necessaries, convenient for a man travelling on horseback, from south Sulawesi, 19th century. The coconut shell and silver container (*pamoneang paleo*) held the lime ingredient in the betel plug.

259–261 A Bugis rectangular amulet box (*tokeng maili*) inscribed in Arabic, and two scallop-edged Bugis *kawari* discs (cf. Pl. 254) found on Riouw island off north Sumatra, one embellished with floral designs in applied filigree and the other with propitious Arabic numerals, 19th–early 20th century.

262 Gold embossed Bugis *kawari* of a type found in south Sulawesi and also in Riouw, where it is called a *koearik*, 19th–early 20th century.

258

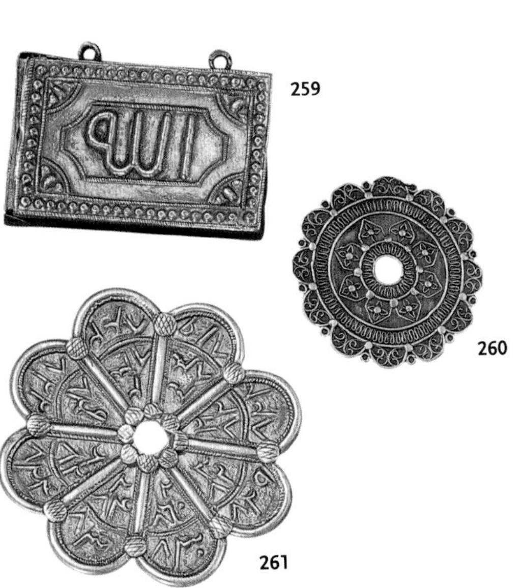

259

260

261

262

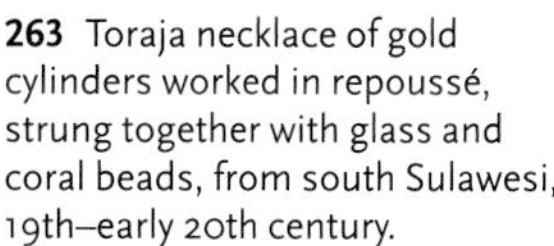

263

263 Toraja necklace of gold cylinders worked in repoussé, strung together with glass and coral beads, from south Sulawesi, 19th–early 20th century.

264 Silver containers (*celepa*) for tobacco and betel equipment worn attached to a man's belt or kerchief, 19th–early 20th century.

The lobed tobacco box on the right with the matching decorative chain is from south Sulawesi (*celepa atarong*). The tobacco boxes in the centre (*celepa poedesi*), with attached boxes for lime and gambir in the shape of mangosteen fruits, are from west Sumatra.

264

265

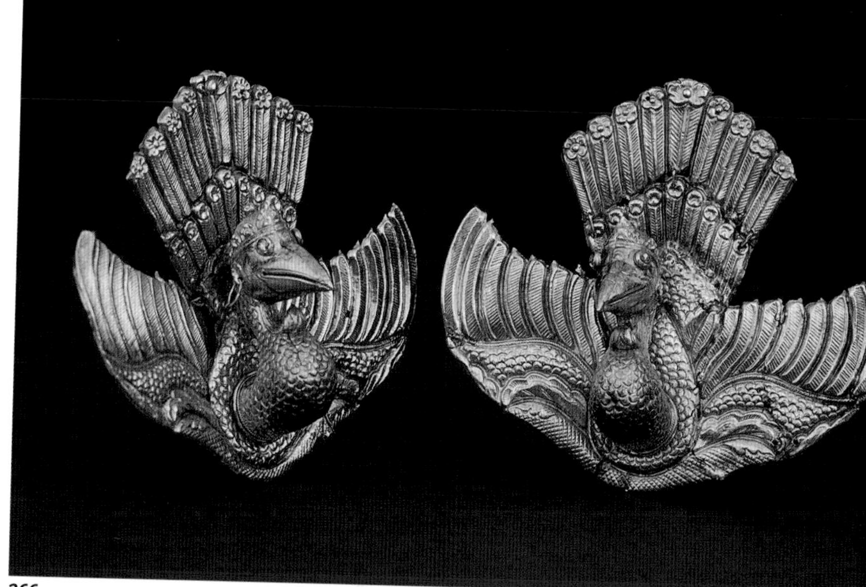

266

267

268

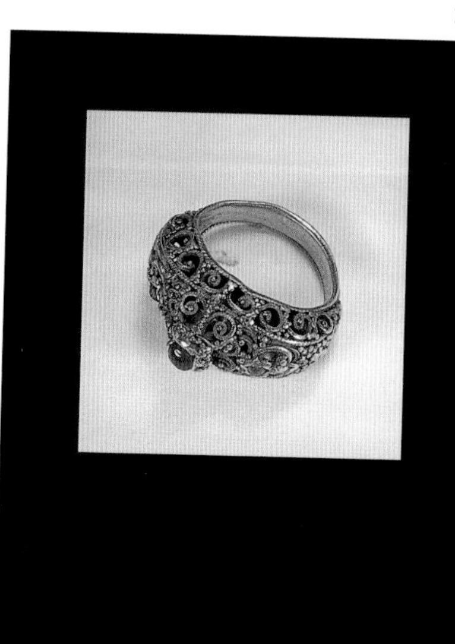

Borneo

265 Embossed pectoral plaque of gold with a copper backing, from Kutai, west Kalimantan, probably 19th century. The paired *nagas* are an important motif locally.

266 Armlets in the form of Garuda, of gold set with diamonds, from Kutai, west Kalimantan, 19th century.

267 Gold bracelets from Kutai, west Kalimantan, 19th century. These have the pointed *gunungan* (mountain) motif as well as the ridged pattern found on the bracelet from Sulawesi (Pl. 257).

268 Gold ring set with emeralds and a ruby, from western Borneo, 18th century or earlier. The notched filigree and the granulation recall medieval Middle-Eastern work.

269

Ornaments were dispersed beyond their place of origin, particularly among trading coastal peoples.

269 The ear-studs lower right, from Aceh, are of *suasa* with rough-cut grey Borneo diamonds and applied filigree. The long ear-cylinders (*subang*), from Makassar, are of an alloy with a low gold content, stained red, and decorated with filigree. The ear-studs at the top have the faceted granular decoration typical of the Malay Peninsula. All are late 19th- or early 20th-century.

270 Gold necklace from Lampung with horn motifs; such filigree pendants are widely employed in Sumatran jewelry. The bracelets display variations on ancient breast/flower and triangle motifs. The engraved red-stained bracelet shows Javanese influence. The *naga* bracelet, of a type widely circulated, was probably made by a Chinese craftsman in Surabaya, east Java.

271 Embossed gilded silver plaques, sewn around the neck opening of a garment for ceremonial occasions. Melanau people, Sarawak, 20th century.

272 An early 20th-century gilded silver necklace in Sumatran style worn by Melanau brides of Sarawak, a 19th-century *dokoh* pendant of gold alloy embossed with vegetal patterns, mounted on copper and set with a clear stone, from the east coast of the Malay Peninsula, and 19th-century Malay wedding anklets of gilded silver with lotus-bud tips.

270

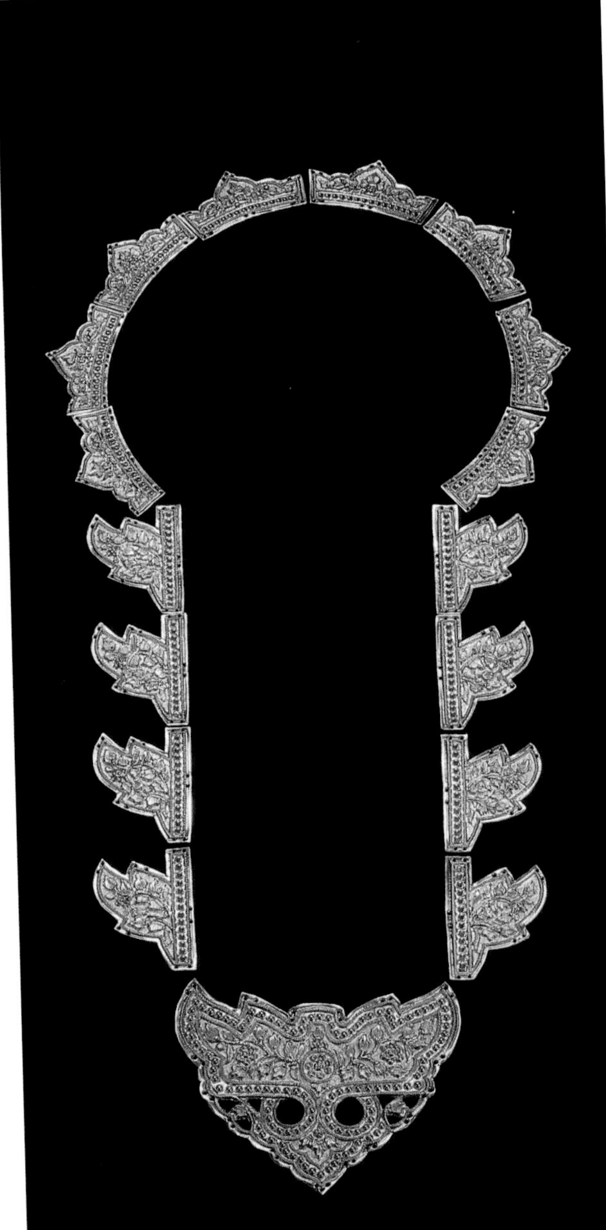

271

273

274

Borneo

273 Brass ear ornaments of the Kenyah and Kayan Dayak peoples of central Kalimantan, Indonesia, and Sarawak, Malaysia, 19th–20th century. The dragon form is that of Aso, the feminine underworld fertility deity.

274 Embossed copper alloy ornament worn as a frontal by the Kenyah and Kayan Dayak peoples of Kalimantan and Sarawak, 19th century. The curvilinear plant-like limbs identify the stylized squatting figure as the Tree of Life deity, often depicted in association with the dragon goddess.

275 Iban Dayak rattan corset and silver wedding crown decorated with silver wire, from Sarawak, 20th century. Sea Dayak traditions of ornament have incorporated aspects of Malay and Chinese decoration.

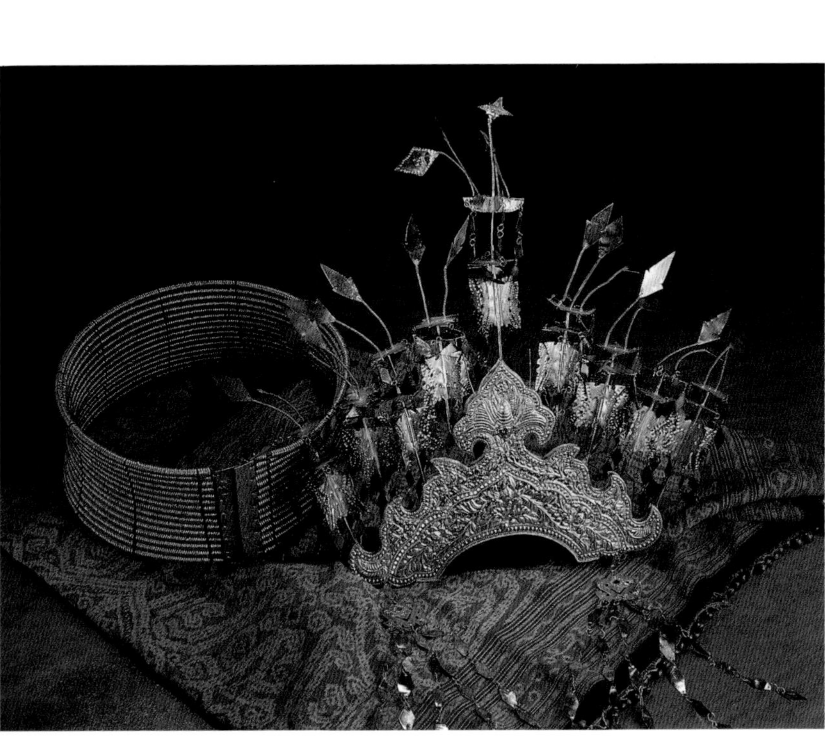

275

276

277

276 Bidayuh Dayak necklace of brass bells, coins, honey-bear teeth and glass beads, from Sarawak, 20th century. The colours reflect the structure and unity of the tiered cosmos, the nexus between male and female, and thus signify fertility. The Chinese glass beads are highly valued by the Bidayuh.

277 Bidayuh Dayak man's necklace of rattan, cowrie shells, blue glass beads and honey-bear teeth. The beads were probably manufactured in Amsterdam, in the 16th century or later.

278

MALAYSIA

278 Buckles (*pending*) and tobacco boxes (*celepa*). Buckles: left, 19th-century niello, with a magically powerful divinatory palindromic square; top right, modern silver embossed and engraved with foliage in a style common in Perak; lower right, 19th-century silver, with a sunburst motif typical of Negeri Sembilan. Tobacco boxes: top left, late 18th–early 19th-century niello from southern Thailand, formerly a Malay state, with a combination of Thai and Malay decorative influences; top centre, early 19th-century silver with embossed palmettes; bottom, 19th–early 20th-century silver tobacco box and lime container from Sumatra.

279 Gold tobacco box, believed to have been the property of Sultan Zainal Abidin III of Terengganu (1725–33). The ten-pointed form probably represents a lotus flower. It is richly decorated with applied filigree, granules and spangles and set with rubies and clear stones. The contrast of yellow and red-stained gold accentuates the complexity of the decoration.

280 Embossed gold buckle (*pending*), 18th–19th century. The central boss is surrounded by flower petals and by concentric vegetal motifs set within borders of punched half-moons forming a water pattern. Buckles were attached by two metal loops at the back to the cloth sashes worn mainly by men to secure their sarongs.

281 Gold buckle opulently decorated with embossed leafy shoots and stems and with gem-set flowers and buds, 18th–19th century. The centre of each four-petalled flower has a tiny floweret composed of gold granules. The eight-pointed star form of the central motif, defined by applied filigree wires, represents a lotus flower.

282 Small rectangular red-stained gold buckle, perhaps for a woman, from Kelentan in north-eastern Malaysia, 18th century. It is embossed with vegetal designs and set with a central green stone and rough-cut rubies.

283 Gold buckle with a central lotus motif, decorated with applied filigree, embossing, and coloured gemstones in box settings, 18th–19th century.

280

281

282

284 Fine gold modesty plaque (*caping*), 19th century. One of this quality would have been worn by a girl from a royal or aristocratic family. The embossed flower motifs represent the breasts, and the bamboo shoot at the bottom the female genitalia. Other motifs include the leaves and fruits of the *mengkudu* plant (*Morinda citrifolia*), which produces a red dye widely used in textiles to indicate high status.

285 Silver *caping* from the east coast of Malaysia, 19th century, enhanced by applied tendrils of gold filigree and beading.

286 Gold *kerongsang rantay* set, Malay, 19th century. Brooches with Islamic motifs of stars and crescent moons, embellished with rows of boldly faceted granules, are linked by chains and foliate elements.

284

285

286

287

287 Large gold Malay ear-studs (*subang*) formed as lotus flowers, with applied filigree, faceted granules and spangles accentuated with red staining, 19th century.

288 Gold jacket button with Chinese floral motifs, 19th century.

289 Gold embossed crown, probably originally set with precious stones, 19th century. The *mahkota* was worn with a white headcloth by young female members of royal families at the ceremony which celebrated the completion of their study and recitation of the Koran.

288

289

290

290 Gold ring set with clear stones to form Islamic crescent moon and star motifs, 19th century.

291 Malay gold ring of elaborate fretwork set with a central ruby and small blue and black sapphires, late 19th century. Similar rings were made in Bali.

292 Gold ring with an eight-sided bezel, decorated with applied filigree and spangles, 19th century. Rings of this type worn by Karo Batak people in north Sumatra were sometimes used by sorcerers as containers for medicines and potions.

291

292

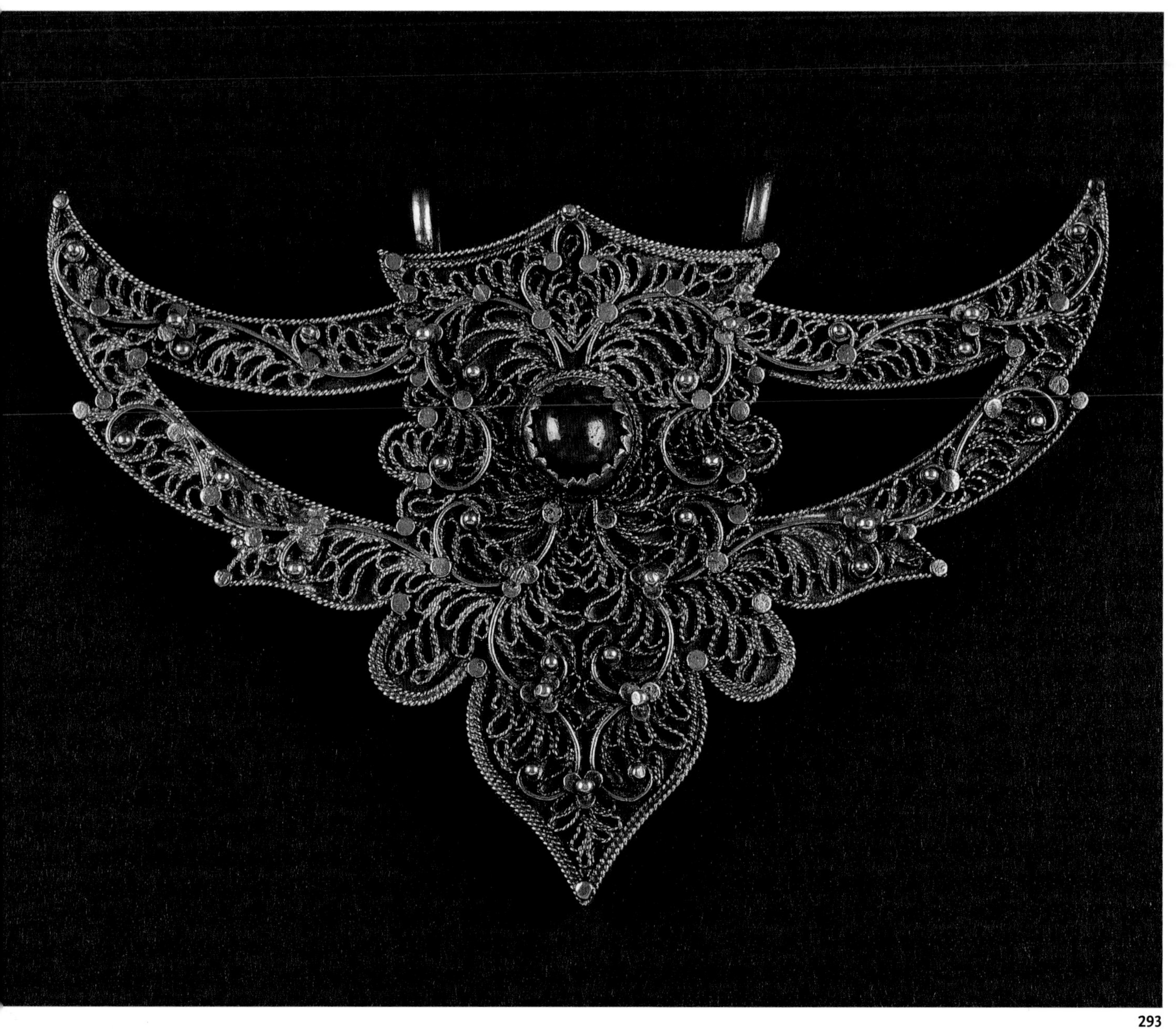

293

293 Gold pendant for a necklace (*dokoh*), 19th century. In breadfruit leaf (*sukun*) form, it is decorated with applied serrated ribbon filigree, granulation, and flat spangles known as *telur ikan* ('fish eggs'), and set with a red stone.

294 Gold *dokoh* necklace elaborated with applied filigree, granulation and slight red staining, 19th century. The central pendant, of breadfruit leaf shape, is set with a large black cabochon stone. One turtle pendant is set with clear quartz and the other with an opaque grey stone; the fish charms are worked in repoussé, and the oval pendants are set with agates. Turtles and fish, both Hindu and Buddhist symbols, were common in necklaces worn by Thai children; this may have been for a child, judging by its short chain.

294

CHINESE COMMUNITIES OF SOUTHEAST ASIA

295 Necklace of very fine granulated and filigree red-stained gold beads of Chinese workmanship, early 20th century, owned by a Nonya of Penang, Malaysia, and a set of 19th-century yellow gold and red-stained brooches from the east coast of the Malay Peninsula. The brooch frames are embellished with ribbons surmounted by flowers cut from sheet gold to create a three-dimensional and richly textured effect.

296 Rare gold belt and matching buckle made by the prestigious Da Xing firm of Hong Kong and Singapore in the early 20th century, owned by a Penang Nonya. Its chased panels are elaborated with nuptial and Taoist scenes and flowers.

295

296

297

298

297 Long silver brooch with floral and insect motifs (*peniti tak*) set with small Borneo diamonds, from Tangerang in west Java, Indonesia, early 20th century.

298 Hairpins with symbols of marital felicity such as butterflies and birds, of fine gold filigree, pearls, and imperial jade. They were probably imported from China in the late 19th–early 20th century.

299 Gold and silver *kerongsang* set from Penang of a type popular in 1920 and before, encrusted with brilliant-cut diamonds in the 'Peruzzi' style. The leaf- or heart-shaped *ibu serong* is worn at the top.

299

300

301

300 Gold buckle of outstanding quality made by the Da Xing firm (cf. Pl. 296). The central medallion is surrounded by a band enclosing four Taoist deities and the flowers of the four seasons, separated by a key fret border from a zone of mythical and auspicious animals, floral sprays and prawns.

301 Gilded silver heart-shaped top brooch (*ibu serong*), from Melaka, Indonesia, set with a red stone and decorated with shrimps, phoenixes, leaves and flowers. The curling feelers of the shrimp frame the upper bird, which plunges its beak into an open blossom. Cut work, faceted granulation, filigree, engraving and lost-wax casting have all been employed in producing this technically extravagant ornament.

302

303

304

305

306

302 Matching set of silver and pearl mourning jewelry comprising a hairpin, pendant and bracelet, *c.* 1920 or possibly later. The whiteness of silver and pearls is associated with death in Chinese tradition; sombre blue and white batik sarongs were worn during mourning.

303 Four small gold brooches set with diamonds, formed as insects and a phoenix, 19th–early 20th century. Each would be the central ornament in a set of three brooches, an arrangement especially favoured in Melaka and Singapore.

304 Gold amulet (*sangkut bahu*) in the form of a carp, a symbol of longevity, late 19th century. The enclosed jade is associated with moral virtues and longevity. Ornaments of this type were usually worn by children in the Straits Settlements and in Java.

305 Gold butterfly brooch (*peniti kupon*) with a large diamond in the body and tiny diamond chips set *à jour* in the wings, made in Java by a Chinese goldsmith, early 20th century. Butterfly brooches were worn in sets.

306 A set of three large gold brooches (*kerongsang*) with rose-cut diamonds in open-backed frames creating a lead-light effect, from the Straits Settlements, *c.* 1920 (the chains are a more recent addition). Each includes a bird and crescent moon.

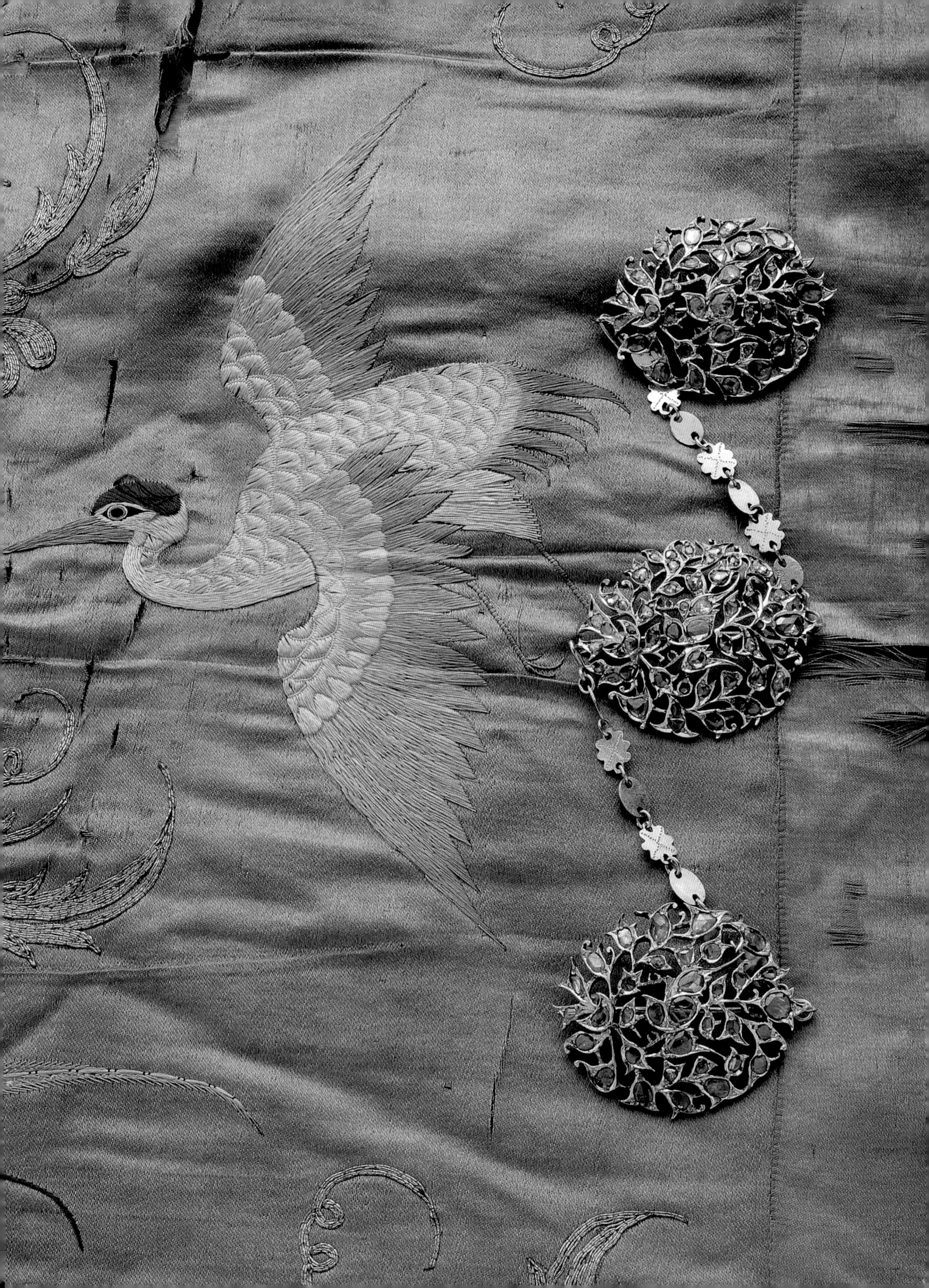

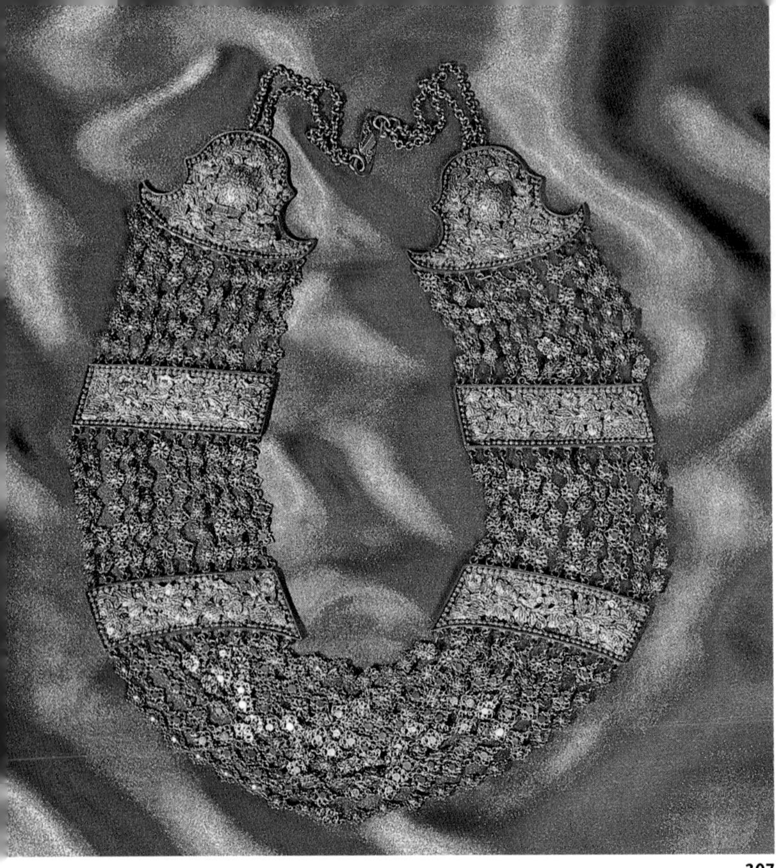

307

308

309

310

307 Gilded silver necklace (*agok*) of Chinese workmanship worn by a Malay bridegroom in coastal west Kalimantan, Indonesia, late 19th century. Similar necklaces with bird and butterfly motifs were made for Chinese brides in the Straits Settlements of Singapore, Melaka and Penang. The form is of ancient Indian origin.

308 A pair of wedding ear pendants (*kraboe gombel*) of gilded silver set with rough-cut Borneo diamonds, early 20th century. The butterflies, symbols of marital joy, and flowers are typical of jewelry made by Chinese artisans in west Java.

309 Heavy gold chain bracelet in the form of a double-headed dragon richly encrusted with rose-cut diamonds and with emerald eyes. This unusual bracelet is representative of ornaments in Chinese style from Penang, Malaysia, 1920.

310 Butterfly ornaments studded with rose-cut diamonds, from Penang, late 19th century. They may have been attached to hairpins or a wedding crown.

311

311 Tortoise- or turtle-shell comb with a gold frame, from the Malay Peninsula, late 19th–early 20th century. The scalloped top with floral embossing and beading suggests a crown. Nonyas wore a single comb of this type, in combination with hairpins.

312 An especially lively gilded and embossed silver belt buckle of Chinese workmanship from Sarawak, Malaysia, early–mid-20th century. Borders include peonies and phoenixes; Taoist Immortals occupy the centre.

313 A pair of gold wedding bracelets stained red and studded with diamonds, probably made in Tangerang, west Java, early 20th century.

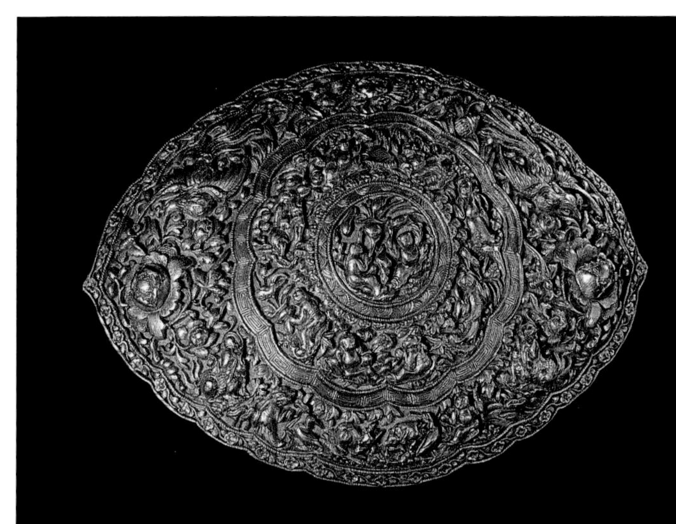

312

313

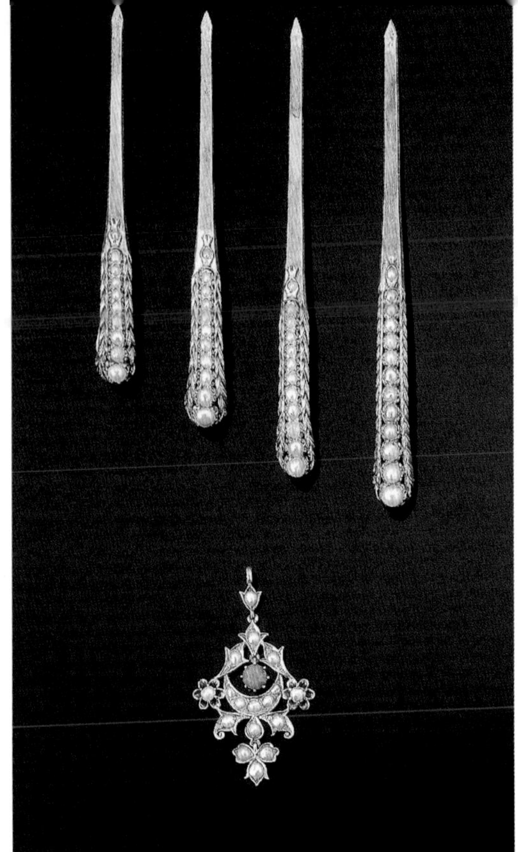

315

314

314 Nonya glass beadwork of outstanding quality, seen in a detail of an early 20th-century velvet mirror cover. Motifs include pomegranates, peonies, peaches and flowers, a monkey, a cockerel and a deer.

315 Engraved silver pearl-set hairpins of graduated size forming part of a set of six, and a necklace pendant set with pearl and green jadeite or Rangoon stone, from Penang, *c.* 1920.

316

316 Gold belt and buckle of the type traditionally worn by Muslim brides in Aceh, Indonesia, but also adopted by Chinese women in north Sumatra and elsewhere, *c.* 1920. The pierced openwork panels depict a peacock perched amid leaves and peonies. Some peacock belts are set with diamonds. Occasionally a different bird is depicted in each panel.

317 Anklets of bright-cut and matt gold decorated with embossed rose and cherry blossom motifs and lotus bud terminals, of Chinese workmanship, *c.* 1950.

318 Richly decorated gold buckle and gold panelled belt. The buckle, *c.* 1920, is set with a brilliant-cut diamond and elaborated with filigree, granulation and appliquéd motifs of birds, peonies and hibiscus leaves within a beaded rim. Appliqué work with large motifs as seen here was practised in west Java, but some of the most elegant examples were made by Chinese goldsmiths in Makassar. Also of a type made both in Java and in Makassar is the embossed belt, *c.* 1940.

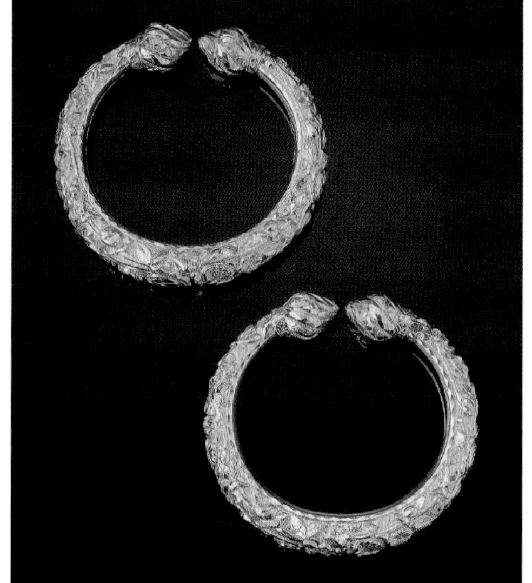

317

318

319, 320 Velvet purses with silver-gilt openwork plaques, worn attached to belts under the folds of wedding clothes, *c.* 1900. The smaller ones were for brides and the larger, longer ones for grooms. Motifs include flowers, Taoist deities and auspicious creatures. A coin was placed inside so that the couple would not enter married life with empty purses. Brides also wore the purses after the wedding, when plainer clothes showed them to advantage.

321 Silver scroll buckle embossed with fine floral sprays, dragons, birds and sea creatures, on a velvet-faced belt very finely beaded with zodiacal animals, flowers and leaves, 19th century.

322 Silver-gilt wedding crown in a style favoured by Straits communities, *c.* 1900, decorated with kingfisher feathers, glass jewels, artificial pearls and red silk pompoms. The Eight Immortals and other deities are set among flowers, dragons and phoenixes. The large Chinese characters mean 'favour bestowed by heaven, sun and moon'; the smaller characters in the little building at the top mean 'compassionate glory'.

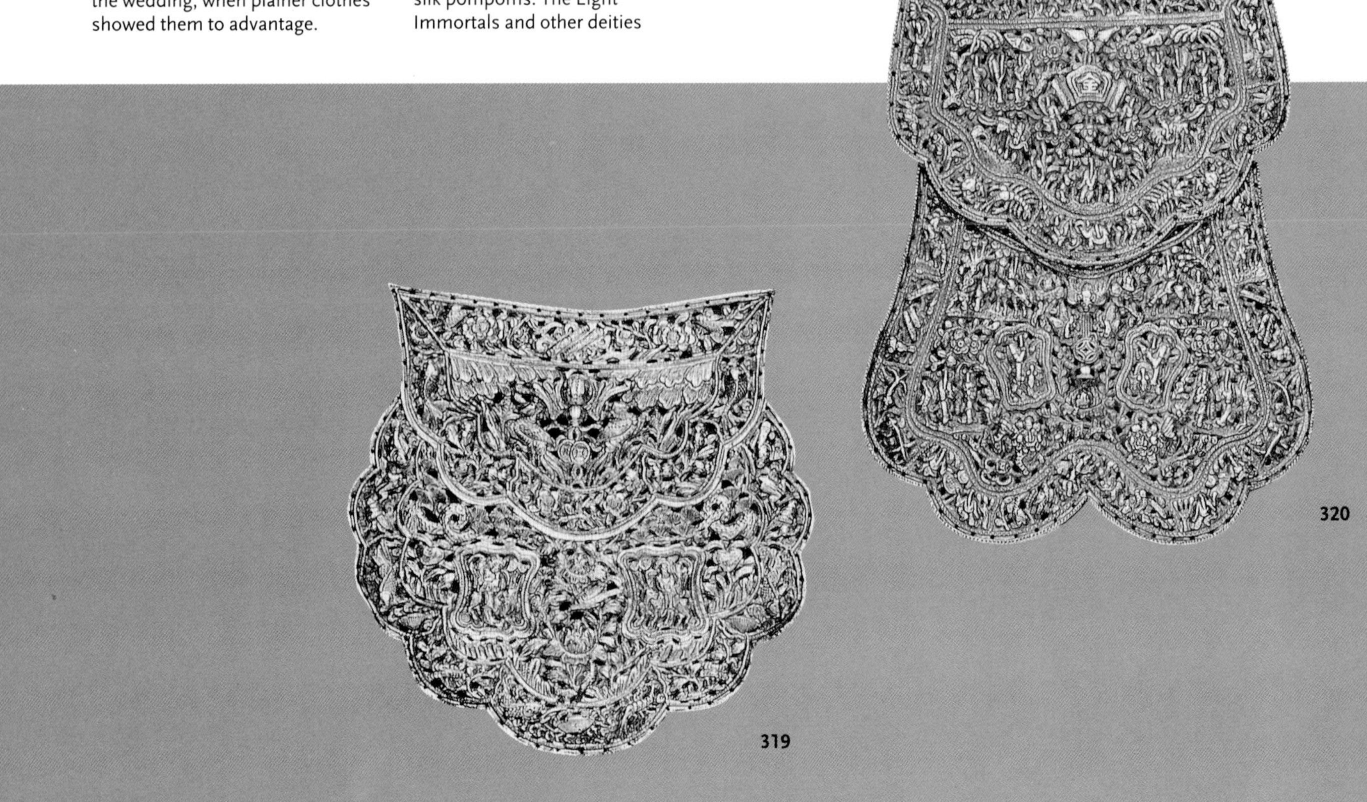

320

319

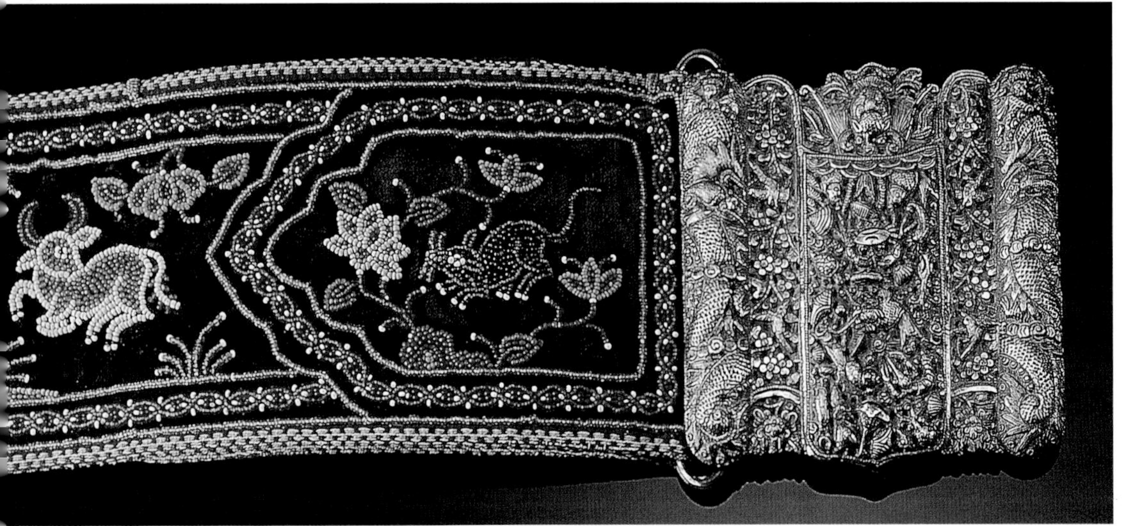

321

322

323

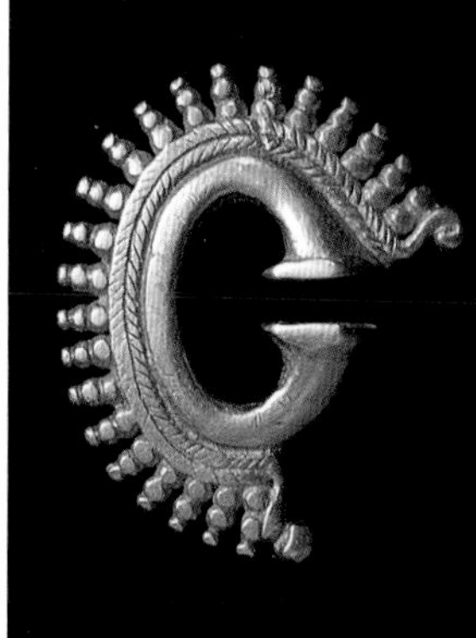

324

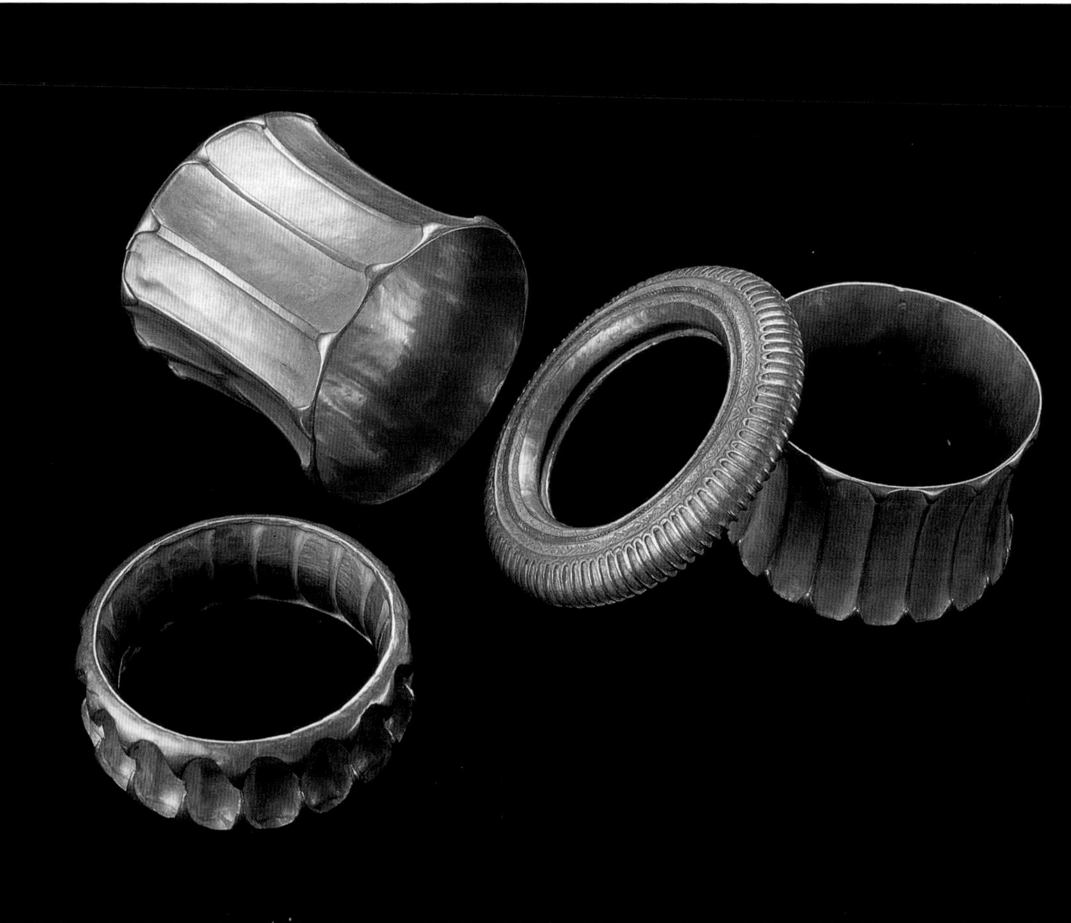

325

326

THE PHILIPPINES

323 Royal sashes of woven gold wire loops with clasps ornamented with fine granulation, from the Surigao hoard, recently discovered in northern Mindanao, 7th–13th century.

324 Gold split-ring ear ornament with a ridge of spines from Butuan, Mindanao, 8th–13th century. The form may represent a stylized *naga*. Similar pieces have been found at Oc Eo, and in Thailand, Java, Maluku and Sumatra (Pls 223, 243).

325 Three gold armlets of beaten gold with ridged ornamentation and a large bangle or anklet with an outer ribbed pattern and inner geometric engravings, from Cagayan valley, northern Luzon, late 1st–early 2nd millennium CE.

326 Royal sash buckles of gold worked in repoussé with central floral motifs surrounded by stylized hummingbirds and vegetal designs, from Butuan, Mindanao, 10th–13th century.

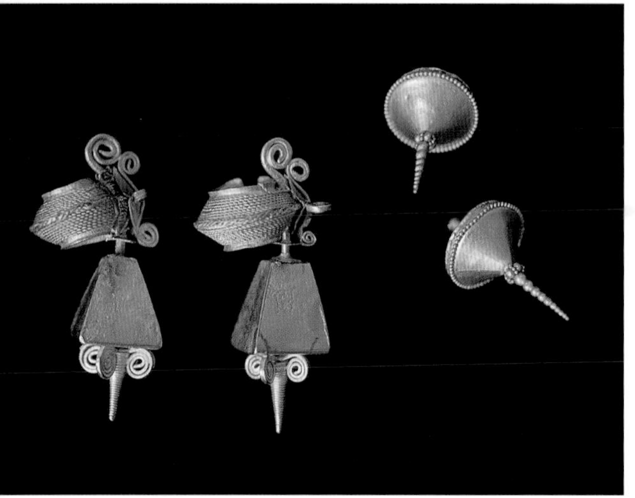

327

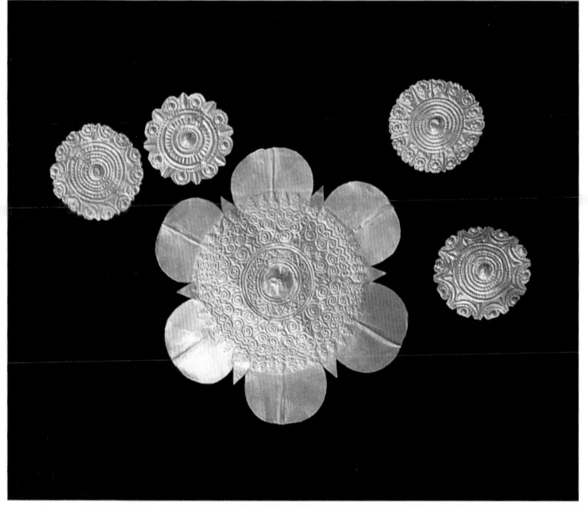

328

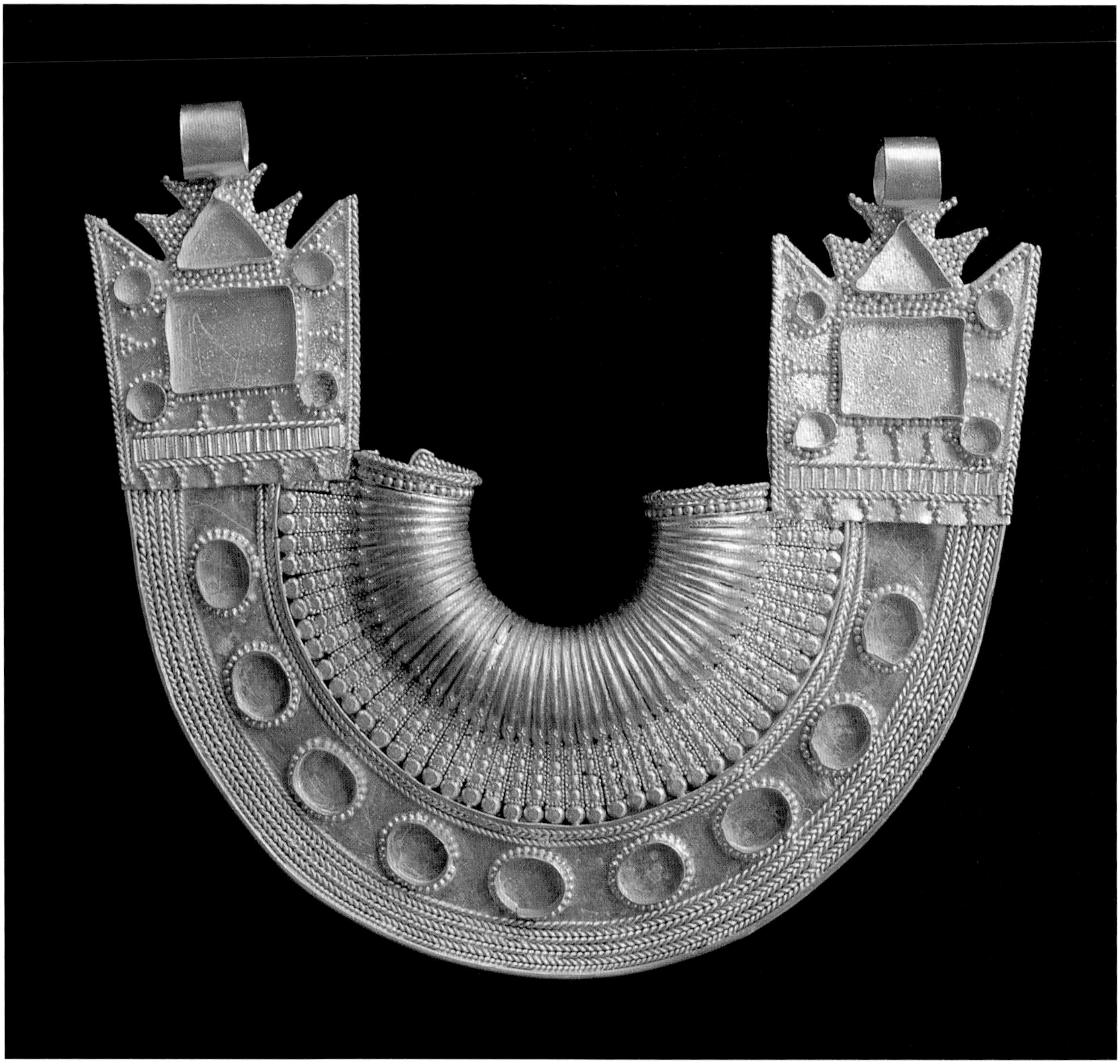

329

330

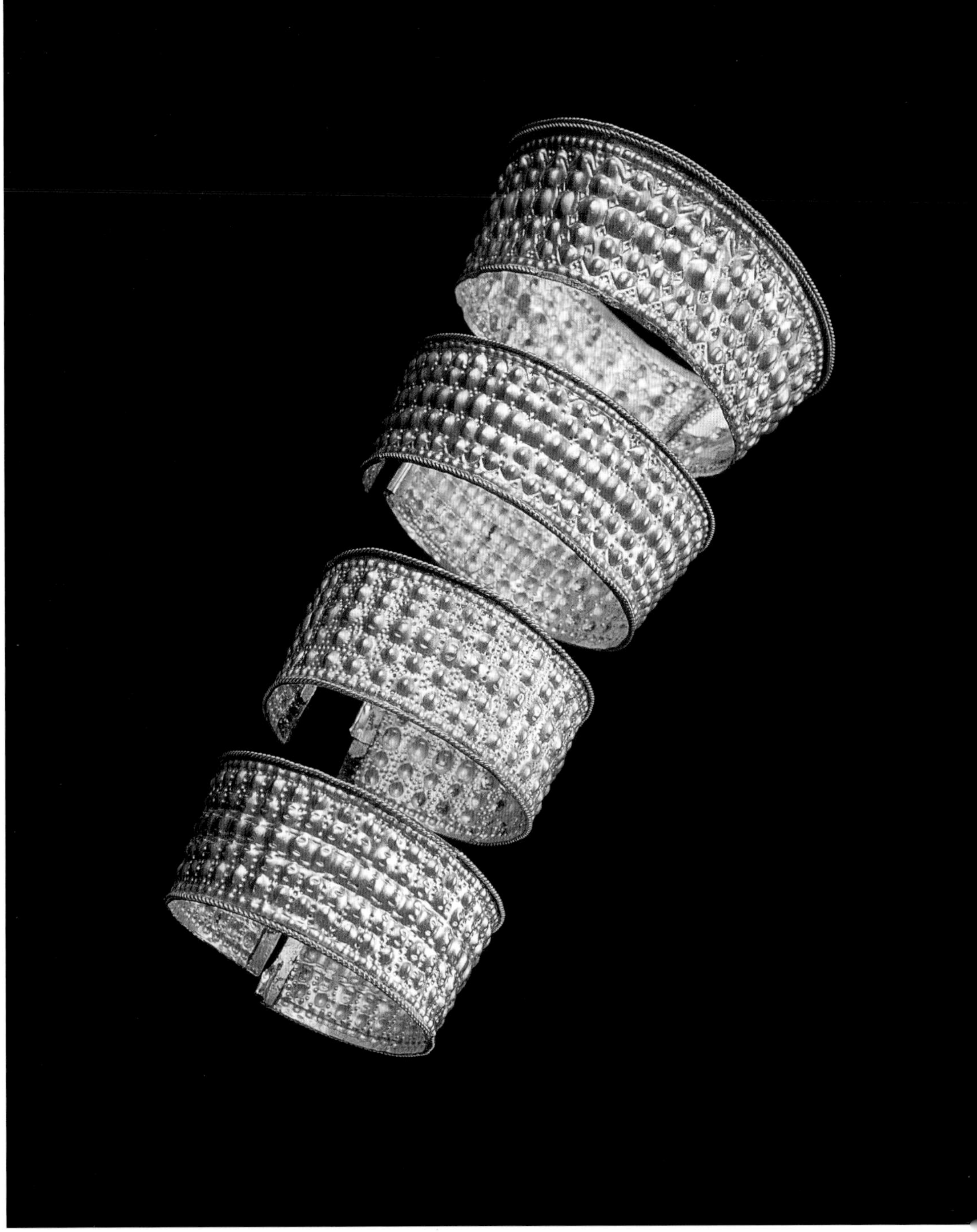

327 Gold ear ornaments decorated with applied filigree and gold wire spirals, from Samar island, 8th–13th century. The small conical umbrella-like ornaments suggest Indonesian influence, since umbrellas signified royal status at Hindu-Buddhist courts.

328 Large floral repoussé ear ornaments of fine gold sheet with simulated granulation, from Iloilo, Panay island, 14th–16th century.

329 Gold U-shaped ornament with applied filigree and granulation, from Butuan, Mindanao, 10th–13th century. The square and circular cells once held gems or coloured glass. The central ribbed section in the form of a stylized caterpillar (*uod*) is slit at the back. This may have enabled the insertion of cloth from a headdress, and it is likely that these ornaments were worn on either side of the face. They are also found on Samar island.

330 Ear pendants of gold sheet with dangling floral and leaf elements, 12th–14th century. This type has been found on Cebu, Bohol and Leyte islands.

331 A set of matching gold repoussé bracelets or arm wraps of graduated size worn from the wrist to the elbow, probably from Mindoro island, *c.* 800.

332 Gold chain with ornamental clasps decorated with applied filigree and granulation, from eastern Mindanao, *c.* 1200–1400.

331

332

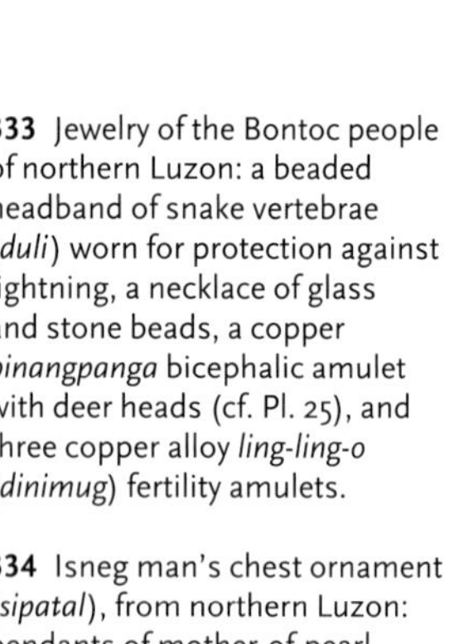

333 Jewelry of the Bontoc people of northern Luzon: a beaded headband of snake vertebrae (*duli*) worn for protection against lightning, a necklace of glass and stone beads, a copper *pinangpanga* bicephalic amulet with deer heads (cf. Pl. 25), and three copper alloy *ling-ling-o* (*dinimug*) fertility amulets.

334 Isneg man's chest ornament (*sipatal*), from northern Luzon: pendants of mother-of-pearl with glass and agate beads are suspended from a beaded collar.

335 Gadang headdress of coloured glass beads, from northern Luzon.

333

334

335

336

336 Bontoc ceremonial armlets (*tankil*), from northern Luzon, early 20th century. Composed of human figures carved in wood, boar's tusks, rattan and horse-hair, they were worn by warriors who had met with success on their first headhunting expedition. The tusks were obtained in advance. The figures are said to represent the victims, or alternatively guardian ancestors.

337 Ear ornaments. Those on the left, made by the T'boli people of Mindanao, early 20th century, have strings of glass beads which are looped under the chin, attached to wooden discs ornamented with engraved silver plaques. Those on the right (*batling*) were made by the Ilongot people of northern Luzon in the early 20th century; of red hornbill beak, mother-of-pearl and copper alloy, they mark prestige acquired through headhunting.

337

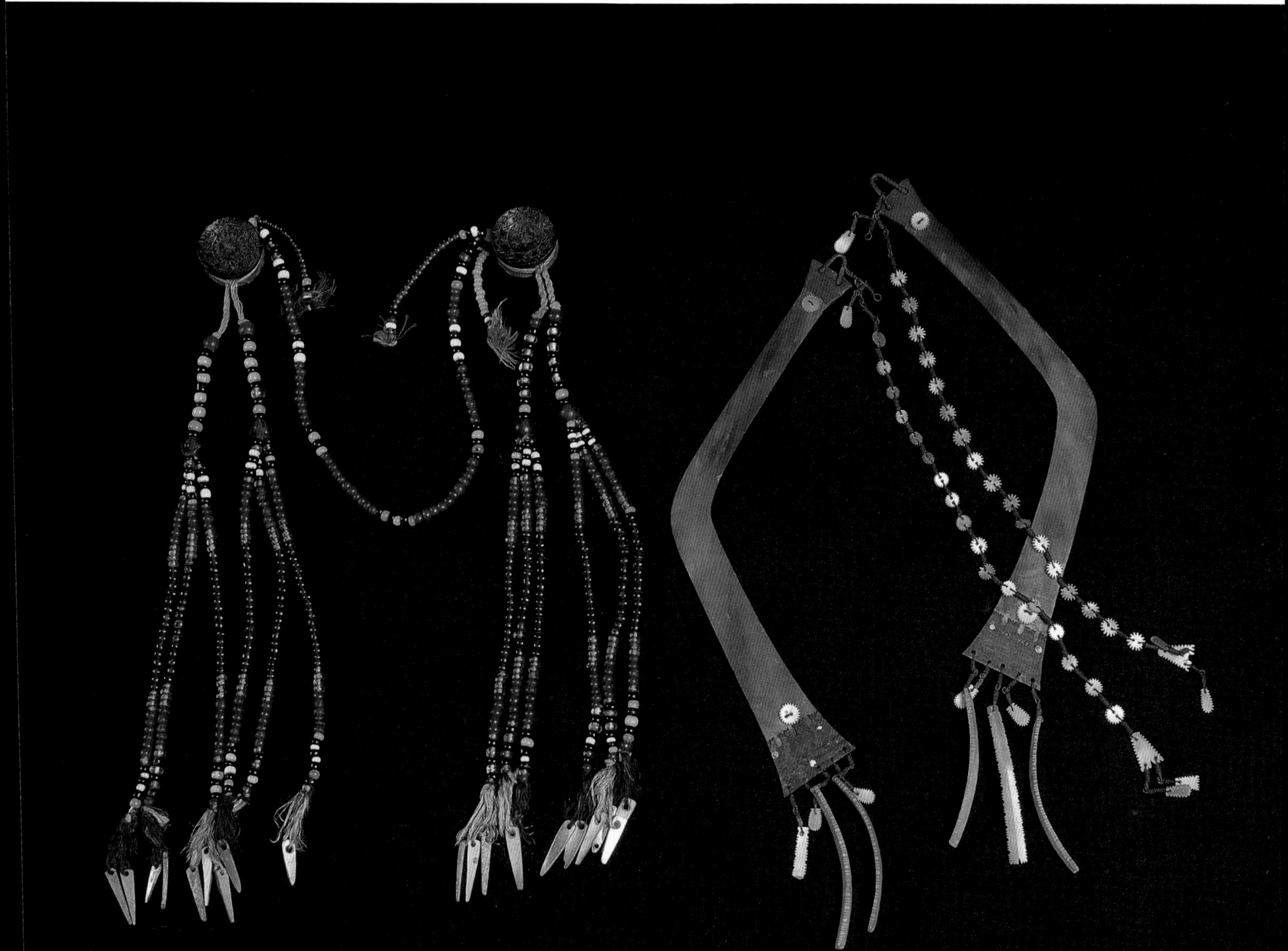

338

339

340

338 Bagobo box for betel and tobacco, cast in brass with a fringed and beaded strap, from Mindanao, early 20th century.

339 Monobo brass anklets with triangular ornamentation and attached jingling rings, from Mindanao, early 20th century.

340 T'boli wooden combs decorated with brass wire and festoons of glass beads, from Mindanao, early–mid-20th century.

341 Mandaya silver pectoral plaques with engraved double spiral decoration, from Mindanao, early 20th century.

341

342

342 Bagobo or T'boli brass belt (*sabitan*) of woven wire with attached bells and a decorative cast buckle, from Mindanao, early 20th century.

343 Bagobo woven necklace of beads with a brass bell, brass anklets with bells, and bracelets decorated with beads and bells, from Mindanao, early 20th century. Bells are widely employed in Bagobo and T'boli jewelry; the tinkling sound contributes to the music accompanying dances performed at festivals.

343

The introduction of ornaments in the Spanish Christian tradition followed the conversion of Filipino people to Christianity.

344 Gold and silver cross suspended on an opulent gold chain, 18th–19th century. The chain is of the *alpajor* ('flat cake') type, consisting of flattened square, circular or lozenge-shaped double-linked panels which often display Islamic influence. Such necklaces were the pride of the upper classes of Manila, the Cagayan valley and Ilocos on Luzon.

345 Baroque crucifix lavishly ornamented with distinctive thorny projections (*tinik*), suspended on a necklace of gold beads, from Luzon, 18th century.

346 Scapular (*scapulario* or *kalmin*), with a border of gold twining leaves and pomegranates and a gold image of Calvary set against red cloth, from Luzon, 18th–19th century.

347 Rosary (*tamborin*) of coral and gold beads, with a gold medallion containing a figurine of the Christ Child in a frame decorated with filigree and granulation, from Luzon, early–mid-19th century. The stylized butterfly from which the medallion hangs is elaborated with filigree and embossing. *Tamborin* composed largely of bright red coral rather than gold filigree beads were especially favoured by Chinese mestizo women who intermarried with Spanish and indigenous families of high status.

344

345

346

347

348

349

348 Among the earliest examples of Christian ornaments in the Philippines are the gold crosses (*krus na baligtad*) of the Cagayan valley, northern Luzon. Many are richly decorated with granulation and applied filigree. Examples from the 17th and 18th centuries were suspended on a long chain upside down, so they could be raised to the face for prayer and contemplation; 19th-century examples hang from a chain by the top.

349 The highly expressive figure of the crucified Christ is set against dark tortoiseshell in the late 18th-century crucifixes of Ilocos, north-western Luzon (left). The crucifix with granulation and red staining (right) is from Cagayan, northern Luzon, 19th century; the beads are of polished coconut shell.

350

351

350 Gold earrings from Luzon, 19th century. The darker filigree ones (right) are composed of *tembaga*, an alloy of copper, silver and gold. The delicate gold ones set with pearls are typical of Manila and towns on Luzon. The ship reflects the commercial concerns of the period. The blue enamelled earrings were made by an Armenian jeweller in Manila.

351 A hairpin with seed pearls, early 19th century; a larger hairpin with a dangling heart, mid-19th century; and a hairpin embellished with grape leaves and vines from Ilocos, Luzon.

352 Luzon tortoiseshell and silver combs enriched with gems, pearls and gold in repoussage, engraving, filigree and openwork. The small comb with silver teeth decorated with a stylized tamarind pod is in the 18th-century Damortis style. The largest comb, with Chinese-Malay engraving, also dates from the 18th century. Pearl-set combs were worn in the mid-19th century.

352

353 Buttons and finger-rings worn by Islamic coastal people of Mindanao, 19th century. They show an obvious stylistic relationship to the jewelry of the Malay Peninsula and southern Thailand. The triangular arrangement of tiny balls is, however, also typical of the remarkable gold ornaments of the late 1st millennium, as well as those of the later Gujarati style absorbed into Southeast Asian Islamic traditions of jewelry.

353

BIBLIOGRAPHY

AA — *Arts of Asia*
BEFEO — *Bulletin de l'Ecole Française de l'Extrême Orient*
BSEI — *Bulletin de la Société des Études Indochinoises*
FH — *Filipino Heritage*
JBRS — *Journal of the Burma Research Society*
JMBRAS — *Journal of the Malay Branch of the Royal Asiatic Society*
JRAI — *Journal of the Royal Asiatic Society*
JSBRAS — *Journal of the Singapore Branch of the Royal Asiatic Society*

Abadie, M. *Les Races du Haut Tonkin de Phong-Tho à Lang-Son*, Paris 1924
Achjadi, Judi *Pakaian Daerah Wanita Indonesia*, Jakarta 1976
Adams, M. J. *Systems and Meaning in Sumba Textile Design*, New Haven 1969
Adhyatman, Sumarah, and Redjiki Arifin *Manik- manik di Indonesia – Beads in Indonesia*, Jakarta 1993
Al-Jadir, Said *Arab and Islamic Silver*, London 1981
Arkell, R. 'Cambay and the Bead Trade', *Antiquity*, 10, 1936, 292–305
Aung, M. H. *Folk Elements in Burmese Buddhism*, Oxford 1962
Aymonier, É. *Les Tchames et leurs religions*, Paris 1891
—— *Le Cambodge*: I, *Le Royaume Actuel*, II, *Les Provinces Siamoises*, III, *Le Groupe d'Angkor et l'histoire*, Paris 1901–3
Baradas, D. 'Art in Maranao Life', *FH*, IV, 1977, 1045–49
Beaulieu, A. de 'Mémoires du Voyage aux Indes Orientales du Général de Beaulieu, dressés par luy-mesme', in *Relations de divers voyages curieux*, ed. Melchisedech Thévenot, II, Paris 1666
Bellwood, P. *Prehistory of the Indo-Malaysian Archipelago* (rev. edn), Honolulu 1997
Beranose, M. *Les Arts décoratifs au Tonkin*, Paris 1922
Bernet Kempers, A. J. *Ancient Indonesian Art*, Amsterdam 1959
—— 'The Kettledrums of Southeast Asia', *Modern Quaternary Studies in Southeast Asia*, 10, 1988, 1–59
Bezacier, L. *L'Art vietnamien*, Paris 1954
Bird, I. *The Golden Chersonese*, 1883/Singapore 1990
Birdwood, G. *The Industrial Arts of India*, London 1880/1971
Blair, J., and E. Robertson *The Philippine Islands, 1493–1898*, 55 vols, 1903–9/Manila 1973
Bock, C. *Headhunters of Borneo*, London 1881
—— *Temples and Elephants: Travels in Siam*, London 1884
Boisselier, J. 'Évolution du diadème dans la statuaire khmère', *BSEI*, n.s., 25, 2, 1950, 149–70
—— *Statuaire khmère et son évolution*, I and II, Saigon 1955
—— *Manuel d'Archéologie d'Extrême Orient, Asie du Sud-est*, I, 1966, *Le Cambodge*
—— 'Travaux de la Mission archéologique française en Thailande', *Arts Asiatiques*, XXV, 1972, 27–91
Borel, F., and J. B. Taylor *The Splendor of Ethnic Jewelry: The Colette and Jean Pierre Ghysels Collection*, New York 1994
Bosch, F. 'Gouden Vingerringen uit het Hindoe-Javaansche tijdperk', *Djawa*, 7, 1927, 305–20
—— *The Golden Germ*, The Hague 1960
Bowrey, T. *A Geographical Account of Countries round the Bay of Bengal, 1669 to 1679*, ed. R. C. Temple, Cambridge 1905
Bowring, J. *The History and People of Siam*, 2 vols, London 1857
Braddell, R. 'A Note on Sambas and Borneo', *JMBRAS*, XXII, 1949, 4
Brosch, N. (ed.) *Jewellery and Goldsmithing in the Islamic world; International Symposium*, Jerusalem 1987
Brown, D., J. Edwards and R. Moore *The Penis Inserts of Southeast Asia, an Annotated Bibliography with an Overview and Comparative Perspectives*, Berkeley 1988
Brus, R. 'The Royal Regalia of Thailand', *AA*, Sept.–Oct. 1985
—— 'Wedding Jewellery in Malaysia', *AA*, Jan.–Feb. 1988
—— 'Crowns in Asia', *AA*, July–Aug. 1989
Bunker, E. 'Splendour and Sensuality in Angkor Period Khmer Jewellery', *AA*, Mar. 2000
—— and D. A. J. Latchford *Khmer Gold; Gift for the Gods*, Chicago 2008
Butler, J. *Yao Design*, Bangkok 1970
Butor, M., and P.-A. Ferrazzini *Adornment: Jewelry from Africa, Asia and the Pacific*, London 1994
Caballero, E. J. *Gold From the Gods: Traditional Small Scale Miners in the Philippines*, Quezon City 1996
Casal, G. 'The Legacy of Ginton: Metal among the T'boli', *FH*, 2, 1977, 455–60
—— 'The High Fashion World of the T'Boli', *FH*, 3, 1977, 729–37
—— et al. *The People and Art of the Philippines*, Los Angeles 1981
Cawed, C. *The Culture of the Bontoc Igorot*, Manila 1972
Chandler, D. *A History of Cambodia*, St Leonards, N.S.W., 1993
Chang, Q. *Memories of a Nonya*, Singapore 1981
Charoenwongsa, P., and B. Bronson (eds) *Prehistoric Studies: The Stone and Early Metal Ages in Thailand*, Bangkok 1988
Chaumont, A. de *À la Cour du Roi de Siam*, Paris 1686
Chazee, L. *Atlas des Ethnies et des sous-ethnies du Laos*, Bangkok 1995
Chin, E. *Gilding the Phoenix: The Straits Chinese and their Jewellery*, Singapore 1991
—— 'The Straits Chinese and their Jewellery', *AA*, July–Aug. 1993
—— 'Classical Indonesian Gold Jewellery in a Private Collection, Part Two', *AA*, July–Aug. 1994
Chin, L., and V. Mashman (eds) *Cultural Heritage of Sarawak*, Kuching 1980
—— *Sarawak Cultural Legacy*, Kuching 1991
Chira Chonkol 'Jewellery and Other Decorative Arts in Thailand', *AA*, Nov.–Dec. 1982
Ch'ng, D. 'Overseas Chinese Silversmiths', *AA*, Jan.–Feb. 1984
—— 'Malay Silver', *AA*, Mar.–Apr. 1986
Chou, A. A. *Silver; A Guide to the Collections in the National Museum of Singapore*, Singapore 1984
Chou Ta-kuan [Zhou Daguan] *The Customs of Cambodia*, trans. by Paul Pelliot (1902) and by A. Griswold and J. G. D. Paul, Bangkok 1987
Christie's *Southeast Asian Pictures and Straits Chinese Ceramics, Gold and Silver* (auction cat.), Singapore, Mar. 1994
—— *Straits Chinese Ceramics, Gold and Silver* (auction cat.), Singapore, Mar. 1995
Chu Thai Son and Dao Hung *Vietnam: a Multicultural Mosaic*, Hanoi 1991
Chumphengphan, Prathum *Gold Treasures of the Ayutthaya Period*, FADB, Bangkok n.d.
Claeys, J. 'Bijoux Cham appartenant à S.A.R. Prince Bu'u Liem', *BEFEO*, XXX, 1930, 529–32
Cochrane, W. W. *The Shans*, Rangoon 1915
Coedès, G. *The Indianized States of Southeast Asia*, Honolulu 1968
Cole, F. C. *The Wild Tribes of Davao*, Chicago 1913
Commission des Moeurs et Coutumes du Cambodge: *see* Porée-Maspero
Condominas, G. *We Have Eaten the Forest; The Story of a Montagnard Village in Central Vietnam* (trans. by A. Foulke of *Nous avons mangé la forêt de la Pierre Genie Goo*), 1957/New York 1977
Content, D. *Islamic Rings and Gems: The Benjamin Zucker Collection*, London 1987
Conti, N. di *India in the Fifteenth Century*, ed. R. Major, London 1857
Cooper, R., N. Tapp, G. Lee and G. Schwoer-Kol *The Hmong*, Bangkok 1996
Courtney, P., and M. Wronska-Friend *Migrants from the Mountains: The Costume Art of the Hmong people of Mainland Southeast Asia*, Townsville, Qld, 1995
Crawfurd, J. *History of the Indian Archipelago*, 3 vols, Edinburgh 1820
Cuisinier, J. *Les Muong*, Paris 1946
Dang Nghiem Van, Chu Thai Son and Luu Hung *Ethnic Minorities in Vietnam*, Hanoi 1993
Dang Ngoc Oanh *Intronisation de l'empereur Khai Dinh*, 1916/Hue 1996
Deraedt, J. 'The Kalinga Notion of Sacrifice', *FH*, II, 1977, 337–45
—— 'The Soul of the Kalinga', *FH*, II, 1977, 427–33
Dessaint, W., and A. Ngwama *Au sud des nuages: Mythes et contes recueillis oralement chez les montagnards lissou*, Paris 1994
Deydier, H. *Introduction à la connaissance du Laos*, Hanoi 1950
Diguet, E. *Les Montagnards du Tonkin*, Paris 1908
Diran, R. K. *The Vanishing Tribes of Burma*, London 1997
Diskul, M. C. S. *Art in Thailand: A Brief History*, Bangkok 1991
Dodd, W. C. *The Tai Race; Elder Brother of the Chinese*, 1923/Bangkok 1966
Drabbe, P. *Het Leven van den Tanembarees: Ethnografische Studie over het Tanembareesche Volk, Internationales Archiv fur Ethnographie*, suppl. to vol. 37, 1940
Drake, Sir F. *The World Encompassed (Carefully Collected out of the Notes of Master Francis Fletcher, Preacher in his employment and divers Others)*, 1628/New York 1969
Dubin, L. S. *The History of Beads from 3000 BC to the Present*, London 1987
Dulawan, L. 'An Ifugao Album, *FH*, IV, 1977, 968–80
Dung: *see* Nguyen Thi Kim Dung
Dunsmore, S. *Beads*, Kuching, Sarawak Museum Occasional Paper no. 2, 1978
Durand, P., and H. Parmentier 'Le Trésor des rois Chams', *BEFEO* (1), 1905
Eiseman, F. B. *Bali, Sekala and Niskala; Essays on Religion, Ritual and Art*, Singapore 1989
Enage, Milagros 'Folk Heritage in Christian Jewellery', *AA*, Sept.–Oct. 1977
Eng Lee Seok Chee *Festive Expressions; Nonya Beadwork and Embroidery*, Singapore 1989
Evans, I. H. N. 'Excavations at Tanjong Rawa, Kuala Selinsing, Perak', *Jnl of the Federated Malay States Museums*, 15/3, 1932
FADB [Fine Arts Department, Bangkok] *Adornment* [in Thai]: essays by Patchrin Sakramul (on prehistory, Dvaravati and Lopburi, and Bangkok), Manon Klipthon (Sukhothai), Kritsada Pinnasri (Ayutthaya), and Songsri Prapathong (Lanna), 1992
Fessler, L. W. 'Maranao Art and the Aga Khan Museum', *AA*, Sept.–Oct. 1977
Filipino Book Guild *Travel Accounts of the Islands*, 1971
Flower, M. *Victorian Jewelry*, New York 1967
Fontein, J., et al. *The Sculpture of Indonesia*, Washington, D.C., 1990
Forest, A. *Le Culte des génies protecteurs au Cambodge*, Paris 1992
Forsythe, M. 'Modern Mien Silver', *AA*, May–June 1984
Fox, J. (ed.) *The Flow of Life: Essays on Eastern Indonesia*, Cambridge, Mass., 1980
Fox, R. *The Tabon Caves; Archaeological Excavation on Palawan Island, Philippines*, Manila 1970
—— 'The Jade Mystique – some evidence of Philippine prehistoric jade', *FH*, II, 1977, 303–8
—— 'Ancient beads – unstringing the history of old beads', *FH*, III, 1977, 757–66
Francis, P. *Bead Emporium; A Guide to the Beads from Arikmedu in the Pondicherry Museum*, Pondicherry 1987
—— 'Beads of India', *AA*, Mar.–Apr. 1988
—— *The Type Collection of Beads from Archaeological Contexts in the Philippines National Museum as Developed and Maintained by Rey Santiago Under the Inspiration and Guidance of Robert B. Fox*, Lake Placid, N.Y., 1989
—— 'Beads in the Islamic World', *The Margaretologist*, 2, 3, 1989
—— 'Beads of the Philippines', *AA*, Nov.–Dec. 1990
—— 'Glass Beads in Asia, Part II: Indo-Pacific Beads', *Asian Perspectives*, 29, 1, 1990, 1–23
—— *Beads and People I; Southeast Asia; Heirlooms of the Hills*, Lake Placid, N.Y., 1992
—— 'Mutisalah Beads; What is Their true Story', *The Margaretologist*, 5, 1, 1992, 5–8
—— 'Pumtek Beads', *The Margaretologist*, 5, 1, 1992, 3–5
—— 'Range of Dates for Coil Beads, *The Margaretologist*, 5, 1, 1992, 11–12
—— 'What About the Gaps in Indo-Pacific Bead History', *The Margaretologist*, 5, 1, 1992, 9–11
—— 'Southeast Asian Glass Beads and the Western Connection, *The Margaretologist*, 6, 2, 1993, 7–9
Frank Sternberg: *see* Stark, *Gold of Asia*
Frape, C. 'Ancient Hardstone Earrings of Vietnam', *AA*, Sept.–Oct. 1997
Fraser, D. (ed.) *The Many Faces of Primitive Art*, Englewood Cliffs, N.J., 1966
Fraser Lu, S. 'Burmese Silverware', *AA*, Apr.–May 1980
—— *Silverware of Southeast Asia*, Singapore 1989
—— *Burmese Crafts, Past and Present*, Kuala Lumpur 1994
Frédéric, L. *La Vie quotidienne dans la péninsule indochinoise à l'époque d'Angkor*, Paris 1981
Funnell, S. 'Ifugao Social Justice', *FH*, IX, 1977, 2458–62

Gervaise, N. *The Natural and Political History of Siam*, trans. J. Villiers, Bangkok 1989
Gilhodes, A. *The Kachins, Religion and Customs*, 1922/Bangkok 1996
Girard-Geslan, M., and J.-F. Jarrige (eds) *Les Ors de l'archipel indonésien*, Paris 1995
—— et al. *Art of Southeast Asia*, New York 1998
Gittinger, M. *Splendid Symbols: Textiles and Tradition in Indonesia*, Washington, D.C., 1979
—— (ed.) *Indonesian Textiles: Irene Emery Roundtable on Museum Textiles 1979 Proceedings*, Washington, D.C., 1980
—— *To Speak with Cloth: Studies in Indonesian Textiles*, Los Angeles 1989
Glass Palace Chronicles of the Kings of Burma, trans. Pe Maung Tin and G. Luce, London 1923
Glover, I. (ed.) *Southeast Asian Archeology 1990*, Proceedings of the Third Conference of the European Association of South-east Asian Archeologists, Hull 1992
——, Pornchai Succhitta and J. Villiers (eds) *Early Metallurgy, Trade and Urban Centres in Thailand and Southeast Asia*, Bangkok 1992
Gosling, B. *Sukhothai; its History, Culture and Art*, Singapore 1991
Groslier, G. *Danseuses cambodgiennes*, Paris 1913
—— *Recherches sur les Cambodgiens*, Paris 1921
—— 'Les Collections khmer du Musée Albert Sarraut à Phnom Penh', *Arts Asiatica*, Paris 1931
Grunfeld, F. V. *Wayfarers of the Thai Forest: the Akkha*, Amsterdam 1982
Guerrero, M., and C. Quirino 'Old Chinatown', *FH*, IV, 1977, 1009–14
Gullick, J. M. 'A Survey of the Malay Weavers and Silversmiths in Kelantan in 1951' *JMBRAS*, XXV (1), 1952, 134–48
Gwee Thian Hock *A Nonya Mosaic; My Mother's Childhood*, Singapore 1985
Gyllensvard, B. *Chinese Gold and Silver in the Karl Kempe Collection*, Stockholm 1953
Harrisson, T. 'Gold and Indian Influences in West Borneo', *JMBRAS*, XXII, 4, 1949
—— 'Kelabit, Land Dayak and Related Glass Beads in Sarawak', *Sarawak Museum Jnl*, V, 1950
—— 'The Golden Hoard of Limbang', *Brunei Museum Jnl*, I, 1969, 57–71
—— *The Malays of South West Sarawak before Malaysia*, Glasgow 1970
—— and S. J. O' Connor *Gold and Megalithic Activity in Prehistoric and Recent West Borneo*, Ithaca, N.Y., 1970
Hautecloque-Howe, A. de *Les Rhades: une société de droit maternel*, Paris 1985
Heine-Geldern, R. 'Some Tribal Art Styles of Southeast Asia', in D. Fraser, *The Many Faces of Primitive Art*, Englewood Cliffs, N.J., 1966
Hemmet, C. (ed.) *Montagnards des Pays d'Indochine*, Paris 1995
Higham, C. *The Archaeology of Mainland Southeast Asia*, Cambridge 1989
—— *The Bronze Age of Southeast Asia*, Cambridge 1996
—— and R. Thosarat (eds) *The Excavations at Khok Phanom Di, A Prehistoric site in Central Thailand*, III: *The Material Culture*, pt i, Society of Antiquaries of London, 1993
Hill, A. H. 'Kelantan Silverwork', *JMBRAS*, XXIV (1), 1951, 100–108
Ho, Wing Meng *Straits Chinese Silver: A Collector's Guide*, Singapore 1984
—— *Straits Chinese Beadwork and Embroidery: A Collector's Guide*, Singapore 1987
Hose, C., and W. McDougall *The Pagan Tribes of Borneo*, 2 vols, 1912/Singapore 1993
Hoskin, J., and J.-L. Dugast *The Supernatural in Thai Life*, Bangkok 1996
Huard, P., and M. Durand *Vietnam: Civilization and Culture* (rev. Engl. edn of *Connaissance du Vietnam*), Hanoi 1994
Imao, Abdulmari 'Muslim Brassware', *FH*, III, 1977, 679–85
—— 'Okkil Art; Our Middle Eastern Tradition', *FH*, IV, 1977, 849–53
Jacobs, J. *The Nagas: Hill Peoples of Northern India*, London 1990
Jasper, J., and M. Pirngadie *De Goud en Zilversmeedkunst* (vol. IV of *De Inlandsche Kunstnijverheid in Nederlandsch Indie*), The Hague 1927
Jessup, H. *Court Arts of Indonesia*, New York 1990
—— and Thierry Zephir (eds) *The Sculpture of Angkor and Ancient Cambodia: Millennium of Glory*, Washington, D.C., 1997
De Jong, N., and T. van Dijk *Forgotten Islands of Indonesia*, Singapore 1995
Kartik, K. 'The Gold Treasure of Wonoboyo at the Jakarta National Museum', *AA*, July–Aug. 1995
—— 'The Gold Collection at the Jakarta National Museum', *AA*, Nov.–Dec. 1995
Kassim Hj. Ali, M. *Caping: Modesty Disk*, Muzium Negara, Kuala Lumpur 1983
—— *Gold Jewellery and Ornaments in the Collection of the Muzium Negara Malaysia*, Kuala Lumpur 1988
—— *Barang Kemas Melayu Tradisi*, Kuala Lumpur 1990
Katigbak, M. S. 'When Coffee Boomed in Lipa, *FH*, VII, 1977, 1760–64
Kaudern, W. *Ethnographical Studies in Celebes; The Results of the Author's Expedition to Celebes 1917–20*, 6 vols, Göteborg 1929
Keene, W. 'Shadows of Men and Spirits: Mamuli of Sumba', in *Tribal Art* (2), 1988
Keesing, F. M. *The Ethnohistory of Northern Luzon*, Stanford 1962
Kennard, S. J. 'Timorese Tribal Bracelets: A Cultural Perspective', *AA*, July–Aug. 1995
King, V. 'Maloh Silversmiths', *The Sarawak Gazette*, June 1975
—— 'Stones and the Mahloh of Indonesian West Borneo', *JMBRAS*, 48, 1975
—— *World Within; The Ethnic Groups of Borneo*, Kuala Lumpur 1994
Kreemer, J. *Atjeh*, Leiden 1922
Kruyt, A. C. *De West-Toradjas op Midden-Celebes*, 4 vols, Amsterdam 1938
Lamb, A. 'Some Observations on Stone and Glass Beads in Early Southeast Asia', *JMBRAS*, 38, 1965, 87–124
Le Ngoc Thang 'Traditional Clothing of the Black Thai Living in Vietnam', *Proceedings of the 4th International Conference of Thai Studies, Kunming*, III, 1990
Le May, R. *An Asian Arcady, The Land and Peoples of Northern Siam*, Cambridge 1926
Lebar, M., G. C. Hickey and K. Musgrave *Ethnic Groups of Mainland Southeast Asia*, New Haven 1964
Legarda, Angelita 'Antique Beads of the Philippines', *AA*, Sept.–Oct. 1977
—— 'Pre-Hispanic Gold in the Philippines', *AA*, Sept.–Oct. 1978
Legeza, L. 'Chinese and Islamic Influences in the Philippines', *AA*, Sept.–Oct. 1977
—— 'Tantric Elements in Pre-Hispanic Gold Art', *AA*, July–Aug. 1988
Leigh, B. *Tangan-tangan Trampil: Seni Kerajinan Aceh. Hands of Time: Crafts of Aceh*, Jakarta 1989
Lemoine, J. *Un Village Hmong Vert du Haut Laos*, Paris 1972
Lewis, P., and E. Lewis *People of the Golden Triangle*, London 1984
Li Tana and A. Reid *Southern Vietnam under the Nguyen: Documents on the Economic History of Cochinchina (1602–1777)*, Singapore 1993
Loofs-Wissowa, H. H. E. 'Prehistoric and protohistoric links between the Indochinese Peninsula and the Philippines, as exemplified by two types of ear-ornaments', *Jnl of the Hong Kong Archaeological Society*, IX, 1980–81, 57–76
Lui, R. K. *A Universal Aesthetic; Collectible Beads*, Vista, Calif., 1995
Ma Huan *Ying-yai-sheng-lan: The Overall Survey of the Ocean's Shores*, trans. J. V. G. Mills, Cambridge 1970
Mackinnon, S. *From a Shattered Sun: Hierarchy, Gender and Alliance in the Tanimbar Islands*, Madison, Wis., 1991
Maheswari, C. S. Uma *Dress and Jewellery of Indian Women: Satavahana to Kakatiya*, Madras 1995
Mak Phoen 'La Communauté Cam au Cambodge du XVe au XIXe siècle', *Actes, Séminaire sur le Champa*, Univ. of Copenhagen 1988
Malay Annals, trans. C. C. Brown, Kuala Lumpur 1970
Malleret, L. 'Intailles et cachets du Cambodge continental', *BEFEO*, XLV, 2, 1951
—— *L'Archéologie du Delta du Mékong*, 4 vols (I, *L'Exploration archéologique et les fouilles d'Oc-eo*; II, *La Civilisation matérielle d'Oc-eo*; III, *La Culture du Funan*; IV, *Le Cisbassac*), Paris 1959–62
Manning, A., T. Mackinnon Edwards and F. E. Treloar 'An Analysis of Gold Jewelry Found at the Kota Cina Site near Medan, Sumatra', *JMBRAS*, 53, 2, 1980
Manrique, S. *Travels of Fray Sebastien Manrique*, trans. C. Luard and F. Hosten, London 1927
Marchal, S. *Costumes et parures Khmer d'après les dewata d'Angkor Wat*, Paris/Brussels 1927
Marr, D., and A. C. Milner (eds) *Southeast Asia in the 9th to 14th Centuries*, Singapore 1986
Marsden, W. *The History of Sumatra*, 1774/Kuala Lumpur 1966
Martowikrido, Wahayono 'The Gold of Wonoboyo, Preliminary Notes', in W. H. Kal (ed.), 'Old Javanese Gold (4th–15th century); An Archaeological Approach', *Bull. Royal Tropical Institute* (Amsterdam), no. 334, 1994
—— and Sutrisno *Gold Treasure of the Museum Nasional*, Jakarta 1992
Maspero, G. *Le Royaume du Champa*, Paris 1928
Matics, K. I. 'Khmer Silver in Animal Shapes', *AA*, July–Aug. 1988
Maurice, A. A. *Les Mnong des Hauts Plateaux*, I, Paris 1993
Maxwell, R. J. *Textiles of Southeast Asia: Tradition, Trade and Transformation*, Melbourne 1990
McCullough, T. 'Gold Jewellery: Pre-Angkor and Angkor Civilization of Cambodia', *AA*, Mar.–Apr. 2000
Mi Mi Khaing *Burmese Family*, London 1946
Miksic, J. *Archaeological Research on the 'Forbidden Hill' of Singapore: Excavations at Fort Canning 1984*, 1985
—— *Small Finds; Ancient Javanese Gold*, Singapore National Museum, 1988
—— *Old Javanese Gold*, Singapore 1990
Milne, L. *The Shans at Home*, London 1910
De Moor, M. 'Gold Jewellery in Nias Culture', *AA*, July–Aug. 1989
—— and W. H. Kal *Indonesische sieraden*, Amsterdam 1983
Moore, E. 'Peranakan Silver in Singapore', *AA*, Jan.–Feb. 1982
Moreno, J. *Philippine Costume*, Manila 1995
Mottin, A. *The History of the Hmong (Meo)*, Bangkok 1980
Mundy, P. *The Travels of Peter Mundy in Europe and Asia 1609–1667*, ed. R. C. Temple, III, pt i, London 1919
Myint Aung 'The Excavations at Halin, *JBRS*, III, pt ii, Dec. 1970
Myint Tun 'Silversmith Craft', *Forward*, Oct. 1978
Naenna, P. C. *Costume and Culture: Vanishing Textiles of some Tai groups of Laos*, Chiang Mai 1990
National Heritage Board, Singapore *Costumes Through Time*, Singapore 1993
National Identity Board, Thailand *Thai Gems and Jewellery*, Bangkok 1987
Nguyen Huu Thong *Hue, nghe va lang nghe thu cong truyen thong: Hue, Its Traditional Handicrafts and Trade Guilds*, Hue 1994
Nguyen Thi Kim Dung 'Research on Stone Augers and Ancient Boring Techniques', *Khao Co Hoc* (2), 1985, 63–80
—— 'Ornaments from Jar Burial Sites in Can Gio District, Ho Chi Minh City', *Khao Co Hoc* (2), 1995, 27–46
—— 'The Trang Kenh Jewelry Making Workshop Site; An Experimental and Microwear Study', *Indo-Pacific History, The Chiangmai Papers*, Canberra, I, 1996, 161–65
Nguyen Van Huyen *La Civilisation annamite*, republ. as *The Ancient Civilization of Vietnam*, 1945/Hanoi 1995
Nooy-Palm, N. 'Dress and Ornament of the Sa'adan Toraja', *Tropical Man*, 2, 1969
Parmentier, H. 'Découverte de bijoux anciens à Mison', *BEFEO* (III), 1903, 664–65
—— *L'Art khmer primitif*, 2 vols, Paris 1927
—— *L'Art du Laos*, Hanoi 1954
Passmore, J. 'Laotian Silver', *AA*, Nov.–Dec. 1963
Patanne, E. P. 'The Romance of Gold; The Quest for Gold in the Philippines', *FH*, II, 1977, 360–64
—— *Philippine Jewelry and Ornaments*, Manila 1991
—— *The Philippines in the 6th to 16th Centuries*, Manila 1996
Pelliot, P. *Le Fou-nan*, *BEFEO*, 3, 1903
Peralta, J. 'Ancient Stone Jewelry', *FH*, II, 1977, 225–27
—— 'Shell Ornaments', *FH*, II, 1977, 500–504
—— 'Feathers, Leaves and other Ornaments', *FH*, II, 1977, 533–38
—— 'Prehistoric Gold Ornaments from the Central Bank of the Philippines', *AA*, Sept.–Oct. 1983
Phan Huy Le, et al. *The Traditional Village in Vietnam*, Hanoi 1993
Pigafetta, A. *First Voyage around the World*, in R. A. Skelton, *Magellan's Voyage: A Narrative Account of the First Navigation*, New Haven 1969

Pigeaud, T. G. 'Javanese Gold', *Bijdragen tot de Taal-, Land- en Volkenkunde* (Leiden), 114, 1958, 192–96
Pirazzoli-t'Serstevens, M. *La Civilisation du Royaume de Dian à l'époque Han*, Paris 1974
Pires, T. *The Summa Oriental of Tomé Pires*, trans. Armando Cortesão, London 1944
Poivre, P. 'Voyage de Pierre Poivre en Cochinchine' [1749–50], *Revue d'Extrême Orient*, III, 1, 1885, 364–510
Polo, M. *The Travels of Marco Polo*, trans. M. Bellonci and T. Waugh, London 1984
Porée-Maspero, E. (ed.) and Commission des Moeurs et Coutumes du Cambodge *Cérémonies privées des Cambodgiens*, Phnom Penh 1958
—— *Cérémonies des douze mois*, Phnom Penh n.d.
Postel, M. *Ear Ornaments of Ancient India; Project for Indian Cultural Studies*, Bombay 1989
Przyluski, J. 'L'Or, son origine et ses pouvoirs magiques: étude et folklore annamite', *BEFEO*, XIV, 5
Punjabhan, Naengnoi *Silverware in Thailand*, Bangkok 1991
Quirino, C. 'Boxer Codex', *FH*, IV, 1977, 1003–8
Raffles, T. S. *The History of Java*, 2 vols, 1817/Kuala Lumpur 1965
Rajahon, Anuman, Phaya *Essays on Thai Folklore*, Bangkok 1988
Rawson, J. *The Chinese Bronzes of Yunnan*, London 1983
—— *Chinese Ornament: The Lotus and the Dragon*, London 1984
—— (ed.) *Mysteries of Ancient China: New Discoveries from the Early Dynasties*, London 1996
Reid, A. *Southeast Asia in the Early Modern Era*, Ithaca, N.Y., 1993
—— *Southeast Asia in the Age of Commerce*, 2 vols, Chiang Mai 1993
—— (ed.) *Witnesses to Sumatra*, New York 1995
—— and K. Rodgers (eds) *Sojourners and Settlers: Histories of Southeast Asia and the Chinese*, St Leonards, N.S.W., 1996
Richter, A. *Arts and Crafts of Indonesia*, London 1993
Rodgers, S. *Power and Gold: Jewelry from Indonesia, Malaysia and the Philippines*, Munich 1990
Rosaldo, R. *Ilongot Headhunting 1883–1974*, Stanford 1980
Roth, L. *Oriental Silverwork: Malay and Chinese*, London 1910
Roveda, V. *Khmer Mythology*, London 1997
Sangermano, V. *The Burmese Empire a Hundred Years Ago*, 1833/Bangkok 1995
Saw Mon Hyin *Myan-ma A-myo-tha-mi Sin Yin Hton Hpa-wa* (Burmese-language historical account of jewelry, hairstyles and costume), Rangoon 1989
Scheurleer, P. L. 'Gold Javanese Jewellery, Part One, Ancient Gold Jewellery from Central Java', *AA*, July–Aug. 1994
Schnitger, F. M. *Forgotten Kingdoms in Sumatra*, Leiden 1939
Schulte Nordholt, H. G. *The Political System of the Atoni of Timor*, The Hague 1971
Scott, W. H. *Looking for the Prehispanic Filipino*, Quezon City 1992
—— *Barangay; Sixteenth-Century Philippine Culture and Society*, Manila 1997
Seidenfaden, E. *The Thai Peoples, Book I*, Bangkok 1967
Sellato, B. *Hornbill and Dragon*, Jakarta 1989
Shangraw, C., et al. *Beauty, Wealth and Power; Jewels and Ornaments of Asia*, San Francisco 1992
Sharam, J. C. *Temples of Champa in Vietnam*, Hanoi 1992
Shelford, R. 'An Illustrated Guide to the Ethnographical Collection of the Sarawak Museum, Pt ii, Personal Ornaments', *JSBRAS* (Singapore), no. 43, Apr. 1905
Sheppard, M. *Taman Indera: Malay Decorative Arts and Pastimes*, Kuala Lumpur 1972
—— *Living Crafts of Malaysia*, Kuala Lumpur 1978
Shway Yoe [Sir James Scott] *The Burman: His Life and Notions*, 1882/New York 1963
Sibeth, A. *The Batak*, London 1991
Sien Mann 'The Insignia of Nobility', *Forward* (Rangoon), XLIV, 4, Oct. 1970
Silice, A. 'Exemples d'art cambodgien contemporain, (II), L'orfèvrerie', *Arts et archéologie khmers* (Paris), II, 2, 1924–26, 241–52
Skeat, W. *Malay Magic: An Introduction to the Folklore and Popular Religion of the Malay Peninsula*, London 1900/1984
Smith, R. B., and W. Watson (eds.) *Early Southeast Asia*, Oxford 1979
Smithies, M. (ed.) *The Mons*, Bangkok 1986
Stargardt, J. *The Ancient Pyu of Burma, I, Early Pyu Cities*, Cambridge 1991
Stark, P. *Important Ancient to Ethnic Works of Art in Precious Metal* (auction cat., Hapsburg Feldman), Geneva 1990
—— *Gold and Silver Auction (Part 1) Ancient to Tribal: Burma (Myanmar), Khmer-Cambodia, Thailand, Philippines, India, China, and Tribal* (auction cat., Taisei Gallery), New York/Singapore 1992
—— *Gold of Asia: Ancient to Tribal, Classical Java, Cambodia, Thailand, China, India, Burma, the Philippines, Island Indonesia* (auction cat., Frank Sternberg), Zurich 1995
Stavorinus, J. S. *Voyage to the East Indies*, trans. S. H. Wilcocke, 3 vols, London 1798
Stronge S., N. Smith and J.C.A. Harle *Golden Treasury: Jewellery from the Indian Subcontinent*, London 1988
Symes, M. *An Account of an Embassy to the Kingdom of Ava Sent by the Governor General of India in the Year 1795*, London 1800
T'ien Ju-K'ang *Religious Cults of the Pai-yi along the Burma–Yunnan Border*, Ithaca, N.Y., 1986
Tait, H. *Seven Thousand Years of Jewellery*, London 1986
Taylor, G., and D. Scarisbrick *Finger Rings from Ancient Egypt to the Present Day*, London 1978
Taylor, K., and J. Whitmore *Essays into Vietnamese Pasts*, Ithaca, N.Y., 1995
Taylor, P., and L. Aragon *Beyond the Java Sea; Art of Indonesia's Outer Islands*, Washington, D.C., 1991
Taylor, P. Y. *Beasts, Birds and Blossoms in Thai Art*, Kuala Lumpur 1994
Tillander, H. *Diamond Cuts in Historic Jewellery 1381–1910*, London 1995
Tineo, M. 'Goldcraft', *FH*, VI, 1977, 1658–65
—— 'The Silver Set', *FH*, VII, 1977, 1718–21
Tran Van Hoang *Recueil d'histoires sur Hué*, Hue 1994
Trin Sinh 'From Stone Ring To Bronze Ring', *Khao Co Hoc* (Hanoi), 23, 1977, 51–56
U Myo Min *Old Burma as Described by Early Travellers*, Rangoon 1948
Untracht, O. *Traditional Jewelry of India*, London 1997
Varthema, Ludovico de *The Travels of Ludovico de Varthema in Egypt, Syria, Arabia Deserta and Arabia Felix, in Persia, India and Ethiopia A.D. 1503 to 1508*, trans. E. Jones and G. Badger, London 1863
Vickers, A. *Travelling to Bali: Four Hundred Years of Journeys*, Kuala Lumpur 1994
Villareal, F. W. *Philippine Prehistoric Gold Bead Catalogue*, Manila 1995
Villegas, R. 'Antique Key Rings: whim and symbol', *Archipelago*, 4, 1977, 32–34
—— *Kayamanan, The Philippine Jewelry Tradition*, Manila 1983
—— *Hiyas: Philippine Jewellery Heritage*, Manila 1997
Wales Quaritch, H. G. *Siamese State Ceremonies*, London 1931
Walker, A. R. *Highland Heritage, Collected Essays on Upland Northern Thailand*, Singapore 1992
Warren, W. *Arts and Crafts of Thailand*, London 1994
Wassing-Visser, R. *Sieraden en Lichaamsversiering uit Indonesie*, Volkenkundig Museum Nusantara, Delft 1984
Wattana Chudhavipata 'Petchburi Goldsmiths Past and Present', in *Regional Issues in the Art and Archeology of Thailand, 5th International Conference of Thai Studies*, London 1993
Webster, R. *Gems, Their Sources, Descriptions and Identification*, rev. B. W. Anderson, London 1990
Wheatley, P. *The Golden Khersonese; Studies in the Historical Geography of the Malay Peninsula before A.D. 1500*, Kuala Lumpur 1961
—— *Nagara and Commandery*, Chicago 1983
Wheeler, R. E. M., A. Gosh and K. Deva 'Arikmedu: an Indo-Roman Trading Station on the East Coast of India, *Ancient India*, 2, 1946, 17–124
White, T. 'Indian and Indigenous Gold', *AA*, Jan.–Feb. 1993
Winstedt, R. O. 'Gold Ornaments Dug up at Fort Canning, Singapore', *JMBRAS*, 6.IV, 1928
—— *The Malays: A Cultural History*, London 1961
—— and R. J. Wilkinson *A History of Perak*, Singapore 1934/Kuala Lumpur 1974
Winters, N. J. 'The Meaning of a Smile', *FH*, II, 1977, 449–54
Wyatt, D. *Thailand: A Short History*, Chiang Mai 1984
Yi Yi Daw 'Life at the Burmese Court under the Konbaung Kings', *JBRS*, XLIV, pt i, 1961; repub. in *JBRS, Silver Jubilee Essays*, Rangoon 1980
Zuraina, M. 'The West Mouth, Niah in the Prehistory of Southeast Asia', *SMJ*, 31, special issue, no. 2, 1982

• • •

MATERIALS AND TECHNIQUES

METALS

SOURCES

Indians described Southeast Asia as 'the golden land' and referred to Java as 'the golden island' as early as the 3rd century BCE, but its **gold** may have been known in more ancient times. It has been suggested that Ophir, the distant land whence the biblical King Solomon (*c.* 1000 BCE) acquired gold for embellishing Jerusalem, was in Southeast Asia. Gold was mined in pre-colonial times in several places. The richest sources were Indonesia and the Philippines. In Indonesia, the most significant sources were the highlands of central and west Sumatra, and also the rivers and river valleys of southern and south-western Borneo; some gold was mined in west Java, west Timor and northern Sulawesi. In the Philippines, important sources include northern Luzon; Davao in the south of Mindanao and Butuan and Surigao in the north; and Mindoro and Masbate islands. Gold was also mined in Pahang on the Malay peninsula; and small deposits and alluvial gold were found in northern Vietnam, Laos, Thailand and Burma/Myanmar.

Southeast Asia was comparatively rich in gold, but poor in **silver**. Silver was mined in Laos and Thailand and was undoubtedly discovered in small quantities elsewhere. The Burmese silver-zinc deposits in Shan state were comparatively large, but the zinc had to be removed by cupellation.

Small deposits of **copper** exist in west Sumatra, central Timor, central Vietnam, northern Burma/Myanmar, northern Laos and central and northern Thailand. Only Luzon in the Philippines has very large deposits.

Tin, which when combined with copper makes bronze, is widely dispersed along the Malay peninsula, in southern Burma/Myanmar and on islands off the east coast of Sumatra. **Bronze** objects made in Southeast Asia have however been found to include a variety of metals and minerals apart from copper and tin. **Brass** is ideally and predominantly an alloy of copper and zinc, but usually includes other metals.

Maps showing locations of major metal deposits in Southeast Asia are provided in Miksic 1990 and Glover et al. 1992.

In communities that traditionally collected alluvial gold or mined it on a small scale, it was customary to perform ceremonies and make offerings to the tutelary spirits or deities who presided over the metal in general and/or local deposits in the hope that deposits would reveal themselves readily (Caballero 1996). The taboos and elaborate ceremonies associated with tin mining on the Malay peninsula are described in Skeat 1900/1984.

METALWORKERS

Many jewellers in small towns and villages continue to use traditional methods. Very fine work in gold and silver is often carried out on top of a tree stump outdoors in a shady place, or at a tiny table in the home or shop. The tools employed are extremely simple and often consist of little more than a hammer, a few punches, some pincers and a bed of charcoal. Heat is intensified by blowing on the charcoal through a bamboo tube. Blowtorches attached to small portable gas cylinders are increasingly employed for some operations, but most artisans work with great care at much lower temperatures than those normally used in the West. When large, heavy metal ornaments of solid silver or iron such as torques are forged, a pair of tall feather-lined pistons made of bamboo or hollow logs may be employed as bellows.

The cost of an item of jewelry is normally reckoned by the prevailing international price of pure gold or silver combined with a fee for workmanship. Gemstones are graded accorded to size, cut, colour and clarity, and are accorded an individual value. In the past it was common for the client to provide the materials. Itinerant jewellers worked at the patron's home under the watchful eye of a family member. Today, gold and gem-set jewelry is available at markets and shops, and jewellers and entrepreneurs with sufficient capital to hold a good stock of gold and gems supervise employee-artisans and apprentices in their homes or shops. Many small jewelry shops are family businesses. Some members make jewelry, while others attend to customers and domestic affairs.

Historically, metalworkers have often been accorded a special, almost separate and often quite high social status, which was usually hereditary. In most traditional communities only men work with fire and metals, but the link between masculinity and metallurgy is no longer so strong. In some places, usually cities and ports, where jewelry manufacture has been more clearly associated historically with commerce, international trade, and increasingly tourism, women assist with finishing and polishing and may perform tasks which require deft fingers such as filigree work.

In the past in Vietnam goldsmiths were indentured court artisans or members of trade guilds. Today they belong to co-operatives; however, the patron saints of their trade are revered as they were in the past. Among Chinese in Southeast Asia only some southern dialect groups, such as the Hokkien, Teochui and Cantonese, specialize in goldsmithing and jewelry-making; they too honour patron saints. In Bali the Hindu-Buddhist goldsmiths (*Pande Mas*) maintain their own temples, meeting houses, ceremonies and *gamelan* orchestras. Urban artisans in Java and Sumatra were often members of Islamic trade guilds. In communities where animist beliefs are still prevalent to a greater or lesser extent, deities or guardian spirits are thought to govern metallurgical processes and ceremonies may be held in their honour.

METALWORKING

• **Beating and forging** Some solid ornaments such as torques and bracelets [**151**, **153**, **325**] are beaten or hammered into the required form much as a blacksmith forges a horseshoe. Soft metals such as gold and silver can be beaten from ingots into sheet form and then stretched, curved and shaped readily. Many early gold ornaments such as funerary masks, and some pieces from outer island Indonesia, are made from gold sheet [**27**, **231**, **235**] cut into appropriate shapes and decorated further by repoussage or embossing. Beating and stretching gold or silver results in brittleness which is then counteracted by the annealing process of repeatedly heating and then cooling the metal object while it is being worked.

• **Casting** Simple bronze and tin ornaments, such as rings and bracelets and decorative plaques and amulets found at early Bronze Age sites in Vietnam and much later Oc Eo, Cambodia and Thailand, were cast in single open or two-part closable moulds of carved stone or hardened clay. Depressions were shaped in matching upper and lower blocks, which were then placed together and secured, and molten metal was poured into channels provided. When the metal cooled and set solid, the moulds were separated and the three-dimensional object was removed, filed and polished. Stone moulds are durable and served to produce numerous identical ornaments. Moulds were found at Oc Eo, in Cambodia, and at various sites in Thailand [**31**, **59**].

Another method of casting metal, employed for many small gold ear ornaments in the 1st millennium and subsequently on the mainland and Java, is the **lost wax** process [**10**]. A wax model is made of the item to be cast. It is encased in a ball of clay, then the ball is dried out and fired. The wax melts from the heat and pours out through tubes provided, leaving a hollow space. This empty space is then filled with molten metal. When the metal cools and solidifies, the mould is broken open and the metal object is retrieved to be filed and polished. A separate model must be made for each item, since the process destroys it. Lost-wax casting is suitable for producing complex three-dimensional ornaments with detailed motifs that can be carved or scratched into the wax with a sharp tool. Sometimes the wax is wrapped around a clay core before being encased in the clay ball, a method that requires less metal. The core may be left in, or dug out so the object is hollow and lighter.

Casting seems to have been employed rarely, if at all, in pre-Hispanic jewelry of the Philippines.

• **Die-stamping** Stone blocks are carved with depressions in decorative shapes, and pieces of sheet metal are beaten from the back into the depressions to form ornaments. The two halves of hollow gold and silver beads, for example, may be beaten into hemispherical depressions and then soldered together. Small dangling necklace and belt pendants depicted in 10th–12th-century and later Cambodian sculpture were probably made this way [**59**]. Large crowns and pectoral ornaments which adorned 10th–11th-century statues of Cambodian divinities were also made by beating gold sheet into carved wooden or stone shapes. Their surface was then engraved and further refined. Some Javanese ornaments look as though they had been formed by the usual process of repoussage, but examination suggests a different process [see the Wonoboyo armlet, **169**]: since the inner face of the gold shows no sign of work, they cannot have been worked in a concave mould. After the thick gold sheet of the armlet had been beaten from the front over a finely carved stone form, the gold front and bronze rear plate were assembled and filled with damp clay, and the gold sheet was folded over the edges to secure the backing. Further decorative work on the outer surface was carried out while the clay was soft but firm enough to offer resistance.

• **Wire work** Wire is made from sheet metal cut into very thin strips. In the distant past it was probably produced by rolling the strips between two stones; but for many hundreds of years, if not the last two millennia, metal strips have been refined and narrowed by being pulled repeatedly through an iron draw plate drilled with holes of decreasing size. In cross-section wire is usually circular, but it may be beaten flat to form a fine ribbon. It can also be twisted, crimped or notched to create the appearance of fine beading and other decorative effects.

Wire is used to form spring-like coils worn as bracelets in Cambodia [**77**], and thick wire was formed into spiral limb ornaments. Small tight circular springs of very fine wire may form a flexible bezel or collar to secure a gemstone or a small metal ball [**272**, single *dokoh* pendant]: this technique was used early in the 1st millennium CE at Oc Eo, and it is frequently employed today by Minangkabau jewellers in west Sumatra, and in Laos, where broad necklace or bracelet bands may be covered with small wire flowers. Some rings derive their form from the sacred Indian *kushu* rings of woven grass [**164**].

In the **open filigree** process, lacy ornaments such as light brooches, pendants, bracelet clasps and beads may be constructed from large and small elements of delicate wire twisted deftly with pincers into scrolling or vegetal patterns [**43**, **208**, **270**]. Smaller elements are usually attached to a stronger wire frame or a series of frames. The decorative sections are placed in position and held by a natural resin adhesive. A tiny particle of solder is usually placed adjacent to each join, and the ornament is subjected to a short burst of heat, which melts the resin and solder but not the wires.

• **Chainmaking** The tradition of making beautiful chains continues today [**69**, **111**], but the gold chains made in the Philippines, Cambodia, Champa and Java between the 7th and 13th centuries deserve special praise. The loop-in-loop type was widespread [**117**, **118**]; this appears to be woven from long strands of wire, but is in fact made from numerous elliptical circlets of wire looped together. Each is first crimped into a figure 8 shape and then bent over into a U shape, and each U-shaped piece is hooked into the next to make a long thin chain. Thick chains are composed of denser looping of a greater number of U-shaped elements. The arrangement of loops may result in a circular or angular cross-section. If the links are looped sideways rather than longitudinally, a herringbone pattern is achieved. Additional decorative wire elements may be woven or looped into the chain. A 10th-century example from Champa displays an especially admirable textural complexity achieved by these methods [**55**].

In boldly three-dimensional Cambodian gold chains which often evoke jasmine blooms [**61**, **65**] each link is constructed from small rods hammered into the required form and soldered together.

Pre-Hispanic gold chains of the Philippines also display unusual complexity. Of special interest are those composed of numerous small gold discs resembling gear cogs. These interlock perfectly to create a chain of great suppleness which from a distance appears smooth and of one piece.

DECORATIVE TECHNIQUES

In most cases a number of decorative techniques are used in combination on a single ornament.

• **Applied filigree** Very fine wire may be arranged in complex, usually vegetal, scrolling patterns and applied to a flat metal surface [**85**, **189**, **218**, **257**, **279**, **285**]. The filigree decoration is placed on the background, secured with an adhesive resin, and soldered, in processes similar to those used for open filigree and granulation. However, in the case of applied filigree it is not necessary to use stronger framing sections, since the backing provides support.

• **Carving** Gold of high purity is extremely soft and may be carved with sharp tools of harder metal such as iron. Some 8th–15th-century ornaments from Java, for example, appear to have been decorated by carving with a sharp chisel.

• **Chasing** This technique creates the appearance of raised surface decoration by depressing the background [**125**, **264**, **280**]. Indented patterns are made by cutting into or beating back some areas of the front surface. Chasing cannot produce very pronounced effects without destroying the integrity of the object, so it is often augmented by embossing or repoussage.

• **Embossing** and **repoussage** In these processes convex protrusions or bosses are formed in sheet metal by beating, stretching and pushing it with punches and a hammer from the rear surface [**90**, **117**, **179**, **262**, **271**, **284**]. During the beating process the object usually rests in a bowl of resin or pitch, just firm enough to offer resistance. When the shaping and decoration from behind are complete, the front is cleaned. It may then be decorated further with chasing and/or engraving.

• **Enamelling** A flux of sand, soda and red lead forms a vitreous base to which metal oxides are added to provide various colours. The compound is applied in powder form; when heated, it liquifies and adheres to the prepared metal surface. In the more common cloisonné process small wire enclosures are applied to the surface and then filled with enamel. With champlevé enamel, the powder is applied to shallow depressions created in the surface. Enamel is especially characteristic of Thai jewelry in the 18th and 19th centuries [**96–98**, **104**]; it was also used in Aceh, north Sumatra [**207**, **209**], and in Cambodia in the 19th and early 20th centuries [**70**] and possibly long before. Although the 18th-century crown of Banten in west Java has exquisite enamelling [**181**], the technique was not widely used in Java. Enamel was also employed by mainland minorities such as the Shan and the Yao [**144**, **147**, **149**].

• **Engraving** Shallow patterns are cut into a metal surface by a tool with a fine sharp tip, which is pushed in a forward direction with a hammer [**102**, **110**, **112**, **114**, **153**, **180**, **278**]. For ornaments such as bracelets made of metal tubing, resin was used as a supportive core while decorative engraving was carried out. It was often removed by melting, but some tubular bracelets retain the filling, which make them less vulnerable to crushing.

• **Granulation** Tiny metal granules or balls are applied to a plain surface, often in scrolls, rows and geometrical patterns such as triangles [**1**, **38**, **108**, **162**, **323**]. The spherical form is created by surface tension when tiny fragments of metal or wire are heated on a charcoal bed. The balls may be flattened to form the spangles which in Malay jewelry are known as 'fish eggs' [**279**], or they may be faceted by filing or hammering [269, 301]. When cool the balls are arranged and secured with resin adhesive. A very small quantity of solder is used and then, as for filigree work, the ornament is subjected to a very carefully applied burst of heat.

• **Matting and ring-matting** The gleam of embossed and chased motifs may be emphasized by contrast with a dull background, created by punches with tips that produce a matt finish. When this is formed by numerous circular indentations it is referred to as ring-matting [120, 128], which is common in Vietnamese silverwork.

• **Niello** Decorative patterns are chased or cut into the front surface of silver; the background is then cut back further, roughened, and filled with a preparation of lead, copper, silver and sulphur in powder form, which melts when heated. Polishing assists in creating a smooth and unified surface of black and silver. In Thailand and northern Malaysia, the silver patterns were sometimes gilded. Some Thai niello may be of a more intense black [278]; Sumatran and Malay niello often has a more greyish colour and greater sheen because the silver content is higher; however, silver content varies in both places. Niello work was carried out in Sumatra and Malaysia until the early 20th century [214, 215, 278], but very little is produced now. In Thailand niello is mostly employed for small objects and souvenirs. Niello items are found in the National Museum in Phnom Penh, Cambodia. Niello was also made in Java, though infrequently, and possibly in south Sulawesi. It is occasionally confused with the *bidri* work of India, which is produced by the very opposite process, as precious metal is inlaid into base. *Bidri* was rarely used for jewelry in Southeast Asia; however, in the 19th and early 20th centuries Javanese iron belt buckles were inlaid with decorative patterns in fine wire or leaf gold [188].

• **Openwork** Sheet metal is pierced or punched to create holes of various shapes and sizes [91, 125, 291, 316]; a metal saw is often used for the purpose today. An entire ornament such as a brooch or pendant may consist of leafy or lacy openwork, or a panel of openwork may be placed over a sheet metal backing to create a double layer [107].

• **Punching** Indented motifs, usually on a border, are achieved by gently hammering with a tool whose metal tip bears a pattern [280].

GOLD AND SILVER PLATING AND GILDING

Creating the effect of a gold or silver surface on an ornament of less valuable and usually more robust metal is largely achieved today by the **galvanic** process (using a small tank and batteries), which was already employed by some jewellers in the early 20th century. In the past, it was carried out by several methods. The first was by the application of **leaf gold** or **gold sheet**, which was glued to the ornament, then polished or burnished to create a smooth unified surface. Some Javanese earrings appear to have been formed in clay [172], and then covered with thin layers of leaf gold or gold sheet. Decorative patterns were worked gently into the gold while the clay beneath was still soft. A similar process was employed with resin for earrings and bracelets well before the 19th century; such ornaments are now extremely fragile because the resin core deteriorates, leaving the gold surface, which is sometimes little more than a paper-thin skin, inadequately supported. Alternatively, a very thin **gold plaque** was attached to a base of copper or another harder, less valuable metal such as an alloy of copper or tin. Usually this was done by means of an eyelet in the gold (often found in the centre of a belt buckle) and a wire loop or clip that fixed the two surfaces together. Alternatively, the surfaces might be secured by small metal clips at the sides; or the soft precious metal of the front might be folded over the edges of the back. The narrow gap between the front and back might be filled with resin to protect delicate embossed patterns. In **fire-gilding**, always used by Chinese goldsmiths, particles of gold or silver were blended with mercury to form a paste which was applied to the metal object to be gilded. The object was heated until the mercury separated as fumes from the paste, leaving a layer of precious metal. **Depletion gilding** or **leaching** involves repeated cleaning and gradual chemical removal of the copper and silver content from the surface of an ornament composed of gold alloy. This leaves a thin layer of purer gold exposed to view and creates the impression that the gold content of the entire ornament is higher. An alloy ornament is sturdier and less prone to damage than one of purer gold.

COLOURING AND STAINING

• **Silver** The pattern and texture of silver jewelry was and is sometimes enhanced by blackening or darkening the ornament with pastes made from plants or a liver of sulphur preparation which reacts with silver to create a black or brown colour. The surface is then polished, and contrasts with the dark colour remaining in depressions. The process is sometimes used, in combination with various procedures of distressing such as scratching and abrasion, to give newly made ornaments a more antique and patinated appearance.

• **Gold** Gold alloys are sometimes given a red stain or transparent coating by one of two methods. Both involve repeated chemical cleaning, drying, very gentle heating, and submersion of the item in chemical compounds. One consists of an acidic paste made from tamarind, or rotted citrus fruits mixed with sulphur. The other is based on potassium nitrate or saltpetre, mixed with rock or sea salt and alum. In Java and Bali, a red clay obtained from volcanic riverbeds, mixed with copper sulphate and rock salt, was occasionally employed. Acidic fruit pulps and sulphur are used in Vietnam, and the potassium nitrate method is still employed in Laos.

Yellow gold ornaments are still given a distinctive and quite intense red sheen, which may range from a bright orange-red to a purplish red-brown [111, 269]. Red staining is sometimes applied to part of an ornament only, to contrast with the yellow gold used elsewhere. It is rarely used in Southeast Asia today except in Laos, where it is still very common, especially in Luang Prabang. It is also employed occasionally for decorative effect by goldsmiths in Hue, central Vietnam. In Java the process is familiar but not often used. Several recipes collected in Indonesia are provided in Jasper and Pirngadie 1927; they are very similar to those used today in Laos, Vietnam and Java.

• **Alloys** Ornaments are occasionally composed of gold alloy, which includes some silver and high levels of copper [205, 206, 226]. This red or pink gold is known in Sumatra as *suasa*, and on the mainland and in the Philippines as *tombac* or *tembaga*. The redness is found throughout the ornament, which thus does not have the appearance of superficial staining or coating. The alloy was prepared by jewellers according to various recipes. Some traditional jewelry is made of gold mixed with significant amounts of silver, and silver ornaments, especially in Indonesia, sometimes contain quite high levels of tin and copper. A bronze or copper alloy mixed with silver and gold, referred to as *samrit* in Cambodia, may not have a red appearance. Red gold is rarely used today.

GEMSTONES

SOURCES

Southeast Asia is a primary source of precious gems, especially the corundums (rubies and sapphires). The highly prized bright crimson 'pigeon's blood' rubies are found only in Burma/Myanmar; Thai and Cambodian rubies may display a more winey colour; less valuable stones have a brown tinge. Good Thai and Cambodian sapphires are a rich deep blue; inferior stones tend towards an opaque blue-black. Imported Sri Lankan corundums may be comparatively pallid, although the best pink rubies and cornflower blue sapphires, which often have a violet tinge, are very highly regarded. Clear sapphires are produced commercially in small quantities in Thailand and Cambodia; those from Sri Lanka were known in the past as *batu Ceylon*. Green sapphires are also found in Thailand and Cambodia. White, grey and some coloured diamonds are still mined and cut on a comparatively small scale in southern Borneo. Garnets, amethysts and rock crystals and many other semi-precious stones occur widely, usually in association with more valuable gems.

USES

In the past, the main goal was to maximize the amount of precious stone available to view in an item of jewelry. Gems were set to emphasize their beauty for those seeing them from afar rather than close up, and in the absence of electric lighting. Irregularity of form was often preserved, and cutting and faceting kept to a minimum.

Before industrialized mining techniques, large and very colourful gems were probably even rarer than they are today. Their value lay in scarcity, size, richness of colour, and the magical and healing powers attributed to them alone and in combination with others. As in India, precious gems worn for medicinal purposes were often set to give contact with the wearer's skin.

In addition to the seven planetary gems, the nine gems of the Indian *nava-ratna* included two further stones to symbolize the ascending and descending phases of the moon. In the Indian symbolic systems current in Southeast Asia, the gems were accorded specific powers and linked to deities, animals, colours, and plants. Precious and semi-precious stones and unusual objects were also regarded as talismans. Jasper and Pirngadie 1927 provide a list of Javanese beliefs about stones and also petrified rose buds, coffee beans, etc.: amethysts, for example, were thought to assist in childbirth and sapphires to deter murderers. The allocation of particular stones to the months of the Western calendar, which is popular in Burma/Myanmar and elsewhere today, is, presumably, a response to Western influences.

GEM-CUTTING

Traditionally gems were not faceted, but abraded mechanically and polished into a rounded cabochon form or left in their natural shape and polished. Cabochons are still more admired in Southeast Asia than in the West, especially when they display the gleaming star form found in some rubies and sapphires. If stones were faceted at all, they were worked in a manner often described as 'rose-cut' because the bottom of the stone is flat and the exposed top or crown is faceted in a regular manner around a central peak; in Southeast Asia as in India, the peak is often off-centre and the faceting irregular. Locally cut gems sometimes display a flat central table instead of a peak. Many old Southeast Asian stones are best described as 'rough-cut'.

European cutting, especially of diamonds, involves a very different approach to the refraction of light. In a modern brilliant-cut diamond, only about 20 per cent of the raw stone may be exposed to full view after cutting and setting. The lower and larger part of the stone, which is obscured by the bezel or claws, acts as a reflector. The practice was traditionally thought wasteful and somewhat pointless in Southeast Asia; but today most gemstones are routinely cut in modern Western styles for export and for local consumption.

GEM-SETTING

Traditionally, stones were box-set rather than held in claws. The box was soldered on, and the rim was pressed gently inwards over the edge of the stone to secure it. Sometimes the rim was partly cut or filed away to leave two or more protruding claws, a technique employed in rings of the 1st millennium CE and subsequently [192]. Sections of metal with claws were also separately soldered to the bezel [54]. Since most stones were of an irregular shape, the box was often made to follow their contours. In some items of jewelry the box was filled with resin and diamond slivers, or irregular precious stones were stuck into the resin before it hardened [211].

Alternatively, a hole or hollow was created in the precious metal to receive the stone, so a separate box or bezel was not required. In this Indian method of gem-setting a collar of very soft pure gold is formed around an irregular stone and then compressed between the stone and the edge of the hole. The base of the hollow was often lined with shiny foil which reflected light back through the stone.

Another method of gem-setting of special appeal to Southeast Asian Chinese communities in the late 19th and early 20th centuries is also of Indian or Sri Lankan origin: rose- or rough-cut diamonds were set into gold frames without a backing to create an impression similar to that of lead lights [306].

GLASS

Many imported and indigenous glass beads were made by drawing [**34, 37, 81**]: glass canes with a central hollow were blown by single craftsmen, the hollow tube was gradually stretched out by a pair of craftsmen facing each other, and the canes were then cut up into small sections. Beads were rounded off by abrasion when cold.

Striped beads were made from canes of coloured glass which were fused together by heat and then cut to shape [**81, 165**]. Decorative effects could be obtained by layering coloured glass and other substances such as leaf gold and by scraping the surface of a newly made bead to create dragged or feathery patterns.

Millefiore and eye patterns were made by inserting thin cross-sections of striped beads into the surface of a freshly made bead which had not quite solidified, and fusing it by re-heating.

Beads exported from China after the early centuries of the 1st millennium CE, which are most common on the mainland and in the Philippines, were usually coiled and contained lead. In this process, molten glass was wound around a metal rod or wire. When sufficiently cool, the soft glass was often shaped and crimped while still on the rod.

It is often possible to detect the method of manufacture and possible origin of a bead by examining it carefully. Protruding coiled ridges are clearly observable on the surface of some beads exported from China. Others have a smooth surface, but the coiled structure and circular dispersion of tiny bubbles can be seen in translucent glass. The bead may seem comparatively heavy due to its lead content. In drawn beads, the longitudinal structure, which runs parallel to the drilled hole, may also be obvious.

Some solid glass ornaments were made in moulds.

SHELL AND STONE ORNAMENTS

Shell and stone ornaments of the Neolithic age were made before the advent of metal tools. It is possible that some jewelry was drilled with bamboo or hard wooden drills. Saws may have been made of string, sharp stone flakes, or bamboo slivers. The tools may have been charged with water and fine sharp sand as an abrasive. At the neolithic Tha Khae site in Thailand, bracelets of giant clam (*Tridacna gigas*) shell were manufactured in the following manner. A shell was cut and then drilled around the perimeter of the intended ring form. The long cylinder was removed, sawn into slices to create several bracelets, and the central discs tapped free and used for pendants, beads, etc. Large hollow *Conus* shells were cut across at points wide enough to serve as bracelets or other ornaments. Shell jewelry was polished with sandstone blocks.

Jade (nephrite and jadeite) is extremely hard and difficult to cut. Research at the Trang Kenh site in north Vietnam has revealed that jade bracelets were made from discs chipped out from a larger block of stone. The central hole was formed with a jasper-tipped drill on a simple hand-operated potter's wheel, working successively on both sides. Smaller bracelets and rings were cut from the discarded central disc. Jade ornaments are cut out and then abraded. Simple belt-driven machines are used in Vietnam.

Carnelian and agate beads, imported from India in the late 1st millennium BCE and after and also manufactured locally from imported and indigenous raw materials, were made from chipped stone which was drilled from both ends of the bead with diamond-tipped bow drills [**6, 34, 37**]. Plain beads were probably polished by lengthy tumbling; those with facets were hand polished against wood or bamboo.

• • •

ACKNOWLEDGMENTS FOR ILLUSTRATIONS

Many institutions, organizations and individuals contributed by generously granting permission for their jewelry to be photographed, or providing photographs.

Museums and institutions

Ayala Museum, Manila **332, 344–346**; Banco Sentral Museum, Manila **1, 323, 325, 326, 331**; British Museum, London **104**; Chao Sam Phraya National Museum, Ayutthaya, Thailand **86–91**; City Museum and Art Gallery, Bristol **144**; Etnografisch Museum, Antwerp **183**; Fine Art Department and National Museum, Bangkok **81, 102, 103**; History Museum, Hanoi **3, 5, 6, 8**; History Museum, Ho Chi Minh City **32–34**; Honolulu Academy of Arts, Gift of Mrs Walter F. Dillingham, 1963 (3164.1) **40, 41**; Linden Museum, Stuttgart **29**; Museum of Ancient Objects, Hue, Vietnam **119–124**; Museum of North Vietnamese Women, Hanoi **132, 140**; Museum of South Vietnamese Women, Ho Chi Minh City **74, 76, 127, 131, 133**; Muzium Negara, Kuala Lumpur **210, 279, 281–290, 292–294, 311**; National Museum, Jakarta **158, 159, 166, 169, 170, 172, 175, 176, 178, 179, 181, 182, 194, 196, 265–267**; National Museum, Manila **333–343**; National Museum, Phnom Penh **19, 59, 68**; National Museum, Rangoon **35, 42, 46, 47, 52**; Museum voor Volkenkunde, Rotterdam **308, 313**; Royal Cambodian Ballet **77**; Sarawak Museum **18, 20, 22, 23**; Shwedagon Paya, Rangoon **48, 49**; Silver Pagoda, Royal Palace, Phnom Penh **69–73**; Sungguminasa Palace Museum, Ujung Pandang, Sulawesi **251, 252**; Thay Nguyen Ethnographic Museum, Vietnam **126, 129, 134, 139**; Tropen Museum, Amsterdam **26, 171, 180, 184, 185, 209**; Uthong National Museum, Thailand **79–83**; Victoria and Albert Museum, London **43–45**.

Private collections

Acacia Tree, Kuala Lumpur **165, 201, 202, 204, 277, 342**; Backman-Cameron collection **197–199, 264, 302, 305**; Betel Box, Bangkok **101**; Collection Ghysels, Brussels **55, 60, 62, 207, 241, 242, 257**; Golden Triangle Gallery, Bangkok **118, 136, 148–151, 153–155, 157**; Mata Tiga Gallery, Bali **186–188, 190**; Nelson Tan Gallery, Kuching **269–272, 275, 276, 298, 303, 312**; Nui collection, Bangkok **137**; Paa Gallery, Bangkok **92, 94, 98, 99, 107**; Private collection, Burma/Myanmar **36, 37, 50, 51, 138**; Private collection, California **7, 9, 12, 21, 31, 38, 39, 54, 56–58, 61, 65, 78, 84, 85, 163, 167, 168, 193, 208, 217, 221–223, 232, 247**; Private collection, Melbourne **24, 28, 135, 145, 146**; Rat Ying, Bangkok **63, 64, 192**; Syamsuddin collection, Indonesia **16, 191, 200, 205, 206, 212, 214, 216, 218–220, 225, 253, 254, 258, 262**; Thai Derm, Bangkok **163, 173, 211**; Talat Sao,Vientiane **111**; Thai Fine Art, Bangkok **105, 109**; Villegas collection, Manila **14, 25, 27, 160, 161, 324, 327–330, 347–349, 350–353**.

All other pieces illustrated are held in private collections.

Credits for photographs

For permission to include their photographs, I am especially indebted to the following institutions : The Asia Society, New York **159, 176, 182, 194, 196, 251, 252, 256, 266, 267**; Christie's, Singapore **314, 315, 317, 318–322**; Musée Guimet, Paris **169, 170, 172, 175, 178, 182**. Credit is also due to the following individual photographers: Dirk Bakker, **158, 179**; Dick Baldovino **1, 323, 325, 326, 331**; H. Dubois **55, 60, 62**; John Gollings **159, 166, 176, 182, 194, 196, 251, 252, 256, 265, 266, 267**; Hilton **204, 277, 342**; Christopher Legget **13, 15, 16, 30, 161, 177, 186–188, 190, 191, 200, 205, 206, 212–216, 218–220, 225, 227–240, 243, 244, 246, 249, 250, 253–255, 258–263, 274, 307**; Hervé Levandowski **169, 170, 172, 175, 178, 181**; Peter Lim **18, 20, 22, 23**; Hugo Maertens **183**; Rick Merry **295, 296, 299, 300, 304, 309, 310**; Jimmy Obleno **2, 4, 14, 16, 24, 27, 160, 162, 324, 327–330, 332–353**; Ping **269–271, 275, 276, 298, 303, 312**; John Storey **11, 28, 51, 66, 106, 116, 117, 125, 128, 135, 141, 142, 146, 189, 197–199, 203, 224, 226, 245, 262, 268, 272, 278, 291, 297, 301, 302, 305, 306**; Zaleha Bt. Tasrib **286, 289, 293, 294**; John Bigelow Taylor **207, 241, 242**. For his unfailing energy and good humour in situations which were not always ideal for photography, I would especially like to thank Darren Campbell **3, 5, 6, 8, 18, 32–37, 42, 46–53, 59, 63, 64, 67–77, 92, 94–101, 105, 107–115, 118–124, 126, 127, 129–134, 136–140, 143, 145, 147–157**.

• • •

INDEX